ENGLISH
MONASTIC LIFE

ST. BENEDICT
PATRIARCH OF WESTERN MONKS

ENGLISH
MONASTIC LIFE

BY

ABBOT GASQUET

WITH NUMEROUS ILLUSTRATIONS, MAPS AND PLANS

KENNIKAT PRESS
Port Washington, N. Y./London

ENGLISH MONASTIC LIFE

First published in 1904
Reissued in 1971 by Kennikat Press
Library of Congress Catalog Card No: 76-118470
ISBN 0-8046-1219-6

Manufactured by Taylor Publishing Company   Dallas, Texas

CONTENTS

CONTENTS

LIST OF ILLUSTRATIONS IN THE TEXT

LIST OF PLATES

PREFACE

THIS volume does not appear to call for any lengthy preface. It should introduce and explain itself, inasmuch as, beyond giving a brief account of the origin and aim of each of the Orders existing in England in pre-Reformation days, and drawing up a general list of the various houses, all I have attempted to do is to set before the reader, in as plain and popular a manner as I could, the general tenor of the life lived by the inmates in any one of those monastic establishments. In one sense the picture is ideal; that is, all the details of the daily observance could not perhaps be justified from an appeal to the annals or custumals of any one single monastery. Regular or religious life was never, it must be borne in mind, such a cast-iron system, or of so stereotyped a form, that it could not be, and for that matter frequently was, modified in this or that particular, according to the needs of places, circumstances, and times. Even in the case of establishments belonging to the same Order or religious body this is true; and it is of course all the more certainly true in regard to houses

belonging to different Orders. Still, as will be explained
later, the general agreement of the life led in all the
monastic establishments is so marked, that it has been
found possible to sketch a picture of that life which,
without being perhaps actually exact in every particular
for any one individual house, is sufficiently near to the
truth in regard to all the houses in general. The purposes
for which the various parts of the monastery were designed and were used, the duties assigned to the numerous
officials, the provisions by which the well-being and order
of the establishment were secured, the disposition of the
hours of the day, and the regulations for carrying out
the common conventual duties, etc., were similar in all
religious bodies in pre-Reformation days ; and, if regard
be paid to the changed circumstances, are still applicable
to the monastic and religious establishments now existing
in England.

It remains for me to publicly record my thanks to
those who have assisted me in the preparation of this
volume.

In regard to the list of the ancient religious houses,
which it is to be hoped may be found of use to the
student of monastic archæology, I have to acknowledge
the kind help of the Rev. Dr. Cox, the general editor of
the series ; of Mr. W. H. St. John Hope ; of Mr. R. C.
Fowler, of the Public Record Office ; of the Rev. R. M.
Serjeantson ; and of the Rev. H. J. D. Astley. My
readers are also indebted to Mr. St. John Hope and to

Mr. H. Brakspear for permission to reproduce three plans giving the typical arrangement of different religious houses ; and lastly, my thanks are due to Dom H. N. Birt for various suggestions, and for his careful reading of the proofs for me.

LIST OF MANUSCRIPTS AND PRINTED BOOKS

BY the advice of the editor of this series, the present list of the principal manuscripts and books used in this volume to describe the life of an English mediæval monastery is here printed, in place of giving multitudinous references at the foot of every page. In the case of the MSS. full transcripts have been made of most of them, in order that all the available evidence bearing on the subject might be fully considered.

Consuetudinarium Monasterii B. Marie, Ebor. St. John's Coll., Cambridge, MS. D. 27.

Consuetudinarium Abbatiæ S. Petri Westmonasteriensis (Abbot Ware's). (4th part only, much burnt.) Cott. MS. Otho c. xi.

Constitutiones pro monasterio de Abingdon. Harl. MSS. 209, ff. 11–12, 85–87.

Ordinale S. Edmundi de Burgo. MS. Harl. 2,977.

Ordinale ecclesiæ S. Augustini Cantuariensis: de disciplina Monachorum, etc. Cott. MS. Vitellius D. xvi.

Consuetudines quædam Abbatiæ S. Edmundi Buriensis. (Stated in a Papal letter in the Marini transcripts). Brit. Mus. Add. MS. 15,358, f. 439 *seqq.*

Traditiones patrum O.S.B. in *Liber albus* of Edmundsbury. Harl. MS. 1005.

Consuetudines quædam Abbatiæ de Reading. MS. Cott. Vesp. E.v. f. 37 *seqq.*

Memoriale qualiter in monasterio conversare debemus.   Harl.
MS. 5,431, f. 114 d.

Officium Senescall. aule Hospitum ecclesie Cantuariensis faciendæ.
MS. Cott. Galba E. v. f. 26 d *seqq.*

Consuetudines Cantuarienses.   Arund. MS. 68, f. 55 *seqq.*

*Traditio Generalis Capituli super mores et observantias mona-
chorum Ordinis S. Benedicti.*   Cott. MS. Faustina C. xii.
f. 181.

*Consuetudines Elemosinæ ecclesiæ Sti. Petri et S. Swithune,
Winton.*   Brit. Mus. Add. MS. 29,436, f. 72 d. *seqq.*

*Walteri de Wykwane, Abb. de Winchcombe, perquisita spiritualia
et temporalia, una cum ejusdem monasterii Constitutionibus et
Ordinationibus per eundem factis.*   Cott. MS. Cleop. B. II.
f. 1.   Printed in *Monasticon.*

Statuta Capituli Generalis O.S.B. (Reading and Abingdon, A.D.
1388).   Cott. MS. Faustina A. II. f. 93 *seqq.*

Westminster Chapter O.S.B. under King Henry V.   Cott. MS.
Vesp. D. ix. f. 193 *seqq.*

Acta Capitulorum Generalium O.S.A.   Brit. Mus. Cotton
Charter xiii. 3.

Acta Capituli Generalis Ordinis Sti. Augustini, A.D. 1506.   R.O.
Exchequer, Q.R. Miscell. $\frac{916}{44}$.

Mortuary Rolls (Norwich).   Brit. Mus. Cotton Charter II. 17
and 18.

Visitationes Abbatiæ de Hayles Ord. Cist.   Brit. Mus., Royal
MS. 12, E. XIV. f. 73 *seqq.*

Visitatio Ecclesiæ Cath. Wynton (Bp. William of Wykham, A.D.
1386).   Harl. MS. 328.

Monasticon Cisterciense.   Julianus, Paris.   ed. nova Hugo
Séjalon.   1892.

Bibliotheca Premonstratensis, 1633.   Le Paige.

*Customary of the Benedictine Monasteries of Saint Augustine,
Canterbury, and Saint Peter, Westminster.*   ed. Sir E.
Maunde Thompson (Henry Bradshaw Soc.).   1902.

The Ancren Riwle.   ed. J. Morton (Camden Soc.).   1853.

*The Observances in use at the Augustinian Priory at Barnwell,
Cambridgeshire.*   ed. J. Willis Clark, M.A., F.S.A.   1897.

Apostolatus Benedictinorum in Anglia. Reyner, Clemens.

Antiquiores Consuetudines Cluniacensis Monasterii—Collectore Udalrico Monacho. Migne, Patr. Lat. vol. 149, col. 635 *seqq.*

The Lausiac History of Palladius. ed. Dom Cuthbert Butler. Part I. Introduction (Texts and Studies, vol. vi.).

De Antiquis Ecclesiæ Ritibus. Martène, III. pp. 253 *seqq.*

Ordinale Conventus Vallis Caulium. ed. W. de Gray Birch. 1900.

De Consuetudinibus Abbendoniæ, Chronicon Monasterii de Abingdon. ed. J. Stevenson (Rolls Series), II. p. 296 *seqq.*

The Ancient English Version of the Rule of St. Francis—Abbreviatio Statutorum. 1451 : in *Monumenta Franciscana.* Vol. ii. (Rolls Series). ed. R. Howlett.

Rouleaux des Morts du ixe au xve Siècle, Léopold Delisle (Soc. de l'Histoire de France). 1866.

Accounts of the Obedientiars of Abingdon Abbey. ed. R. E. G. Kirk (Camden Soc.). 1892.

Compotus Rolls of the Obedientiaries of St. Swithun's Priory, Winchester. ed. G. W. Kitchin (Hampshire Record Soc.). 1892.

De prima Institutione Monachorum in *Monasticon Anglicanum.* (ed. Calley Ellis and Bandinel), I. xix. *seqq.*

Processus electionis Abbatum S. Albani. Mon. Angl. II. 191, *note.*

De Consuetudinibus et Ordinationibus officialium separalium in Abbatia de Evesham. Mon. Angl. II. 23-5.

Literæ Constitutionum Hugonis, Lincoln. Episcopi, Visitatione Monalium de Cotun. Mon. Angl. V. 677.

Tractatus Statutorum Ordinis Cartusiensis pro Noviciis, etc. Mon. Angl. VI. pp. v., xii.

De Canonicorum Ordinis Origine, etc. Mon. Angl. VI. pp. 39-49.

Ordinatio pro coquina conventus Canonicorum de Haghmon. Mon. Angl. VI. 111.

Ordinatio pro officiis Prioris et Subprioris ibidem. Mon. Angl. VI. p. 112.

Institutiones beati Gilberti et successorum ejus, per Capitula Generalia institutæ. Mon. Angl. VI. p. 2, pp. *xxix.- *xcvii.

Regula Monachorum S. Trinitatis. Mon. Angl. VI. p. 3, p. 1,558 *seqq.*

De primordiis et inventione sacræ Religionis Iherosolimorum. Mon. Angl. V. p. 2, pp. 787 *seqq.*

De Canonicorum Ordinis Præmonstratensis Origine, etc. Mon. Angl. V. p. 2, pp. 857 *seqq.*

Consuetudines Abbatiæ Eveshamensis. Mon. Angl. II. 27–32.

De officis Præcentoris. Mon. Angl. II. p. 39.

De Sacrista. Mon. Angl. II. p. 40.

Constitutiones per Decanum et Capitulum Ecclesiæ Cathedralis S. Pauli, Lond., factæ, Moniales Cœnobii S. Helenæ prope Bishop's-gate, infra Civitatem London, tangentes. Mon. Angl. IV. p. 553.

Leges Monachis Hydensibus ab Edgaro Rege datæ. Mon. Angl. II. p. 439 *seqq.*

Constitutiones Capituli Generalis O.S.B. apud Northampton, A.D. 1225, in Mon. Angl. I. pp. xlvi.–li.

A Consuetudinary of the Fourteenth Century for the House of St. Swithin, Winchester. ed. G. W. Kitchen, D.D. 1886.

Collectanea Anglo-Premonstratensia (Camden Soc.). 1904.

Charters and Records of Cluni. G. Duckett.

Visitations of English Cluniac Foundations. G. Duckett.

Two Chartularies of the Priory of St. Peter at Bath. ed. W. Hunt (Somerset Record Soc.). 1893.

Rentalia et Custumaria of Glastonbury. ed. C. Elton (Somerset Record Soc.).

Woman and Monasticism. L. Eckenstein. 1896.

S. Gilbert of Sempringham and the Gilbertines. Rose Graham. 1902.

Gesta Abbatum S. Albani. ed. Riley (Rolls Series), II. pp. 95–107, *Constitutiones Abbatis Johannis de Maryns,* c. 1308. pp. 301–316, *Constitutiones,* c. 1336. pp. 418–466, *Constitutiones Abb. Thomæ de la Mare,* c. 1386. pp. 511–519. *Constitutions for nuns of Sopwell.*

Gesta Abbatum S. Albani. ed. Riley (Rolls Series), III. pp. 470–72. *Constitutiones Abbatis Johannis de la Moote.*

Adam de Domerham. Hearne, p. 123. *De electione Walteri More Abbatis Cenobii Glastoniensis.*

The Register of Ralph of Shrewsbury, Bishop of Bath and Wells (1329–1363). ed. T. S. Holmes (Somerset Record Soc.). 1896.

Episcopal Register of the Diocese of Winchester. William of Wykeham. ed. T. F. Kirby (Hampshire Record Soc.). 1899.

Episcopal Registers of the Diocese of Exeter. Seven vols. ed. F. C. Hingeston-Randolph.

Episcopal Register of the Diocese of Winchester, John de Sandale and Rigaud de Asserio. ed. F. J. Baigent (Hampshire Record Soc.). 1897.

Episcopal Registers of the Diocese of Worcester. ed. J. Willis Bund (Worcester Hist. Soc.).

Visitations of the Diocese of Norwich, A.D. 1492–1532. ed. A. Jessop, D.D. (Camden Soc.). 1888.

Rites and Customs within the Monastical Church of Durham. ed. J. Raine (Surtees Soc.). 1842.

The Durham Household Book. ed. J. Raine (Surtees Soc.). 1844.

Halmota Prioratus Dunelmensis. ed J. Booth (Surtees Soc.) 1886.

Durham Account Rolls. ed. J. T. Fowler (Surtees Soc.). 3 vols. 1898–1900.

ENGLISH MONASTIC LIFE

CHAPTER I

THE MONASTIC LIFE

THE regular or monastic life was instituted to enable
men to attain with greater security to the higher
ideals of the Christian life proposed to them in the
Gospel. In the early ages of the Church the fervour of
the first converts, strengthened and purified by the fierce
persecutions they had to endure for religion, enabled
them, or a considerable number of them, to reach this
high standard without withdrawing from the world, its
business, or society. The belief that, by the means of
regulated labour and strict discipline of the senses and
appetites, it was in the power of man to perfect his moral
nature and rise to heights in the spiritual order, not otherwise attainable, seems almost inherent in man's nature.
Well-regulated practices founded upon this principle have
bee 1 existent in all forms of religious worship other than
Christian, and they can be recognised no less in the observances of ancient Egypt than in those of the lamas of
modern Thibet. In the pagan world this doctrine seems
to have dictated much of the peculiar teaching of the
Stoics; and among the Jews the Essenes governed their

lives in theory and practice upon this belief. Even among
the early Christians there were some, who by striving to
master their lower nature desired to attain the true end of
human life as the Gospel taught them, the knowledge and
love of God and obedience to His will. These were known
as *Ascetae*, and in one of the earliest Christian documents
they are mentioned as a class of Christians between the
laity and the clergy. They were, however, in the world
though not "of the world," and strove to reach their goal
whilst living their ordinary life by means of perseverance
in prayer, voluntary chastity and poverty, as well as by
the exercise of mortification of all kinds.

Though the practice of seeking seclusion from the world
for the purpose of better carrying out these ideals was
apparently not unknown in the third century, it was not
until after the conversion of Constantine that it can be
said to have become general. The triumph of Christianity
not only freed Christians from the spiritual stimulus of
persecution, but it opened the door of the Christian home
to worldly habits and luxury which were hitherto unknown,
and which made the practice of the higher ideals of the
spirit difficult, if not impossible, in the ordinary surround-
ings of the family life. To use the expression of Walter
Hilton, the baptism of Constantine "brought so many
fish into Peter's net that it was well-nigh rent by the very
multitude." Henceforth it became necessary for Christians, who would satisfy the deeply seated instinct of
human nature for the higher life, to seek it mostly in the
solitudes of the desert, or later within the sheltering walls
of the monastery.

For a right understanding of monastic history and
monastic practices in the West generally, and even in

England, it is necessary to have some idea at least of the main features of Eastern monachism. It has been pointed out by Dom Butler, in his masterly introduction to the *Lausiac History of Palladius*,[1] that monachism developed along two lines in Egypt. The first was the system initiated and directed by St. Anthony, when about the year A.D. 305, after living a life of seclusion for some twenty years, he undertook the direction and organisation of the multitude of monks which the reputation of his sanctity had drawn to his neighbourhood. The second was due to St. Pachomius, who, just about the same time, at the beginning of the fourth century, whilst yet quite a young man, founded his first monastery at Tabennisi in the far south of Egypt.

The first system came to prevail over a great portion of the country by the end of the first century after its foundation by St. Anthony. The monks were mostly hermits in the strict sense of the word. They lived apart and "out of earshot of one another,"[2] coming together at certain times for divine worship. In other districts the religious lived together in threes or fours, who, on all days but the Saturdays and Sundays when all assembled in the great church, were used to sing their songs and hymns together in their common cells. Of this system Palladius, who is the first authority on the matter, says: "They have different practices, each as he is able and as he wishes." Dom Butler thus describes it :—

"There was no rule of life. The Elders exercised an authority, but it was mainly personal. . . . The society appears to have been a sort of spiritual democracy, ruled by the personal influence of the leading ascetics, but there was

---

[1] *Texts and Studies, Cambridge*, vol. vi., No. 1, p. 233.   [2] *Ibid.*

no efficient hold upon individuals to keep them from falling into extravagances. . . . A young man would put himself under the guidance of a senior and obey him in all things ; but the bonds between them were wholly voluntary. The purely eremitical life tended to die out, but what took its place continued to be semi-eremitical."[1]

The second system introduced at the beginning of the fourth century may be described as the cenobitical or conventual type of monachism. Pachomius' monks lived together under a complete system of organisation, not, indeed, as a family under a father, but rather as an army under a discipline of a military character. This form of the monastic life spread with great rapidity, and by the time of its founder's death (c. 345) it counted eight monasteries and several hundred monks.

"The most remarkable feature about it," says Dom Butler, "is that (like Citeaux in a later age) it almost at once assumed the shape of a fully organised congregation or order, with a superior general and a system of visitation and general chapters—in short, all the machinery of centralised government, such as does not appear again in the monastic world until the Cistercians and the Mendicant Orders arose in the twelfth and thirteenth centuries."[2]

The various monasteries under the Rule of St. Pachomius existed as separate houses, each with a head or præpositus and other officials of its own, and organised apparently on the basis of the trades followed by the inmates. The numbers in each house naturally varied ; between thirty and forty on an average living together. At the more solemn services all the members of the various houses came together to the common church ;

[1] *Ibid.*, p. 234.   [2] *Ibid.*, p. 235.

but the lesser offices were celebrated by the houses individually. Under this rule, regular organised work was provided for the monk not merely as a discipline and penitential exercise, as was the case under the Antonian system, but as a part of the life itself. The common ideal of asceticism aimed at was not too high.

" The fundamental idea of St. Pachomius' Rule was," says Dom Butler, "to establish a moderate level of observance which might be obligatory upon all; and to leave it open to each—and to, indeed, encourage each—to go beyond the fixed minimum, according as he was prompted by his strength, his courage, and his zeal."[1]

Hence we find the Pachomian monks eating or fasting as they wished. The tables were laid at midday, and dinner was provided every hour till evening; they ate when they liked, or fasted if they felt called on so to do. Some took a meal only in the evening, others every second or even only every fifth day. The Rule allowed them their full freedom; and any idea of what is now understood by " Common Life "—the living together and doing all things together according to rule—was a feature entirely absent from Egyptian monachism.

One other feature must also be noticed, which would seem to be the direct outcome of the liberty allowed in much of the life, and in particular in the matter of austerities, to the individual monk under the systems both of St. Anthony and St. Pachomius. It is a spirit of strongly marked individualism. Each worked for his personal advance in virtue; each strove to do his utmost in all kinds of ascetical exercises and austerities—in prolonging his fasts, his prayers, his silence. The favourite

[1] *Ibid.*, p. 236.

name used to describe any of the prominent monks was
"great athlete." They loved "to make a record" in
austerities, and to contend with one another in mortifica-
tions ; and they would freely boast of their spiritual
achievements. This being so, penances and austerities
tended to multiply and increase in severity, and this
freedom of the individual in regard to his asceticism
accounts for the very severe and often incongruous morti-
fications undertaken by the monks of Egypt.

Monachism was introduced into Western Europe from
Egypt by way of Rome. The first monks who settled in
the Eternal City were known as "Egyptians," and the
Latin translation of the *Vita Antonii* (*c.* 380) became "the
recognised embodiment of the monastic ideal." It preserved its primitive character in the matter of austerities
during the fourth century, and St. Augustine declares that
he knew of religious bodies of both sexes, which exercised
themselves "in incredible fastings," passing not merely
one day without food or drink, which was "a common
practice," but often going "for three days or more without
anything."

During this same century the monastic life made its
appearance in Gaul. About A.D. 360 St. Martin founded
a religious house at Ligugé, near Poitiers ; and when
about A.D. 371 he became Bishop of Tours, he established
another monastic centre in a retired position near his
episcopal city, which he made his usual residence. The
life led by the monks was a simple reproduction of that of
St. Anthony's followers. Cassian, the great organiser of
monachism in Gaul, also followed closely the primitive
Egyptian ideals both in theory and practice, whilst what
is known of the early history of the monastery at Lerins,

founded by Honoratus, to whom Cassian dedicated the second part of his Conferences, points to the fact that here too the eremitical life was regarded as the monastic ideal. On the whole, therefore, it may be said that the available evidence "amply justifies the statement that Gallic monachism during the fifth and sixth centuries was thoroughly Egyptian in both theory and practice."[1]

It is now possible to understand the position of St. Benedict in regard to monasticism. The great Patriarch of Western monks was born probably about A.D. 480, and it was during that century that the knowledge of Eastern rules of regular life was increased greatly in Italy by the translation of an abridgment of Saint Basil's code into Latin by Rufinus. St. Basil had introduced for his monks in Cappadocia and the neighbouring provinces certain modifications of the Egyptian monastic observances. There was more common life for his religious : they lived together and ate together ; and not when they pleased, but when the superior ordained. They prayed always in common, and generally depended upon the will of a common superior. About the same time St. Jerome translated the Rule of Pachomius, and the influence of these two Rules upon the monastic life of Italy at the period when St. Benedict comes upon the scene is manifest. Whatever changes had been introduced into the local observances, and however varied were the practices of individual monasteries, it is at least certain that at this period the monastic system in use in Italy was founded upon and drew its chief inspirations from Egyptian models. What was wholly successful in the East proved, however, unsuitable to Western imitators, and, owing to the climatic

[1] *Ibid.*, p. 247.

conditions, impossible. This much seems certain even from the mention made of the Gyrovagi and Sarabites by St. Benedict, since he describes them as existing kinds of monks whose example was to be avoided. That he had practical knowledge and experience of the Egyptian and the Eastern types of monachism clearly appears in his reference to Cassian and to the Rule of "Our Holy Father Saint Basil," as he calls him, and in the fact that he made his own first essay in the monastic life as a solitary.

When, some time about the beginning of the sixth century, St. Benedict came to write his Rule, with full knowledge and experience both of the systems then in vogue and of the existing need of some reconstitution, it is noteworthy that he did not attempt to restore the lapsed practices of primitive asceticism, or insist upon any very different scheme of regular discipline. On the contrary, "he deliberately turned his back on the austerities that had hitherto been regarded as the chief means for attaining the spiritual end of the monastic life." He calls his Rule "a very little rule for beginners"—*minima inchoationis regula*, and says that though there may be in it some things "a little severe," still he hopes that he will establish "nothing harsh, nothing heavy." The most cursory comparison between this new Rule and those which previously existed will make it abundantly clear that St. Benedict's legislation was conceived in a spirit of moderation in regard to every detail of the monastic life. Common-sense, and the wise consideration of the superior in tempering any possible severity, according to the needs of times, places, and circumstances were, by his desire, to preside over the spiritual growth of those trained in his "school of divine service."

In addition to this St. Benedict broke with the past in another and not less important way, and in one which, if rightly considered and acted upon, more than compensated for the mitigation of corporal austerities introduced into his rule of life. The strong note of individualism characteristic of Egyptian monachism, which gave rise to what Dom Butler calls the "rivalry in ascetical achievement," gave place in St. Benedict's code to the common practices of the community, and to the entire submission of the individual will, even in matters of personal austerity and mortification, to the judgment of the superior.

"This two-fold break with the past, in the elimination of austerity and in the sinking of the individual in the community, made St. Benedict's Rule less a development than a revolution in monachism. It may be almost called a new creation; and it was destined to prove, as the subsequent history shows, peculiarly adapted to the new races that were peopling Western Europe."[1]

We are now in a position to turn to England. When, less than half a century after St. Benedict's death, St. Augustine and his fellow monks in A.D. 597 first brought this Rule of Life to our country, a system of monasticism had been long established in the land. It was Celtic in its immediate origin; but whether it had been imported originally from Egypt or the East generally, or whether, as some recent scholars have thought, it was a natural and spontaneous growth, is extremely doubtful. The method of life pursued by the Celtic monks and the austerities practised by them bear a singular resemblance to the main features of Egyptian monachism; so close, indeed, is this likeness that it is hard to believe there could have been no connection between them. One

[1] *Ibid.*, p. 256.

characteristic feature of Celtic monasticism, on the other
hand, appears to be unique and to divide it off from
every other type.   The Celtic monasteries included
among their officials one, and in some cases many
bishops.   At the head was the abbot, and the episcopal
office was held by members of the house subordinate to
him.   In certain monasteries the number of bishops was
so numerous as to suggest that they must have really
occupied the position of priests at the subordinate
churches.   Thus St. Columba went in A.D. 590 from
Iona to a synod at Drumcheatt, accompanied by as many
as twenty bishops ; and in some of the Irish ecclesiastical
meetings the bishops, as in the case of some of the
African synods, could be counted by hundreds.   This
Celtic system appears to be without parallel in other parts
of the Christian Church, and scholars have suggested
that it was a purely indigenous growth.   One writer, Mr.
Willis Bund, is of the opinion that the origin was tribal
and that the first "monasteries" were mere settlements
of Christians—clergy and laity, men, women, and children—who for the sake of protection lived together.   It
was at some subsequent date that a division was made
between the male and female portions of the settlement,
and later still the eremitical idea was grafted on the
already existing system.   If the tribal settlement was the
origin of the Celtic monastery, it affords some explanation
of the position occupied by the bishops as subjects of the
abbots.   The latter were in the first instance the chiefs or
governors of the settlements, which would include the
bishop or bishops of the churches comprised in the settlement.   By degrees, according to the theory advanced,
the head received a recognised ecclesiastical position as

abbot, the bishop still continuing to occupy a subordinate position, although there is evidence in the lives of the early Irish saints to show that the holder of the office was certainly treated with special dignity and honour.

The Celtic monastic system was apparently in vogue among the remnant of the ancient British Church in Wales and the West Country on the coming of St. Augustine. Little is known with certainty, but as the British Church was Celtic in origin it may be presumed that the Celtic type of monachism prevailed amongst the Christians in this country after the Saxon conquest. Whether it followed the distinctive practice of Irish monasticism in regard to the position of the abbot and the subject bishops may perhaps be doubted, as this does not appear to have been the practice of the Celtic Church of Gaul, with which there was a close early connection.

It has usually been supposed that the Rule of St. Columbanus represented the normal life of a Celtic monastery, but it has been lately shown that, so far as regards the Irish or Welsh houses, this Rule was never taken as a guide. It had its origin apparently in the fact that the Celtic monks on the Continent were induced, almost in spite of themselves, to adopt a mitigated rule of life by their close contact with Latin monasticism, which was then organising itself on the lines of the Rule of St. Benedict.[1] The Columban Rule was a code of great rigour, and "would, if carried out in its entirety, have made the Celtic monks almost, if not quite,, the most austere of men." Even if it was not actually in use, the Rule of St. Columbanus may safely be taken to indicate the tendencies of Celtic monasticism generally, and the

[1] *The Celtic Church of Wales*, J. J. Willis Bund, p. 166.

impracticable nature of much of the legislation and the hard spirit which characterises it goes far to explain how it came to pass that whenever it was brought face to face with the wider, milder, and more flexible code of St. Benedict, invariably, sooner or later, it gave place to it. In some monasteries, for a time, the two Rules seem to have been combined, or at least to have existed side by side, as at Luxeuil and Bobbio, in Italy, in the seventh century ; but when the abbot of the former monastery was called upon to defend the Celtic rule, at the Synod of Macon in A.D. 625, the Columban code may be said to have ceased to exist anywhere as a separate rule of life.

For the present purpose it will be sufficient to consider English monasticism from the coming of St. Augustine at the close of the sixth century as Benedictine. There was, it is true, a brief period when in Northumberland the Celtic form of regular observance established itself at Lindisfarne and elsewhere. This was due to the direct appeal made by King Edwy of Northumbria to the monks of Iona to come into Northumbria, and continue in the North the work of St. Paulinus, which had been interrupted by the incursions of Penda. Iona, the foundation and home of St. Columba, was a large monastic and missionary centre regulated according to the true type of Celtic monachism under the abbatial superior ; and from Iona came St. Aidan and the other Celtic apostles of the northern parts. In one point, so far as the evidence exists for forming any judgment at all, the new foundation of Lindisfarne differed from the parent house at Iona. At the Northumbrian monastery the bishop was the head and took the place of the abbot, and did not occupy the subordinate position held by the bishops at Iona and its dependencies.

CHAPTER II

THE MATERIAL PARTS OF A MONASTERY

I. THE CHURCH

IN any account of the parts of a monastic establishment the church obviously finds the first place. As St. Benedict laid down the principle that "nothing is to be preferred to the *Opus Dei*," or Divine Service, so in every well-regulated religious establishment the church must of necessity be the very centre of the regular life as being, in fact no less than in word, the "House of God."

In northern climates the church was situated, as a rule, upon the northern side of the monastic buildings. With its high and massive walls it afforded to those who lived there a good shelter from the rough north winds. As the northern cloister usually stretched along the nave wall of the church and terminated at the south transept, the buildings of the choir and presbytery and also the retrochapels, if there were any, gave some protection from the east wind. Sometimes, of course, there were exceptions, caused by the natural lie of the ground or other reason, which did not allow of the church being placed in the ordinary English position. Canterbury itself and Chester are examples of this, the church being in each case on the southern side, where also it is found very frequently

in warm and sunny climates, with the obvious intention
of obtaining from its high walls some shelter from the
excessive heat of the sun.   Convenience, therefore, and
not any very recondite symbolism, may be considered to
have usually dictated the position of "God's house."

Christian churches, especially the great cathedral and
monastic churches, were originally designed and built
upon lines which had much symbolism in them ; the
main body of the church with its transepts was to all, of
course, a representation of Christ upon the cross.   To the
builders of these old sanctuaries the work was one of faith
and love rather than a matter of mere mercenary business.
They designed and worshipped whilst they wrought.   To
them, says one writer, the building "was instinct with
speech, a tree of life planted in paradise ; sending its
roots deep down into the crypt ; rising with stems in
pillar and shaft ; branching out into boughs over the
vaulting ; blossoming in diaper and mural flora ; breaking out into foliage, flower, and fruit, on corbel, capital,
and boss."   It was all real and true to them, for it sprang
out of their strong belief that in the church they had
"the House of God" and "the Gate of heaven," into
which at the moment of the solemn dedication "the King
of Glory" had come to take lasting possession of His home.
For this reason, to those who worshipped in any such
sanctuary the idea that they stood in the "courts of the
Lord" as His chosen ministers was ever present in their
daily service, as with the eyes of their simple faith they
could almost penetrate the veil that hid His majesty from
their sight.   As St. Benedict taught his disciples, mediæval monks believed "without any doubt" that God
was present to them "in a special manner" when they

NORWICH CATHEDRAL, WITH CLOISTERS

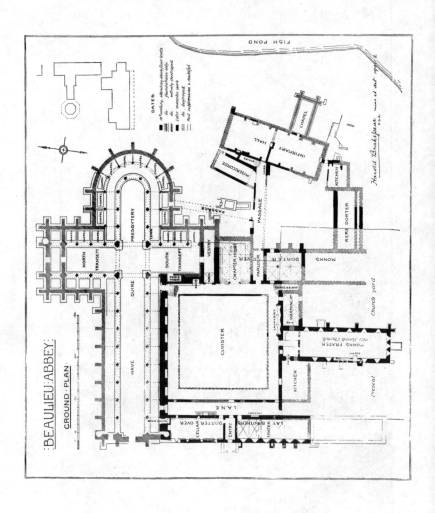

BEAULIEU ABBEY.
GROUND PLAN.

DATES

FISH POND

Harold Brakspear mens et del 1906-7

"assisted at their divine service." "Therefore," says the great master of the regular observance, "let us consider in what manner and with what reverence it behoveth us to be in the sight of God and of the Angels, and so let us sing in choir, that mind and voice may accord together."

So far as the religious life was concerned, the most important part of the church was of course the presbytery with the High Altar and the choir. Here all, or nearly all, public services were performed. The choir frequently, if not generally, stretched beyond the transepts and took up one, if not two, bays of the nave ; being enclosed and divided off from that more public part by the great screen. Other gates of ironwork, across the aisle above the presbytery and in a line with the choir screen, kept the public from the south transept. Privacy was thus secured for the monks, whilst by this arrangement the people had full access to all parts of the sacred building except the choir and the transept nearest to the monastery.

The choir was entered, when the buildings were in the normal English position, from a door in the southern wall of the church at the juncture of the northern and eastern walks of the cloister. At the western end of the same northern cloister there was generally another door into the church reserved for the more solemn processions. The first, however, was the ordinary entrance used by the monks, and passing through it they found themselves in the area reserved for them within the screens which stretched across the choir and aisle.

In the centre of the choir stood the great raised lectern or reading-desk, from which the lessons were chanted, and from which, also, the singing was directed by the cantor and his assistant. The stalls were arranged in two or

more rows slightly raised one above the other. The
superior and the second in command usually occupied the
two stalls on each side of the main entrance furthest from
the altar, the juniors being ranged nearest to the presbytery. This was the common practice except at the time
of the celebration of the Sacrifice of the Holy Mass, or
during such portion of the Office which preceded the
Mass. On these occasions the elders took their places
nearest to the altar, for the purpose of making the
necessary oblations at the Holy Sacrifice. In many
monastic choirs, for this reason, the abbot and prior had
each two places reserved for their special use, one on
either side near the altar, and the others at the entrance
of the choir. Besides the great lectern of the choir there
was likewise a second standing-desk for the reading of
the Gospel at Matins, usually placed near to the steps of
the presbytery. In some cases, apparently, this was
always in its place, but more frequently it was brought
into the choir for the occasion, and removed afterwards by
the servers of the church.

There were in every church, besides the High Altar,
several, and frequently numerous, smaller altars. The
Rites of Durham describes minutely the nine altars arranged along the eastern wall of the church and facing
the shrine of St. Cuthbert.

"They," says the author, "each had their several shrines
and covers of wainscot over-head, in very decent and comely
form, having likewise betwixt every altar a very fair and
large partition of wainscot, all varnished over, with very fine
branches and flowers and other imagery work most finely and
artificially pictured and gilded, containing the several lockers
or ambers for the safe keeping of the vestments and orna-

CANONS IN CHOIR

ments belonging to every altar ; with three or four aumbries in the wall pertaining to some of the said altars."

It would be now quite impossible to describe the rich adornments of an English mediæval monastic church. The *Rites of Durham* give some idea of the wealth of plate, vestments and hangings, and the art treasures, mural paintings and stained windows, with which generations of benefactors had enriched that great northern sanctuary. What we know of other monastic houses shows that Durham was not an exception in any way ; but that almost any one, at any rate of the greater houses, could challenge comparison with it. A foreign traveller almost on the eve of their destruction speaks of the artistic wealth of the monastic churches of England as unrivalled by that of any other religious establishments in the whole of Europe.

2. THE CLOISTERS

In every monastery next in public importance to the church came the cloisters. The very name has become a synonym for the monastery itself. The four walks of the cloister formed the dwelling-place of the community. With the progress of time there came into existence certain private rooms in which the officials transacted their business, and later still the use of private cells or cubicles became common, but these were the exception ; and, at any rate, in England till the dissolution of the religious houses, the common life of the cloister was in full vigour.

In the normal position of the church on the north side of the monastic buildings, the north cloister with its openings looking south was the warmest of the four divisions. Here, in the first place, next the door of the church, was the prior's seat, and the rest of the seniors in their order sat after him, not necessarily in order of seniority, but in the positions that best suited their work.

THE CLOISTERS, WORCESTER

The abbot's place, "since his dignity demands," as the Westminster Custumal puts it, was somewhat apart from the rest. He had his fixed seat at the end of the eastern cloister nearest to the church door. In the same cloister, but more towards the other, or southern end, the novice-master taught his novices, and the walk immediately opposite, namely, the western side of the cloister, was devoted to the junior monks, who were, as the Rule of St. Benedict says, *"adhuc in custodia"*: still under stricter discipline. The southern walk, which would have been in ordinary circumstances the sunless, cold side of the quadrangle, was not usually occupied in the daily life of the community. This was the common position for the refectory, with the lavatory close at hand, and the aumbries or cupboards for the towels, etc. It was here also that the door from the outside world into the monastic precincts was usually to be found. At Durham, for example, we are told that—

"there was on the south side of the cloister door, a stool, or seat with four feet, and a back of wood joined to the said stool, which was made fast in the wall for the porter to sit on, which did keep the cloister door. And before the said stool it was boarded in under foot, for warmness. And he that was the last porter there was called Edward Pattinson."

The same account describes the cupboards near to the refectory door in which the monks kept their towels—

"All the forepart of the aumbry was thorough carved work, to give air to the towels." There were "three doors in the forepart of either aumbry and a lock on every door, and every monk had a key for the said aumbries, wherein did hang in every one clean towels for the monks to dry their hands on, when they washed and went to dinner."

We who see the cold damp-stained cloisters of the old monastic buildings as they are to-day, as at Westminster for example, may well feel a difficulty in realising what they were in the time of their glory. Day after day for centuries the cloister was the centre of the activity of the religious establishment. The quadrangle was the place where the monks lived and studied and wrote. In the three sides—the northern, eastern, and western walks—were transacted the chief business of the house, other than what was merely external. Here the older monks laboured at the tasks appointed them by obedience, or discussed questions relating to ecclesiastical learning or regular observance, or at permitted times joined in re-creative conversation. Here, too, in the parts set aside for the purpose, the younger members toiled at their studies under the eye of their teacher, learnt the monastic observance from the lips of the novice-master, or practised the chants and melodies of the Divine Office with the cantor or his assistant. How the work was done in the winter time, even supposing that the great windows look-ing out on to the cloister-garth were glazed or closed with wooden shutters, must ever remain a mystery. In some places, it is true, certain screenwork divisions appear to have been devised, so as to afford some shelter and pro-tection to the elder members and scribes of the monastery from the sharper draughts inevitable in an open cloister. The account given in the *Rites of Durham* on this point is worth quoting at length :—

"In the cloister," says the writer—and he is speaking of the northern walk, set apart for the seniors—"in the cloister there were carrels finely wainscotted and very close, all but the fore-part, which had carved work to give light in at their carrel doors. And in every carrel was a desk to lie their books on, and the carrel was no greater than from one stanchell (centre-bar) of the window to another. And over against the carrels, against the church wall, did stand certain great aumbries of wainscot all full of books, with great store of ancient manu-scripts to help them in their study." In these cupboards, "did lie as well the old ancient written Doctors of the Church as

THE CLOISTERS, GLOUCESTER, SHEWING CARRELS

other profane authors, with divers other holy men's works, so
that every one did study what doctor pleased him best, having
the Library at all times to go and study in besides these carrels."

In speaking of the novices the same writer tells us that—

"over against the said treasury door was a fair seat of wainscot, where the novices were taught. And the master of the
novices had a pretty seat of wainscot adjoining to the south
side of the treasury door, over against the seat where the
novices sat; and there he taught the novices both forenoon
and afternoon. No strangers or other persons were suffered
to molest, or trouble the said novices, or monks in their carrels
while they were at their books within the cloister. For to this
purpose there was a porter appointed to keep the cloister
door."

In other monasteries, such for example as Westminster
and St. Augustine's, Canterbury, these enclosed wooden
sitting-places seem to have been very few in number, and
allowed only to those officers of the house who had much
business to transact for the common good. At Durham,
however, we are told that "every one of the old monks"
had his own special seat, and in each window of the
south cloister there were set "three of these pews or
carrels."

3. THE REFECTORY

The refectory, sometimes called the *fratry* or *fraterhouse*, was the common hall for all conventual meals.
Its situation in the plan of a monastic establishment was
almost always as far removed from the church as possible,
that is, it was on the opposite side of the cloister quadrangle and, according to the usual plan, in the southern
walk of the cloister. The reason for this arrangement is
obvious. It was to secure that the church and its pre-

cincts might be kept as free as possible from the annoyance caused by the noise and smells necessarily connected with the preparation and consumption of the meals.

As a rule, the walls of the hall would no doubt have been wainscotted. At one end, probably, great presses would have been placed to receive the plate and linen, with the salt-cellars, cups, and other ordinary requirements for the common meals. The floor of a monastic refectory was spread with hay or rushes, which covering was changed three or four times in the year; and the tables were ranged in single rows lengthways, with the benches for the monks upon the inside, where they sat with their backs to the panelled walls. At the east end, under some sacred figure, or painting of the crucifix, or of our Lord in glory, called the *Majestas,* was the *mensa major*, or high table for the superior. Above this the *scylla* or small signal-bell was suspended. This was sounded by the president of the meal as a sign that the community might begin their refection, and for the commencement of each of the new courses. The pulpit, or reading-desk, was, as a rule, placed upon the south side of the hall, and below it was usually placed the table for the novices, presided over by their master.

"At which time (of meals)," says the *Rites of Durham,* "the master observed this wholesome order for the continual instructing of their youth in virtue and learning; that is, one of the novices, at the election and appointment of the master, did read some part of the Old and New Testament, in Latin, in dinner-time, having a convenient place at the south end of the high table within a fair glass window, environed with iron, and certain steps of stone with iron rails of the one side to go up into it and to support an iron desk there placed, upon which lay the Holy Bible."

In most cases the kitchens and offices would have been situated near the western end of the refectory, across which a screen pierced with doors would probably have somewhat veiled the serving-hatch, the dresser, and the passages to the butteries, cellars, and pantry.

Besides the great refectory there was frequently a smaller hall, called by various names such as the "misericord," or "oriel" at St. Alban's, the "disport" (*deportus*)

THE REFECTORY, CLEVE ABBEY

at Canterbury, and the "spane" at Peterborough. In this smaller dining-place those who had been bled and others, who by the dispensation of the superior were to have different or better food than that served in the common refectory, came to their meals. At Durham, apparently, the ordinary dining-place was called the "loft," and was at the west end of a larger hall entered from the south alley of the cloister, called the "fraterhouse." In this hall "the great feast of Saint Cuthbert's day in Lent was holden." In an aumbry in the wainscot, on the left-hand of the door, says the author of the *Rites of Durham*, was kept the great mazer, called the *grace-cup*, "which did service to the monks every day, after grace was said, to drink in round the table."

4. THE KITCHEN

Near to the refectory was, of course, the conventual kitchen. At Canterbury this kitchen was a square of some forty-five feet; at Durham it was somewhat smaller; and at Glastonbury, Worcester, and Chester the hall was some thirty-five feet square. A small courtyard with the usual offices adjoined it; and this sometimes, as at Westminster and Chester, had a tower and a larder on the western side. According to the Cluniac constitutions there were to be two kitchens: the one served in weekly turns by the brethren, the other in which a good deal of the food was prepared by paid servants. The first was chiefly used for the preparation of the soup or pottage, which formed the foundation of the monastic dinner. The furniture of this kitchen is minutely described in the Custumals: there were to be three *caldaria* or cauldrons for boiling water: one for cooking the beans, a second for the vegetables, and a third, with an iron tripod to stand it upon, to furnish hot water for washing plates, dishes, cloths, etc. Secondly, there were to be four great dishes or vessels: one for half-cooked beans; another and much larger one, into which water was always to be kept running, for washing vegetables; a third for washing up plates and dishes; and a fourth to be reserved for holding a supply of hot water required for the weekly feet-washing, and for the shaving of faces and tonsures, etc.

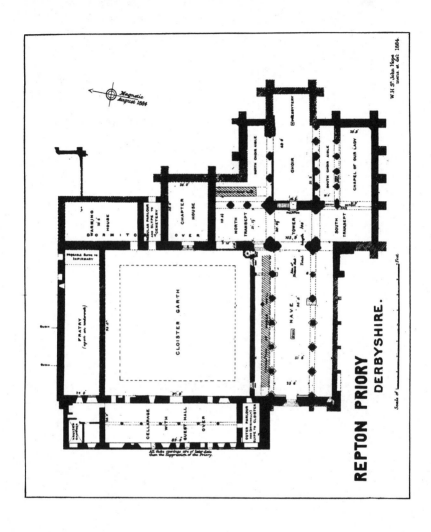

REPTON PRIORY
DERBYSHIRE.

Magnetic
August 1884

W.H. St John Hope
mens. et del. 1884.

Scale of _____ Feet.

All these openings are of later date
than the Suppression of the Priory.

In the same way there were to be always in the kitchen
four spoons : the first for beans, the second for vegetables,
the third (a small one naturally) for seasoning the soup,
and the fourth (an iron one of large size) for shovelling
coals on to the fire. Besides these necessary articles, the
superior was to see that there were to be always at hand
four pairs of sleeves for the use of the servers, that they
might not soil their ordinary habits ; two pairs of gloves
for moving hot vessels, and three napkins for wiping
dishes, etc., which were to be changed every Thursday.
Besides these things there were, of course, to be knives,
and a stone wherewith to sharpen them ; a small dish to
get hot water quickly when required ; a strainer ; an urn
to draw hot water from ; two ladles ; a fan to blow the fire
up when needed, and stands to set the pots upon, etc.

The work of the weekly cooks is also carefully set
out in these constitutions. These officials were four in
number, and, upon the sign for vespers, after making
their prayer, they were to proceed to the kitchen and
obtain the necessary measure of beans for the following
day. They then said their vespers together, and proceeded to wash the beans in three waters, putting them
afterwards into the great boiling-pot with water ready for
the next day. After Lauds on the following day, when
they had received the usual blessing for the servers, after
washing themselves they proceeded to the kitchen and set
the cauldron of beans on the fire. The pot was to be
watched most carefully lest the contents should be burnt.
The skins were to be taken off as they became loosened,
and the beans were to be removed as they were cooked.
When all had been finished, the great cauldron was to be
scoured and cleaned "*usque ad nitidum.*" Directly the

beans had been removed from the fire, another pot was to be put in its place, so that there might always be a good supply of water for washing plates and dishes. These, when cleaned, were to be put into a rack to dry; this rack was to be constantly and thoroughly scoured and kept clean and sweet.

When the cooking of this bean soup had progressed so far, the four cooks were to sit down and say their Divine Office together whilst the hot water was being boiled. A third pot, with vegetables in cold water, was to be then made ready to take its place on the fire, after the Gospel of the morning Mass. When the daily Chapter, at which all had to be present, was finished, the beans were again to be put on the fire and boiled with more water, whilst the vegetables also were set to cook; and when these were done the cooks got the lard and seasoning, and, having melted it, poured it over them. Two of the four weekly cooks now went to the High Mass, the other two remaining behind to watch the dinner and to put more water into the cooking-pots when needed. When the community were ready for their meal, the first cook ladled out the soup into dishes, and the other three carried them to the refectory. In the same way the vegetables were to be served to the community, and when this had been done the four weekly cooks proceeded at once to wash with hot water the dishes and plates which had been used for beans and vegetables, lest by delay any remains should stick to the substance of the plate and be afterwards difficult to remove.

THE CHAPTER HOUSE, WESTMINSTER

5. THE CHAPTER-HOUSE

The chapter-hall, or house, was situated on the eastern side of the cloister, as near to the church as possible. Its shape, usually rectangular, sometimes varied according to circumstances and places. At Worcester and Westminster, for example, it was octagonal; at Canterbury and Chester rectangular; at Durham and Norwich rectangular with an apsidal termination. Seats were arranged along the walls for the monks, sometimes in two rows, one raised above the other, and at the easternmost part of the hall was the chair of the superior, with the crucifix or *Majestas* over it. In the centre a raised desk or pulpit was arranged for the reader of the Martyrology, etc., at that part of Prime which preceded the daily Chapter, and at the evening Collation before Compline.

6. THE DORMITORY

The position of the dormitory among the claustral buildings was apparently not so determined either by rule or custom, as some of the other parts of the religious house. Normally, it may be taken to have communicated with the southern transept, for the purpose of giving easy access to the choir for the night offices. In two cases it stood at right angles to the cloister—at Worcester on the western side, and at Winchester on the east. The *Rites of Durham* says that "on the west side of the cloister was a large house called the Dortor, where the monks and novices lay. Every monk had a little chamber to himself. Each chamber had a window towards the Chapter, and the partition betwixt every chamber was close wainscotted, and in each window was a desk to support their books."

The place itself at Durham, and, indeed, no doubt, usually, was raised upon an undercroft and divided into various chambers and rooms. Amongst these were the treasury at Durham and Westminster, and the passage to the chapter-hall in the latter. The dormitory-hall was originally one open apartment, in which the beds of the monks were placed without screens or dividing hangings. In process of time, however, divisions became introduced such as are described by the author of the *Rites of Durham*, and such as we know existed elsewhere. The cubicles or cells thus formed came to be used for the purpose of study as well as for sleeping, which accounts for the presence of the "desk to support their books" spoken of above. The dormitory also communicated with the latrine or *rere-dortor*, which was lighted, partitioned, and provided with clean hay.

For the purpose of easy access, as for instance at Worcester, the dormitory frequently communicated directly with the church through the south-western turret; at Canterbury a gallery was formed in the west gable-wall of the chapter-house, over the doorway, and continuing over the cloister roof, came out into an upper chapel in the northern part of the transept; at Westminster a bridge crossed the west end of the sacristy, and at St. Alban's and Winchester passages in the wall of the transept gave communication by stairs into the church.

7. THE INFIRMARY

In the disposition of the parts of the religious house no fixed locality was apparently assigned by rule or custom to the infirmary, or house for the sick and aged. Usually it appears to have been to the east of the dor-

mitory ; but there were undoubtedly numerous exceptions.
At Worcester it faced the west front of the church, and
at Durham and Rochester apparently it joined it ; whilst
at Norwich and Gloucester it was in a position parallel to
the refectory. Adjoining the infirmary was sometimes
the *herbarium,* or garden for herbs ; and occasionally, as
at Westminister, Gloucester, and Canterbury, this was
surrounded by little cloisters. The main hall, or large
room, of the infirmary often included a chapel at the
easternmost point, where the sick could say their Hours
and other Offices when able to do so, and where the
infirmarian could say Mass· for those under his charge.
According to the constitutions of all religious bodies
the care of the sick was enjoined upon the superior
of every religious house as one of his most important
duties.

"Before all things, and above all things," says St. Benedict in
his Rule, "special care must be taken of the sick, so that they
be served in very deed, as Christ Himself, for He saith : ' I was
sick, and ye visited me ' ; and, ' What ye did to one of these
My least Brethren, ye did to Me.' "

On this principle not only was a special official appointed in every monastery, whose first duty it was to
look to the care and comfort of those who were infirm and
sick, but the officials of the house generally were charged
with seeing that they were supplied with what was needed
for their comfort and cure. Above all, says the great
legislator, "let the abbot take special care they be not
neglected," that they have what they require at the hands
of the cellarer, and that the attendants do not neglect
them, "because," he adds, "whatever is done amiss by
his disciples is imputed to him." For this reason, at stated

times, as for instance immediately after the midday meal,
the superior, who had presided in the common refectory,
was charged to visit the sick brethren in the infirmary, in
order to be sure that they had been served properly and
in no ways neglected.

8. THE GUEST-HOUSE

The guest-house (*hostellary, hostry,* etc.) was a necessary
part of every great religious house. It was presided over
by a senior monk, whose duty it was to keep the hall and
chambers ready for the reception of guests, and to be ever
prepared to receive those who came to ask for hospitality.
Naturally the guest-house was situated where it would be
least likely to interfere with the privacy of the monastery.
The guest-place at Canterbury was of great size, measur-
ing forty feet broad by a hundred and fifty feet long.
The main building was a big hall, resembling a church
with columns, having on each side bedrooms or cubicles
leading out of it. In the thirteenth century John de
Hertford, abbot of St. Alban's, built a noble hall for the
use of guests frequenting his abbey, with an inner parlour
having a fireplace in it, and many chambers arranged for
the use of various kinds of guests. It had also a *pro-aula*,
or reception-room, in which the guest-master first received
the pilgrim or traveller, before conducting him to the
church, or arranging for a reception corresponding to his
rank and position.

In the greater monastic establishments there were frequently several places for the reception of guests. The
abbot, or superior, had rooms to accommodate distinguished or honoured guests and benefactors of the
establishment. The cellarer's department, too, frequently
had to entertain merchants and others who came upon

business of the house : a third shelter was provided near the gate of the monastery for the poorer folk, and a fourth for the monks of other religious houses, who had their meals in the common refectory, and joined in many of the exercises of the community.

The *Rites of Durham* thus describes the guest-house which the author remembered in the great cathedral monastery of the North :—

"There was a famous house of hospitality, called the Guest Hall, within the Abbey garth of Durham, on the west side, towards the water, the Terrar of the house being master thereof, as one appointed to give entertainment to all states, both noble, gentle, and whatsoever degree that came thither as strangers, their entertainment not being inferior to any place in England, both for the goodness of their diet, the sweet and dainty furniture of their lodgings, and generally all things necessary for travellers. And, withal, this entertainment continuing, (the monks) not willing or commanding any man to depart, upon his honest and good behaviour. This hall is a goodly, brave place, much like unto the body of a church, with very fair pillars supporting it on either side, and in the midst of the hall a most large range for the fire. The chambers and lodgings belonging to it were sweetly kept and so richly furnished that they were not unpleasant to lie in, especially one chamber called the 'king's chamber,' deserving that name, in that the king himself might very well have lain in it, for the princely linen thereof. . . . The prior (whose hospitality was such as that there needed no guest-hall, but that they (the Convent) were desirous to abound in all liberal and free almsgiving) did keep a most honourable house and very noble entertainment, being attended upon both with gentlemen and yeomen, of the best in the country, as the honourable service of his house deserved no less. The benevolence thereof, with the relief and alms of the whole Convent, was always open and free, not only to the poor of the city of Durham, but to all the poor people of the country besides."

In most monastic statutes, the time during which a
visitor was to be allowed free hospitality was not un-
limited, as, according to the recollection of the author of
the *Rites of Durham,* appears to have been the case in
that monastery. The usual period was apparently two
days and nights, and in ordinary cases after dinner on the
third day the guest was expected to take his departure.
If for any reason a visitor desired to prolong his stay,
permission had to be obtained from the superior by the
guest-master. Unless prevented by sickness, after that
time the guest had to rise for Matins, and otherwise
follow the exercises of the community. With the Franciscans, a visitor who asked for hospitality from the
convent beyond three days, had to beg pardon in the
conventual chapter before he departed for his excessive
demand upon the hospitality of the house.

9. THE PARLOUR OR LOCUTORIUM

In most Custumals of monastic observance mention is
made of a *Parlour*, and in some of more than one such
place. Here the monks could be sent for by the superiors
to discuss necessary matters of business, when strict silence
had to be observed in the cloister itself. Here, too—it
may be in the same, or in another such room—visitors
could converse with the religious they had come to see.
Sometimes, apparently, among the Cistercians, the place
where the monastic schools were held, other than the
cloister, was called the *auditorium* or *locutorium*. At
Durham, the room called the parlour stood between the
chapter-house and the church door, and is described as
"a place for merchants to utter their wares." It apparently
had a door which gave access to the monastic cemetery,

as the religious were directed to pass through it for the funeral of any of the brethren. During the times of silence, when anything had to be settled without unnecessary delay, the officials could summon any of the religious to the parlour for the purpose ; but they were warned not to make any long stay, and to take great care that no sound of their voices disturbed the quiet of the cloister.

10. THE ALMONRY

No religious house was complete without a place where the poor could come and beg alms in the name of Christ. The convent doles of food and clothing were administered by one of the senior monks, who, by his office of almoner, had to interview the crowds of poor who daily flocked to the gate in search of relief. His charity was to be wider than his means ; and where he could not satisfy the actual needs of all, he was at least to manifest his Christian sympathy for their sufferings. The house or room, from which the monastic relief was given, frequently stood near the church, as showing the necessary connection between charity and religion. In most of the almonries, at any rate in those of the larger monasteries, there was a free school for poor boys. It was in these that most of the students who were presented for Ordination by the religious houses in such number during the fourteenth and fifteenth centuries, (as is shown by the episcopal registers of the English dioceses), were prepared to exercise their sacred ministry in the ranks of the parochial clergy.

11. THE COMMON-ROOM OR CALEFACTORY

The common-room, sometimes called the calefactory or warming-place, was a room to which the religious resorted, especially in winter, for the purpose of warming themselves at the common fire, which was lighted on the feast of All Saints, November 1st, and kept burning daily until Easter. On certain occasions, such as Christmas night, when the Offices in the church were specially long, the caretaker was warned to be particularly careful to have a bright fire burning for the community to go to when they came out of the choir. The common-room was also used at times for the purpose of recreation.

"On the right hand, as you go out of the cloisters into the infirmary," says the *Rites of Durham*, "was the Common House and a master thereof. This house was intended to this end, to have a fire kept in it all the winter, for the monks to come and warm them at, being allowed no fire but that only, except the masters and officers of the house, who had their several fires. There was belonging to the Common House a garden and a bowling alley, on the back-side of the said house, towards the water, for the novices sometimes to recreate themselves, when they had leave of their master; he standing by to see their good order.

"Also, within this house did the master thereof keep his *O Sapientia* once a year—namely, between Martinmas and Christmas—a solemn banquet that the prior and convent did use at that time of the year only, when their banquet was of figs and raisins, ale and cakes; and thereof no superfluity or excess, but a scholastical and moderate congratulation amongst themselves."

12. THE LIBRARY

"A monastery without a library is like a castle without an armoury" was an old monastic saying. At first, and in most places in England probably to the end, there was no special hall, room, or place which was set aside for the reception of the books belonging to the monastery. In the church and in the cloister there were generally cup-

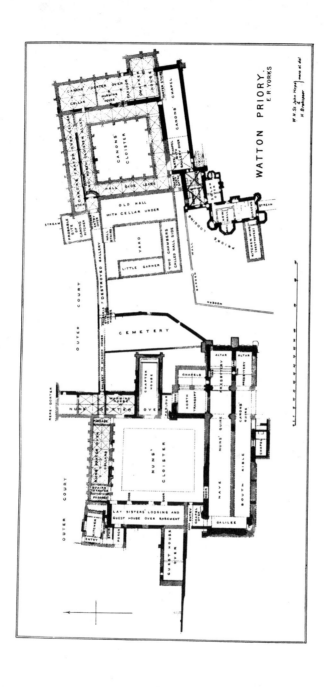

WATTON PRIORY.
E R YORKS

W H St John Hope } mens et del
H Brakspear

boards to hold the manuscripts in constant use. It was not till the later middle ages that the practice of gathering together the books of an establishment into one place or room became at all common. At Durham, about 1446, Prior Wessington made a *library*, "well replenished with old written doctors and other Histories and Ecclesiastical writers," to which henceforth the monks could always repair to study in, "besides their carrels" in the cloister. So, too, at St. Alban's, Michael de Mentmore, who was abbot from 1335 to 1349, besides enriching the presses in the cloister with books, made a collection of special volumes in what he called his study. This collection grew; but it was not till 1452 that Abbot Whethamstede finally completed the *library*, which had long been projected. About the same time, at Canterbury, Prior Thomas Goldstone finished a library there, which was enriched by the celebrated Prior William Sellyng with many precious classical manuscripts brought back from Italy. In the same way many other religious houses in the fifteenth century erected, or set apart, special places for their collections of books, whilst still retaining the great cloister presses for those volumes which were in daily and constant use.

In addition to the above-named parts of every religious house, there were in most monasteries, and especially in the larger ones, a great number of offices. The officials, or obedientiaries, for instance, had their chequer or *scaccarium*, where the accounts of the various estates assigned to the support of the burdens of their special offices were rendered and checked. There were also the usual workrooms for tailors, shoemakers, etc., under the management of the chamberlain, or camerarius, and for the servants of the church, under the sacrist and his assistant. The above, however, will be sufficient to give some general idea of the material parts which composed the ordinary English religious house. More, however, will be learnt of them, and especially of their use, when the work of the officials, and the daily life led by the monks in the cloister is discussed.

CHAPTER III

THE MONASTERY AND ITS RULERS

THE monastic rule, at least after the days of St. Benedict, was eminently social. Both in theory and in practice the regular observance of the great abbeys and other religious houses was based upon the principle of common life. Monks and other religious were not solitaries or hermits, but they lived and worked and prayed together in an association as close as it is possible to conceive. The community or corporation was the sole entity; individual interests were merged in that of the general body, and the life of an individual member was in reality merely an item in the common life of the convent as a whole. This is practically true in all forms of regular life, without regard to any variety of observance or rule. Some regulations for English pre-Reformation houses lay great stress upon this great principle of monastic life. To emphasise it, they require from all outward signs of respect for the community as a whole, and especially at such times and on such occasions as the convent was gathered together in its corporate capacity. Should the religious, for example, be passing in procession, either through the cloister or elsewhere, anyone meeting them, even were it the superior himself, was bound to turn aside to avoid them altogether, or to draw on one side and salute them with a bow as they went by. When they were gathered together for any public duty no noise of any kind likely to reach their ears was to be permitted. When the religious were sitting in the cloister, strangers in the parlour were to be warned to speak in low tones, and above all to avoid laughter which might penetrate to them in their seclusion. If the superior was prevented from taking his meals in the common refectory, he was charged to acquaint the next in office beforehand, so that the community might not be kept waiting by expecting him. So, too, the servers, who remained behind in the refectory after meals, were to show their respect for the community by bowing towards its members, as they passed in procession before them. For the same reason officials, like the cellarer, the kitchener, and the refectorian were bound to see that all was ready in their various departments, so that the convent should never be kept waiting for a meal. In these and numberless other ways monastic regulations emphasised the respect that must be paid to the community as a corporate whole.

As the end and object of all forms of religious life was one and the same, the general tenor of that life was practically identical in all religious houses. The main features of the observances were the same, not merely in houses of the same Order, which naturally would be the case, but in every religious establishment irrespective of rule. A comparison of the various Custumals or Consuetudinaries which set forth the details of the religious life in the English houses of various Orders, will show that there is sometimes actual verbal agreement in these directions, even in the case of bodies so different as the Benedictines

and the Cistercians on the one hand, and the Premonstratensians or White Canons and the Canons Regular on the
other. Moreover, where no actual verbal agreement can
now be detected, the rules of life are more than similar
even in minute points of observance. This is, of course,
precisely what anyone possessing a knowledge of the
meaning and object of regular life, especially when the
number of the community was considerable, would be led
to expect. And, it is this fact which makes it possible to
describe the life led in an English pre-Reformation
monastery in such a way as to present a fairly correct
picture of the life, whether in a Benedictine or Cistercian
abbey, or in a house of Canons Regular, or, with certain
allowances, in a Franciscan or Dominican friary.

This is true also in respect to convents of women. The
life led by these ladies who had dedicated themselves to
God in the cloister, was for practical purposes the same as
that lived by the monks, with a few necessary exceptions.
Its end, and the means by which that end was sought to
be obtained, were the same. The abbess, like the abbot,
had jurisdiction over the lives of her subjects, and like
him she bore a crosier as a symbol of her office and of
her rank. She took tithes from churches impropriated
to her house, presented the secular vicars to serve the
parochial churches, and had all the privileges of a land-
lord over the temporal estates attached to her abbey. The
abbess of Shaftesbury, for instance, at one time, found
seven knights' fees for the king's service and held her
own manor courts. Wilton, Barking, and Nunnaminster
as well as Shaftesbury "held of the king by an entire
barony," and by the right of this tenure had, for a period,
the privilege of being summoned to Parliament. As

regards the interior arrangements of the house, a convent followed very closely that of a monastery, and practically what is said of the officials and life of the latter is true also of the former.

In order to understand this regular life the inquirer must know something of the offices and position of the various superiors and officials, and must understand the parts, and the disposition of the various parts, of the material buildings in which that life was led. Moreover, he must realise the divisions of the day, and the meaning of the regulations, which were intended to control the day's work in general, and in a special manner, the ecclesiastical side of it, which occupied so considerable a portion of every conventual day. After the description of the main portion of the monastic buildings given in the last chapter, the reader's attention is now directed to the officials of the monastery and their duties.

In most Benedictine and Cistercian houses the superior was an abbot. By the constitution of St. Norbert for his White canons, in Premonstratensian establishments as in the larger houses of Augustinian, or Black, canons, the head also received the title and dignity of abbot. In English Benedictine monasteries which were attached to cathedral churches, such as Canterbury, Winchester, Durham and elsewhere, the superiors, although hardly inferior in position and dignity to the heads of the great abbeys, were priors. This constitution of cathedrals with monastic chapters was practically peculiar to this country. It had grown up with the life of the church from the days of its first founders, the monastic followers of St. Augustine. No fewer than nine of the old cathedral foundations were Benedictine, whilst one, Carlisle, belonged to the Canons Regular. Chester, Gloucester, and Peterborough, made into cathedrals by Henry VIII., were previously Benedictine abbeys.

In the case of these cathedral monasteries the bishop was in many ways regarded as holding the place of the abbot. He was frequently addressed as such, and in some instances at least he exercised a certain limited jurisdiction over the convent and claimed to appoint some of the officials, notably those who had most to do with his cathedral church, like the sacrist and the precentor. Such claims, however, when made were often successfully resisted, like the further claim to appoint the superior, put forward at times by a bishop with a monastic chapter. So far, then, as the practical management of the cathedral monasteries is concerned, the priors ruled with an authority equal to that of an abbot, and whatever legislation applies to the latter would apply equally to the former. The same may be said of the superior of those houses of Canons Regular, and other bodies, where the chief official was a prior. This will only partially be true in the case of the heads of dependent monasteries, such as Tynemouth, which was a cell of St. Alban's Abbey, and whose superior, although a prior ruling the house with full jurisdiction, was nominated by the abbot of the mother house, and held office not for life, but at his will and pleasure. The same may be said of the priors of Dominican houses, and of the guardians of Franciscan friaries, whose office was temporary ; and of the heads of alien monasteries, who were dependent to a greater or less extent upon their foreign superiors.

Roughly speaking, then, the office of superior was the same in all religious houses ; and if proper allowance be made for different circumstances, and for the especial ecclesiastical position necessarily secured by the abbatial dignity, any description of the duties and functions of an abbot in one of the great English houses will be found to apply to other religious superiors under whatever name they may be designated.

<h2 align="center">I. THE ABBOT</h2>

The title abbot (*abbas*) means father, and was used from the earliest times as a title appropriate to designate the superior of a religious house, as expressing the paternal qualities which should characterise his rule. St. Benedict says that "an abbot who is worthy to have charge of a monastery ought always to remember by what title he is called," and that "in the monastery he is considered to represent the person of Christ, seeing that he is called by His name." The monastic system established by St. Benedict was based entirely upon the supremacy of the abbot. Though the Rule gives directions as to an abbot's government, and furnishes him with principles upon which to act, and binds him to carry out certain prescriptions as to consultation with others in difficult matters, etc., the subject is told to obey without question or hesitation the decision of the superior. It is of course needless to say that this obedience did not extend to the commission of evil, even were any such a command ever imposed. Upon this principle of implicit obedience to authority depended the power and success of the monastic system, and in acknowledging the supreme jurisdiction of the superior, whether abbot or prior, all pre-Reformation religious Orders agreed.

It is useful at the outset to understand how the abbot

THOMAS, ABBOT OF ST. ALBAN'S

was chosen.   According to the monastic rule, he was to be elected by the universal suffrages of his future subjects. In practice these could be made known in one of three ways : (1) By individual voting, *per viam scrutinii;* (2) by the choice of a certain number, or even of one eminent person, to elect in the name of the community, a mode of election known as *electio per compromissum;* and (3) by acclamation, or the uncontradicted declaration of the common wish of the body.   Prior, however, to this formal election there were certain preliminaries to be gone through, which varied according to circumstances.   Very frequently the founder or patron, who was the descendant of the original founder of the religious house, had to be consulted, and his leave obtained for the community to proceed to an election.   In the case of many of the small houses, and, of course, of the greater monasteries, the sovereign was regarded as the founder ; and not unfrequently one condition imposed upon a would-be founder for leave to endow a religious house with lands exempt from the Mortmain Acts, was that, on the death of the superior, the convent should be bound to ask permission from the king to elect his successor.   This requirement of a royal *congé d'élire* was frequently regarded as an infringement of the right of the actual founder, but in practice it appears to have been maintained very generally in the case of houses largely endowed with lands, as a legal check upon them, rendered fitting by the provision of the Mortmain Acts.   Moreover, on the death of the superior, the king took possession of the revenues of his office, which were administered by his officials till, on the confirmation of his successor, the temporalities were restored by a royal writ.   In some cases this

administration pertained only to the portion of the
revenues specially assigned to the office of superior;
in others it appears to have included the entire revenue
of the house, the community having to look to the royal
receiver for the money necessary for their support.

In practice the process of election in one of the greater
monasteries on the death of the abbot was as follows.
In the first place the community assembled together and
made choice of two of their number to carry their common
letter to the king, to announce the death and to beg leave
to proceed to the election of a successor. This *congé
d'élire* was usually granted without much difficulty, the
Crown at the same time appointing the official charged
with guarding the revenues of the house or office during
the vacancy. On the return of the conventual ambassa-
dors to their monastery, the day of election was first
determined, and notice to attend was sent to all the
religious not present who were possessed of what was
called an "active voice," or the right of voting, in the
election. At the appointed time, after a Mass *De Spiritu
Sancto* had been celebrated to beg the help of the Holy
Ghost, the community assembled in the chapter-house
for the process of election. In the first place was read
the constitution of the General Council—*Quia propter*—
in which the conditions of a valid election were set forth,
and all who might be under ecclesiastical censure or
suspension were warned that they not only had no right
to take part in the business, but that their votes might
render the election null and void.

After this formal preparation the community determined
by which of the various legitimate modes of election they
would proceed, either the first or second method being

usually followed. When all this actual process of election had been properly carried out and attested in a formal document, the community accompanied the newly chosen superior in procession to the church, where his election was proclaimed to the people, and the *Te Deum* was sung. The elect was subsequently taken to the prior's lodgings, or elsewhere, to await the result of the subsequent examination as to fitness, and the confirmation. Meantime, if the newly chosen had been the acting superior, he could still continue to administer in his office, but could not hold conventual chapter, or perform other functions peculiar to the superior, until such time as he had been confirmed and installed. If he was not the acting superior, he was required to remain in seclusion, and to take no part in administration until after his installation.

Immediately after the process of election had been duly accomplished and the necessary documents had been drawn up, some of the religious were despatched to the king to obtain his assent to the choice of the community. In the event of this petition being successful, the next step was to obtain confirmation from the ecclesiastical authority, which might either be the bishop of the diocese, or in the case of exempt houses, the pope. In either case the delegates of the community would have to present a long series of documents to prove that the process had been carried out correctly. First came the royal licence to choose; then the formal appointment of the day of election; the result of the election, and the method by which it was effected; the letter signed by the whole community, requesting confirmation of the elect in his office, and sealed by the convent seal; the royal assent to the election, and finally an attested statement of the entire process by which it had been made.

The ecclesiastical authority, upon the reception of these documents, proceeded to an examination of the formal process, and questioned the delegates both as to this, and as to their knowledge of the fitness of the elect for the office. If the result was not satisfactory, the pope or bishop, as the case might be, either cancelled the election or called for the candidate in order to examine him personally as to "doctrine and morals," and as to his capability of ruling a religious house in spirituals and temporals. In the event of the election being quashed, the authority either ordered a new election, or, on the ground of the failure of the community to elect within a definite period a fit and proper superior, appointed someone to the office.

The ecclesiastical confirmation of the election was followed, after as brief an interval as possible, by the installation. In the case of an exempt abbey, a delay of some weeks was inevitable, sometimes until the return of the messengers from the Curia, and thus occasionally the office of superior was necessarily kept a long time vacant. If the superior was to hold the abbatial dignity, before his installation he received the rite of solemn benediction at the hands of the diocesan. This was generally conferred in some other than the monastic church, probably because until after installation, which was subsequent to the abbatial blessing, the new abbot was not supposed legally to have any position in the house he was afterwards to rule.

On the day appointed for the solemn installation, the abbot, walking with bare feet, presented himself at the church door. He was there met by the community and conducted to the High Altar, where, during the singing of the *Te Deum*, he remained prostrate on the ground. At the conclusion of the hymn, he was conducted to his seat, the process of his election and confirmation was read, together with the episcopal or papal mandate, charging all the religious to render him every canonical obedience and service. Then one by one the community came, and, kneeling before their new superior, received from him the kiss of peace. The ceremony was concluded by a solemn blessing bestowed by the newly-installed abbot standing at the High Altar.

The position of the abbot among his community may be summed up in the expression made use of by St. Benedict. He takes Christ's place. All the exterior respect shown to him, which to modern ideas may perhaps seem exaggerated, if not ridiculous, presupposes this idea as existing in the mind of the religious. Just as the great Patriarch of Western monachism ordered that obedience was to be shown to a superior as if it were obedience paid to God himself, and "as if the command had come from God," so reverence and respect was paid him for Christ's love, because as abbot—father—he was the representative of Christ in the midst of the brethren. In all places, for this reason, external honour was to be shown to him. When he passed by, all were to stand and bow towards him. In Chapter and refectory none might sit in their places until he had taken his seat; when he sat in the cloister no one might take the seat next to him, unless he invited him so to do. In his presence conversation was to be moderated and unobtrusive, and no one might break in upon anything that he might be saying with remarks of his own. Familiarity with him was to be avoided, as it would be with our Lord himself; and he, on his part, must be careful not to lower the dignity of his office by too much condescending to those who might be disposed to take advantage of his good nature; nor might he omit to correct any want of respect manifested towards his person. He was in this to consider his office and not his natural inclinations.

The abbot is to occupy the first place in the choir on the right-hand side. During the Office his stall is to be furthest from the altar, the juniors being in front of him, and placed nearest to the sanctuary steps. At Mass, however, the position is changed, the abbot and seniors being closest to the altar, for the purpose of making the oblations at the Holy Sacrifice, and giving the blessings. Whenever a book or other thing is brought to him, the book and his hand are to be kissed. When he gives out an Antiphon, or sings a Responsory, he does so, not as the others perform the duty in the middle of the choir, but at his own stall; and the precentor, coming with the other cantors and his chaplain, stand round about him to help him, if need be, and to show him honour. When the abbot makes a mistake and, according to religious custom, stoops to touch the ground as a penance, those near about him rise and bow to him, as if to prevent him in this act of humiliation. He reads the Gospel at Matins, the Sacred Text and lights being brought to him. He gives the blessings whenever he is present, and at Mass he puts the incense into the thurible for the priest, and blesses it; gives the blessing to the deacon before the Gospel, and kisses the book after it has been sung. The altar, at which he offers the Holy Sacrifice of the Mass, is to be better ornamented than the other altars,

and he is to have more lights to burn upon it during the
Holy Sacrifice. If his name is mentioned in any list of
duties all bow on hearing it read out in the Chapter, and
they do the same when he orders any prayers to be said
or any duty to be performed, even should he not be
present when the order is published.

The whole government of every religious house depended upon the abbot, as described by St. Benedict in
the second chapter of his Rule. He was the mainspring
of the entire machine, and his will in all things was
supreme. His permission was required in all cases. All
the officials, from the prior downward, were appointed by
him, and had their authority from him : they were his
assistants in the government of the house. In the refectory he alone could send for anything, and could allow
anyone to be admitted to the common table. The meal
was not to begin till after the reading had commenced and
he had given the sign to the refectorian to ring the signal-
bell. He might send a dish to any one of the brethren
whom he thought stood in need of it, and the brother on
receiving it was to rise and bow his acknowledgment.

In early times the abbot slept in the common dormitory in the midst of the monks. His duty it was to ring
the bell for the community to rise ; and, indeed, when any
ringing was required for a public duty, he either himself
rang the call, or stood by the side of the ringer till all
were assembled for the duty, and he gave the sign to
cease the signal. To emphasise this part of his duty, in
some Orders, at the abbot's installation the ropes of the
church bells were placed in his hands. It was naturally
the abbot's place to entertain the guests that came to the
monastery, and he frequently had to have his meals

served in his private hall. To these repasts he could, if he wished, invite some of the brethren, giving notice of this to the superior who was to preside in his place in the refectory. On great days in some houses, like St. Mary's, York, after the abbot had been celebrating the Office and Mass in full pontificals, it was the custom for him to send his chaplain to the door of the refectory to ask the sacred ministers who had served him, with the precentor and the organists, to dine with him.

When the abbot had been away from the monastery for more than three days, it was the custom for the brethren to kneel for his blessing and kiss his hand the first time they met him after his return. When business had taken him to the Roman Curia or elsewhere, for any length of time, on his home-coming he was met in solemn procession by the entire community who, having presented him with holy water, were sprinkled, in their turn, by him. They conducted him to the High Altar, chanting the *Te Deum* for his safe return, and received his solemn blessing.

Whilst all reverence was directed to be given to him, he on his part was warned by the Rule and by every declaration, that he must always remember the fact that all this honour was paid not to him personally, but to his office and to Christ who was regarded and reverenced in him.

He, above all others, was to be careful to keep every rule and regulation, since it was certain that where he did not obey himself, he could not look for the obedience of others; and that though he had no one set over him, he was, for that reason, all the more bound to claustral discipline. As superior, he had to stand aloof from the rest, so as not unduly to encourage familiarity in his subjects. He was to show no respect for persons ; not favouring one of his sons more than another, as this could not fail to be fatal to true observance and to religious obedience. "In giving help he should be a father," says one Custumal ; "in giving instruction, he should speak as a teacher." He should be "ever ready to help those who are striving after the higher paths of virtue." He should not hesitate " to stimulate the indifferent to earnestness, and to use every means to rouse the slothful." To him specially the sick are committed, that he may by his visits console and strengthen them to bear the trials God has sent them.

He must, in a word, "study with paternal solicitude the character, actions, and needs of all the brethren ; never forgetting that he will one day have to render to God an account of them all."

2. THE CLAUSTRAL PRIOR

The prior, or second superior of the house, is above all things concerned with the observance and internal discipline of the monastery. He is appointed by the abbot after hearing the opinions of the seniors. Sometimes, as at Westminster and St. Augustine's, Canterbury, he was chosen with great deliberation. In the first place, three names were selected by the precentor and by each of the two divisions of the house, the abbot's side of the choir and the prior's side. These selected names were then considered by a committee of three appointed by the abbot, who reported their opinion to him. Finally, the abbot appointed whom he pleased.

In all places and duties the prior's place is next after the

JOHN STOKE
ABBOT OF ST. ALBANS

PRIOR REYMUND
ST. ALBANS

abbot. He is to be honoured by all; when he enters the Chapter or comes to the Collation, all rise and continue standing until he has sat down; when the community are incensed in choir, he is to have that mark of respect paid to him, next after the priest who is vested in a cope. "The prior," says one Custumal, "ought to be humble, kindly in disposition, a living example of religious observance, excellent in everything, doing all things like the rest of the brethren. He should be first among the first, and last with the last."

The reader will perhaps here recall Jocelin of Brakelond's analysis of the reasons which prompted the choice of Prior Herbert at Bury, in the closing years of Abbot Sampson's rule :—

"The chapter being over, I being guest-master," says Jocelin, "sat in the porch of the Guest-hall, stupefied, and revolving in my mind the things I had heard and seen; and I began to consider closely for what cause and for what particular merits such a man should be advanced to so high a dignity. And I began to reflect that the man is of comely stature and of (good) personal appearance; a man of handsome face and amiable aspect; always in good temper; of a smiling countenance, be it early or late; kind to all; a man calm in his bearing and grave in his demeanour; pleasant in speech, possessing a sweet voice in chanting and impressive in reading; young, brave, of a healthy body, and always in readiness to undergo travail for the need of the church; skilful in conforming himself to every circumstance of place and time, either with ecclesiastics or laymen; liberal and social, and gentle in reproof; not spiteful, not suspicious, not covetous, not drawling, not slothful; sober and fluent of tongue in the French idiom, as being a Norman by birth; a man of moderate capacity whom if too much learning should make (one) mad, might be said to be a perfectly accomplished man."

The prior's main duty, besides taking the abbot's place whenever he was absent, and generally looking after the government of the monastery, was to see to the discipline of the house and to maintain the general excellence of observance. This he was to do as much by example as by precept, and he was to make himself loved rather than feared. He was told to endeavour to occupy in a community, what is called in one rule, "the position of the mother of the family." He stood, as it were, between the father and his sons; and so long as discipline was not harmed, he should not hesitate to be prodigal in kindness and ready to open his heart in friendly intercourse with all who sought his help. "Let him remember," says one rule, "that the peace of the house depends on him."

In monasteries where no other disposition was made, after the triple prayer before the night Office had been said, it was the prior's duty to take a lighted lantern and go first to the dormitory to see that all were up and that none had overslept themselves, and then to perambulate the cloister and the chapels to see that no one had fallen asleep there, and that the altars were ready for Mass. After Compline at night, having given the sign for leaving the church, he himself went out first, and after receiving the holy water at the door from the hebdomadarian, or priest appointed for the weekly duty, stood aside whilst the community filed out into the cloister, and each in their turn, after being sprinkled with the holy water, put on his hood and passed up to the dormitory. When all were gone, the prior was directed to go round the house and cloister, with a lantern if necessary, to see that all the doors were fastened, that the lights were safe for the night, and that all was well and quiet "in the time of the great silence." He then took the keys of the outer doors with him to the dormitory, and sitting by his bed, waited to retire until all the rest were lying down.

The prior had his regular week for acting as hebdomadarian priest like the rest; but he did not take his turn with the others in reading in the refectory or serving at meals. When he passed along the cloister the brethren were not bound to rise and bow as they had to do to the abbot; but should he wish to sit down anywhere, those near the place were to rise and remain standing until he was seated. As his office was chiefly concerned with the regular discipline, all permissions to be absent from conventual duties, even if granted by the abbot himself, were to be notified to him.

A true prior, it is frequently remarked in the old Custumals, is a blessing to a religious house, and his presence is like that of an angel of peace.

"He should show," says one English writer, "an example of the patience of holy Job and of the devotion of David. To his subjects he should manifest the religious observance of our holy fathers, so that he, who is first in name, may be ever first in the virtues of patience, devotion, and, indeed, in all the virtues of the religious life."

3. THE SUB-PRIOR

The sub-prior was the prior's assistant in the duties of his office. Like the rest of the monastic officials, he was appointed by the abbot with the advice of the prior. Ordinarily this third superior did not take any special position in the community. He usually occupied the

place of his profession, except when he was called upon
to preside over the religious exercises instead of the
abbot or prior.   All the duties which had to be performed by the prior, in his absence devolved upon the
sub-prior.

Besides this, the sub-prior was often charged with
specially looking to certain matters of discipline, and
with giving certain permissions, even when the prior was
present.   All permissions given and arrangements made
by the sub-prior, during the absence of either the abbot
or prior, were to be reported to them on their return to
claustral duties.

"The sub-prior should be remarkable for his holiness," says
one English writer, "his charity should be overflowing, his
sympathy should be abundant.   He must be careful to ex-
tirpate evil tendencies, to be unwearied in his duties, and
tender to those in trouble.   In a word, he should set before all
the example of our Lord."

Besides the prior and sub-prior, in most large monasteries
there were third and fourth priors, called also *circas* or
circatores claustri, that is, watchers over the discipline of
the cloister.   Their duty chiefly consisted in going round
about the house and specially the cloister in times of
silence, to see that there was nothing amiss or contrary
to the usual observance.   They had no authority to
correct, but they kept their eyes and ears open in order
to report.   They did not go about necessarily together,
but according as special duties might have been assigned
to them by the abbot.   When, in the course of their
official investigations, they found any of the brethren
engaged in conversation or work out of the ordinary

course, it was the duty of one of those so engaged to inform the official of the permission they had received. The usual time for the exercise of their functions was after Compline, before Matins, after dinner and supper, and whenever the community were gathered together in the cloister.

CHAPTER IV

THE OBEDIENTIARIES

THE officials of a monastery were frequently known by the name of *obedientiaries*. Sometimes under this name were included even the prior and sub-prior, as they also were appointed by the abbot, and were, of course, equally with the others in subjection and obedience to him. But as usually understood, by the word obedientiaries was signified the other officials, and not the prior and sub-prior, who assisted in the general government of the monastery. Various duties were assigned to all obedientiaries, and they possessed extensive powers in their own spheres. Very frequently in mediæval times they had the full management of the property assigned to the special support of the burdens of their offices. Their number naturally varied considerably in different monasteries; but here it may be well to describe briefly the duties of each of the ordinary officials, as they are set forth in the monastic Custumals that have come down to us.

I. THE CANTOR OR PRECENTOR

The cantor was one of the most important officials in the monastery. He was appointed, of course, by the abbot, but with a necessary regard to the varied qualifications required for the office; for the cantor was both

singer, chief librarian, and archivist. He should be a
priest, says one English Custumal, of proved, upright
character, wise and well instructed in all knowledge pertaining to his office, as well as thoroughly conversant
with ecclesiastical customs. Under his management all
the church services were arranged and performed: the
names of those who were to take part in the singing
of Lessons or Responsories at Matins or other parts of
the daily Office were set down by him on the table, or
official programme, and no one could refuse any duty
assigned to him in this way. In everything regarding
the church services the cantor had no superior except the
abbot, although in certain cases, where the Divine Office,
for example, had been delayed for some reason or other,
the sacrist might sign to him in suggestion that he
should cause the singers to chant more briskly. What
he arranged to be sung had to be sung, what he settled
to be read in the refectory had to be read; the portion
of Sacred Scripture, or other book that he had marked
for the evening Collation, had to be used, and no other.

The place of the cantor in the church was always on
the right hand of the choir; that of his assistant, the
succentor, or sub-cantor, was on the left. It was part of
the cantor's duty to move about the choir when it was
necessary to regulate the singing, and especially when
any Prose, or long *Magnificat* with difficult music was
being sung. Above all things, he had to guard against
mistakes, or even the possibility of mistakes, in the divine
service by every means in his power. With this end in
view, he was instructed to select only music that was
known to all, and to see that it was sung in the traditional
manner. To guard against faults in reading and singing

he was obliged by his office to go over the Lessons for
Matins with the younger monks, and to hear the reader
in the refectory before the meals, in order to point out
defects of pronunciation and quantity, as well as to regulate the tone of the voice and the rate of reading.

When the abbot had to give out an Antiphon or
Responsory on one of the greater feasts, the cantor always
attended him, and helped him if there were need. If
the abbot was unable to take any of his duties in church
in the way of singing, such as celebrating the High
Mass or intoning the Antiphons at the *Benedictus* and
Magnificat, the cantor took them as part of the duties of
his office. On all greater feasts of the second class, the
cantor, by virtue of his office, gave out the Antiphon at
the *Benedictus* and at the *Magnificat*. At the Mass and
other solemn parts of the Divine Office on these occasions,
he directed the choir with his staff of office : assisted on
first-class days by six of the brethren in copes, and on
feasts of the second class by four. His side of the choir
was always to take up any psalm he had intoned ; the
other side of the choir, under the direction of the sub-
cantor, doing the same in regard to what he intoned.

Even when the cantor himself was not directing the
choir, as on ordinary days, he had to be always ready to
come to the assistance of the community, in the case of
any breakdown in the singing or hesitation as to the
correct Antiphons to be used, etc. If an Antiphon was
not given out, or given out wrongly, or if the brethren
got astray in the music, he was to set it right with as
little delay as possible. If the tone of the chanting had
to be raised or to be lowered, it was to be done only by
him, and all had to follow his lead without hesitation.

On festivals it was his duty to select the singers of the
Epistle and Gospel, and he was to be ever guided in his
choice of deacon and sub-deacon by his knowledge of
their capacity to do honour to the feast by their good
singing.   When the community were walking in procession through the cloisters or elsewhere, it was his duty
to walk up and down, between the ranks of the brethren,
to see that the singing was correctly rendered, and that
it was kept together.   The brethren were charged un-
hesitatingly to follow his suggestion and his leading.

Besides this, the cantor was naturally the instructor of
music in the community, and at certain times he took the
novices and trained them in the proper mode of ecclesiastical chanting and in the traditional music of the
house.   In many monasteries he had also to teach the
boys of the cloister-school to read, and the exasperating
nature of this part of his office may be perhaps gauged
from a provision inserted in some statutes, that he was on
no account to slap their heads or pull their hair, this
privilege being permitted only to their special master.

On account of the cantor's care of the church services
and the necessary labour entailed thereby upon him, some
indulgence was generally accorded to him in regard to
his attendance at the parts of the Divine Office where his
presence was not specially required.   He was, however,
forbidden to absent himself from two consecutive canonical
hours, and was not to stay away from Matins, Vespers, or
Compline.   On Saturdays, like the rest, he had to wash
his feet in the cloister.

So much with regard to the duties of the precentor, as
chief singer of the monastery.   He was also the librarian,
or *armarius;* the two offices, somewhat strangely, perhaps,

to our modern notion, always going together. In this capacity he had charge of all the books contained in the aumbry, or book-cupboard, or later in the book-room, or library. Moreover, he had to prepare the ink for the various writers of manuscripts and charters, etc., and to procure the necessary parchment for book-making. He had to watch that the books did not suffer from ill use, or misuse, and to see to the mending and binding of them all. As keeper of the bookshelves, the cantor was supposed to know the position and titles of the volumes, and by constant attention to protect them from dust, and injury from insects, damp, or decay. When they required repair or cleaning, he was to see to it; and also to judge when the binding had to be repaired or renewed. For the purpose of thus renovating the manuscripts under his care, he had, of course, frequently to employ skilled labour. At such times he received an allowance of food for the workmen engaged "on cleaning the bindings of the choir books," etc. Special revenues also were at his disposal "for making new books and keeping up the organs."

At the beginning of Lent the cantor was to remind the community in Chapter of those who had given the books to their house, or had written them; and subsequently it was his duty to request that an Office and Mass for the Dead should be said for such benefactors. And, during the morning Mass of the first Sunday of Lent, he was to bring a collection of volumes into the Chapter-house, that the abbot might distribute one volume to each monk as his special Lenten reading. In the ordinary course, the precentor was bound to give out whatever books were required or asked for, taking care always to enter their titles and the names of the borrowers in his register. He was permitted sometimes to lend the less precious manuscripts; but if the loan was made to someone outside the monastery, he had to see that he received a sufficient pledge for its safe return.

All writings of the church, or made for the church, came under the charge of the precentor. He made, for example, the *tabulae*, or lists of those taking any part in the services. These were graven on waxen tablets, the writing on which could easily be changed, and for making and repairing of which the sacrist had to furnish the wax. Moreover, the precentor had to supply the writers with the parchment, ink, etc., for their work, and personally to hire the scribes and rubricators who laboured for money. Also, he was supposed to provide those in the cloister who could write and desired to do so, with whatever materials they required; but before receiving these the religious had first to obtain leave from the abbot or superior, and then only to signify their wants to the precentor. He was told to give them what they needed, remembering that none of the brethren wrote or copied for their own personal good, but for the general utility of the monastery.

The precentor also, in his capacity of librarian, had to provide the books used for reading and singing in the church and for reading in the refectory and at Collation. He had personally to see that the public reader had his volume ready, and that it was replaced in the aumbry at night. To prevent mistakes, as far as it was possible so to do, the cantor was supposed to go over the book to be read carefully, and to put a point at the places where the pauses in public reading should be made. It was also his duty as archivist to enter the names of deceased members of the community and their relatives in the necrology of the house, that they might be remembered on their anniversaries. In this same capacity, at the time of the profession of any brother, he received from the abbot the written charter of the vows that had been pronounced, so that the document itself might be placed in the archives of the house. He was also required to draw up the "Brief" or "Mortuary Roll," wherewith to announce the death of any brother to other monasteries, etc., and to ask for prayers for his soul. This document, often executed in an elaborate manner and illuminated, after it had received the sanction of the Chapter was handed to the almoner, who sent it by special messenger, called a "breviator," to the other religious houses. In like manner the cantor received from the almoner all such notices of deaths as came to hand, and presented them to the conventual Chapter to obtain the suffrages asked for. If, as was frequently the case, the roll had to be endorsed with the name of the monastery, with the assurance of prayers, or some Latin verses in praise of the dead or expressive of sympathy with the living at their loss, it was the precentor's duty to see that all this was done fittingly before the roll was committed again into the almoner's hand, to be returned to the "breviator" by whom it had been brought.

The cantor also was one of the three custodians of the convent seal, and he held one of the three keys of the chest which contained it. When the die, often in the shape of single or double mould, was needed for the purpose of sealing a document he was responsible for bringing it to the Chapter with the necessary wax in order

HEADING OF MORTUARY ROLL.
THOMAS BROWN, BISHOP OF NORWICH, D. 1445

to affix the common seal to the document, in the presence of the whole convent, and for then returning it to its place of safe custody.

Such an important office as that of precentor obviously required many high qualities for its due discharge. According to one English Custumal, he should "ever comport himself with regularity, reverence, and modesty, since his office, when exercised with the characteristic virtues, is a source of delight and pleasure to God, to the angels, and to men. He should bow down before the altar with all reverence; he should salute the brethren with all respect; he should in walking manifest his modesty; he should sing with such sweetness, recollection, and devotion that all the brethren, both old and young, might find in his behaviour and demeanour a living pattern to help them in their own religious life and in carrying out the observances required by their Rule from each one."

The succentor, or sub-cantor, was the cantor's assistant in everything. When the precentor was absent he took his place and performed his duties. In ordinary course he regulated the singing on the left-hand side of the choir, and attended to such details of the cantor's administration as might be committed to him. It was part, however, of his own duty, as fixed by rule, to see that all the brethren who were tabulated for any duty, or who were involved in any change made in the daily *tabula*, had knowledge of it, in order to prevent the possibility of mistakes, which would interfere with the solemnity of the divine service, and by such carelessness manifest a want of that respect due to the community as a body. Moreover, before the morning Mass and the High Mass the succentor was to be at hand to point out to the celebrants the Collects that had to be said in the Holy Sacrifice, and the order in which they came. If, whilst at the altar, notwithstanding all his care, the priest could not find the proper place, or made delay from some other reason, he was at once to come to his assistance. Lastly, to take one more instance of the succentor's duty : if during the course of the night Office he should see any of the brethren drowsy or forgetting to recite, it was his duty to take his lantern and go towards them, in order to remind them that they were to be more alert as "watchmen keeping their vigil in the Lord's service."

2. THE SACRIST

Next in importance to the office of cantor, especially in regard to the church services which formed so integral a part in the daily life of a monastery, was the sacrist. To him, with his several assistants, was committed the care of the church fabric, with its sacred plate and vestments, as well as of the various reliquaries, shrines, and precious ornaments, which the monastery possessed. It was his duty to provide for the cleansing and lighting of the church, to prepare the choir and altars for the various services, to see that on feast days they were decked out with the appropriate hangings and ornaments; to provide that the vestments for the sacred ministers were ready for use as required, and that, on days when the community were vested in albs or in copes, these were rightly distributed to the brethren. The High Altar was specially in his own personal care : he had to see that it was becomingly decked for the great feasts, and he was particularly enjoined never to leave it without a frontal of some kind, that he might not seem to neglect the place where the daily Sacrifice was offered.

Upon the sacrist was specially enjoined the necessary virtue of cleanliness. Every Saturday he had to see that the sconces of the candlesticks were all scoured out, and that the pavements before the altars were washed and cleaned. The floor of the presbytery was, like the High Altar, to be his own special charge. He was directed constantly to change the linen cloths of the altar and all those otherwise used in the Holy Sacrifice, remembering as a guiding principle that it was " unbecoming to minister to God, with things unsuitable for profane use." The corporals he was also to wash and prepare himself, polishing them with a stone, known as "*lisca*"—"lischa," or glass-stone. For this and the making of the altar breads —concerning which work the minute legislation of the Custumals testifies to the care required in the production of the bread for the Holy Eucharist—the sacrist and his assistants had to be vested in albs and were required to take every precaution in order to secure spotless cleanness of hands and person. During the operation psalms and other prayers were to be said. Once a week, also on Saturdays, if he were a priest or deacon, the sacrist was ordered to wash thoroughly all the chalices and sacred vessels used at the Holy Sacrifice, and to see that no stains of wine, or marks of use, were left on them. If he were not in Sacred Orders he had to get one of the brethren who was to do this office for him. On the Wednesday of each week all the cruets were to be thoroughly cleansed at the lavatory, as also all the jugs and utensils under his care or belonging to his office.

Another function of the sacrist was the care of the

cemetery where the dead brethren were laid to their last rest.   He was to keep it neat and tidy, with the grass cut and trimmed, and the walks free from weeds.   No animals were ever to be allowed to feed among the graves or to disturb the peace of "God's acre."   This evidence of his care was intended to show to all that it was here that the bodies of the holy departed were laid to their peaceful repose to "await the day of the great Resurrection."   In some places the sacrist also had care of the bells, especially of those which summoned the brethren to the church ; and of the clock, where there was one, and this last could be touched by no one but himself or one of his assistants on any pretence whatsoever.

Perhaps his most important duty, however, was that of looking after the lighting of the entire establishment. His office in this matter, somewhat curiously as it may appear to us, was not confined to the church ; but from him the officers of other departments had to obtain the candles or other lights they needed.   He had to purchase the supply of wax for making the best candles, and the tallow or mutton fat for the cressets and the commoner sort of lights, together with the cotton for making the wicks.   At certain periods of the year, it was his province to hire the itinerant candle-makers and, having provided the necessary material, to preside over the process of manufacturing the waxen and other lights that would be needed by the community.   From his store he had to supply the church with all necessary lights for the altars, for the choir, and for illuminating the candle-beams and candelabra on feast days.   To light up the dormitory and church cloister, the sacrist had to rise before the others were called for Matins, so that all might be in readiness for the beginning of the service. For those who had to read the Lessons, he was warned to provide plenty of lights, especially in view of the difficulty experienced by "old men and those with weak sight," if the light was poor. Moreover, he had to furnish the novices, who as yet did not know the psalms by heart, with candles to read by. At Matins, he himself was always to have a lighted lantern ready in case of any difficulty, and at the verse of the *Te Deum*, "The heavens and the earth are full of Thy glory," he took this lantern and, going to the priest whose duty it was to read the Gospel, bowed, and gave it to him so that he might hold it to throw its light on the sacred text. At the conclusion of Matins he received back his lantern, and going out from the choir rang the bells for Lauds.

For the use of the monastery, as has been said, the sacrist had to find the material for lighting the cloister. When it was dark he had to light the four cressets, or bowls of tallow with wicks, which, one in each part of the cloister, can have done very little more than help to make the darkness visible. When more light was needed the sacrist found tallow or wax candles for particular purposes. He did the same in the church, where also great cressets, one in the nave, one at the choir-gates, one at the steps of the sanctuary at the top of the choir, and one in the treasury, were always kept burning during the hours of darkness. Moreover, the sacrist had to furnish the two candles for the abbot's Mass, and to give a certain specified amount of wax to each of the community to make their candles. At St. Augustine's, Canterbury, and Westminster, for instance, the abbot had to receive 40 lbs. of wax for his yearly supply of candles;

the prior had 15 lbs.; the precentor, 7 lbs.; each of the senior priests, 6 lbs.; the junior priests, 5 lbs.; and the juniors, 4 lbs. He had likewise to find all the candles necessary to light the refectory and chapter-room, and to give the cellarer and the infirmarian what they needed for the purposes of their offices. In winter, after the evening Collation, the sacrist waited in the chapter-room after the community, standing aside and bowing as they passed out. When all had departed, he extinguished the lights and locked the door. As one amongst the many minor duties of his office, the sacrist had each Sunday to obtain from the cellarer the platter of salt to be blessed for the holy water. For this he could either himself enter the kitchen, otherwise out of the enclosure, or send another to fetch it. After the Sunday blessing of the salt, he was himself to place a pinch of the blessed salt in every salt-cellar used in the refectory.

In brief, the sacrist, as one of the English Custumals has it, "should be of well-tried character, grave at his work, faithful in all his duties, careful in keeping the brethren to traditions, and watchful over the things committed to his care." "If he love our Lord," says another, "he will love the church, and the more spiritual his office is, the more careful should he be to make the church becoming and attractive for use, and to study to make it in every way more fitting" to be called "the House of God."

The sacrist in most of the greater monasteries appears to have had under him four principal assistants: the sub-sacrist, called in some places the *secretary*, in others the *matricularius*, in others, again, the *master of works;* the *treasurer;* the *revestiarius;* and the assistant sacristan. The first named, the secretary, had charge of the offerings made to the church, and was to look after the fabric of the church. He was entrusted also with the general bell-ringing, and was exhorted by the Custumals to endeavour by study to master the traditional system of the peals, which in most monasteries was very elaborate. The secretary also had to see that wine was provided for the altar, and that a supply of incense was procured when it was needed ; also that the store of charcoal, wax, and tallow was replenished and not allowed to fall too low. He had to purchase these, and the materials, such as lead, glass, etc., for the repair of the fabric, at the neighbouring fairs ; and he was warned to keep an eye to the building so that it might not suffer by neglect.

Besides these duties, he was the official chiefly concerned in the opening and closing of the church doors at the appointed times, and in seeing to the safe custody of the monastic treasures. For this purpose, he with two other under-sacristans always slept in the church, or close at hand, whilst the treasurer and one other monk slept in the treasury, and even took their meals near at hand, so that the church was never left without guardians either day or night.

The *revestiarius*, as his name implies, was mainly concerned with the vestments, the copes, albs, curtains, and other hangings belonging to the church. He was responsible for their care and mending, and for setting them out for use according to their proper colour, and as their varied richness was appropriate to the order and dignity of the ecclesiastical feasts. By his office he was also charged with giving the albs to the brethren when they were to be vested in them, and also with bringing to the precentor in the choir sufficient copes for him to distribute one to each of the community on festivals when the Office was celebrated "*in cappis*"; or at other times to the *schola cantorum*, who assisted him in the singing at the lectern.

The *treasurer* was appointed for the purpose of looking after the shrines, the sacred vessels, and other church plate under the orders of the sacrist. He assisted also in other duties of the sacrist as he might be required; for example, after Compline he, with the others, when the community had retired to bed, prepared whatever lights would be necessary for the night Office. Several times a year it was the general duty of the officials of the sacristy to sweep the church and remove the hay with which it was mostly carpeted, and to put fresh hay in its place. Once a year also they had to find new rush mats for the choir, for the altars, for the steps of the choir, to place under the feet of the monks in their stalls, and before the benches, and at the reading-place in the chapter-house. Various farmsteads, belonging to the monastery, were usually bound at certain times to find the hay, straw, and rushes necessary for this part of the sacrist's work.

3. THE CELLARER

The cellarer was the monastic purveyor of all food-stuffs for the community. His chief duty, perhaps, was to look ahead and to see that the stores were not running low; that the corn had come in from the granges, and flour from the mill, and that it was ready for use by the bakers; that what was needed of flesh, fish, and vege-tables for immediate use was ready at hand. He had to provide all that was necessary for the kitchen ; but was to make no great purchases without the knowledge and consent of the abbot. In some places it was enjoined that every Saturday he was to consult with the prior as to the requirements for the coming week, so as to be prepared with the changes of diet associated by custom with certain times and feasts.

To procure the necessary stores, the cellarer had of course to be frequently away at the granges and at neighbouring fairs and markets ; but he had to inform the abbot and prior when he would be absent, and to leave the keys of his office with his assistant. As the "Martha" of the establishment, always busy with many things in the service of the brethren, he was exempt from much of the ordinary choir duty, but when not present at the public Office, he had to say his own privately in a side chapel. He did not sleep usually in the common dormitory, but in the infirmary, as he was frequently wanted at all hours.

As part of his duty the cellarer had charge of all the servants, whom he alone could engage, dismiss, or punish. He presided at their table after the conventual meals, unless he had to be present in the abbot's chamber to entertain guests, when the under-cellarer took his place. At dinner, the cellarer stood by the kitchen hatch to see the dishes as they came in, and that the serving was properly done. On days when the community had dishes of large fish, or great joints of meat, or other portions from which many had to be served before the dinner, the dishes, after being divided in the kitchen, were set in the vestibule of the cellarer's office, and there the prior inspected them to see that the portions were fairly equal.   At supper it was his duty to serve out the cheese and cut it into pieces for the brethren.

In the case of Westminster and St. Augustine's, Canterbury, the cellarer was urged to look well to the supply of fish, both fresh and salt.   In the case of the first, he was to be careful that it had not been caught longer than a couple of days or so, and that it was always properly cooked.   In regard to all the meals he was to see that the cooks were prepared and in time with their work, since, says the Custumal, " it were better to let the cook wait to serve up the dinner, than to oblige the brethren to sit wanting for their meal."

In Benedictine monasteries, on those days when, in the daily reading of the Rule, the part dealing with the duties and qualifications of the cellarer was read, he was supposed to furnish something extra to the brethren in the refectory.   On those occasions he was to be present when the passage of the Rule was read out, and to make sure that he might not be away, was to ask the cantor to let him know a few days beforehand.

Besides the main part of his office as caterer to the community, on the cellarer devolved many other duties. In fact, the general management of the establishment, except what was specially assigned to other officials, or given to any individual by the superior, was in his hands. In this way, besides the question of food and drink, the cellarer had to see to fuel, the carriage of goods, the general repairs of the house, and the purchases of all materials, such as wood, iron, glass, nails, etc.   Some of the Obedientiary accounts which have survived show the multitude and variety of the cellarer's cares.   At one time, on one such Roll, beyond the ordinary expenses

ADAM THE CELLARER
ST. ALBANS

there is noted the purchase of three hundred and eighty quarters of coal for the kitchen, the carriage of one hundredweight of wax from London, the process of making torches and candles, the purchase of cotton for the wicks, the employment of women to make oatmeal, the purchase of "blanket-cloth" for jelly strainers, and the employment of "the pudding wife" on great feast days to make the pastry. He had, of course, frequently to visit the granges and manors under his care, to look that the overseer knew his business and did not neglect it, to see that the servants and labourers did not misconduct themselves, and that the shepherds spent the nights watching with their flocks, and did not wander off to any neighbouring tavern. Besides this he was charged to see that the granary doors were sound and the locks in good order, and in the time of threshing out the corn he was to keep a watch over the men engaged in the work and the women who were winnowing. He was constantly warned by the Custumals that he should frequently discuss the details of his work with his superior, and take his advice, and get to know his wishes. Finally, in one English Custumal at least, he is warned, in the midst of all his numberless duties undertaken for the community, not to let it affect his character as a religious. He should avoid, he is told, ever getting into the habit of trafficking like a tradesman, of striving too eagerly after some slender profit, or of grinding out a hard bargain from those who could ill afford it.

As chief assistant the cellarer had an under official, called the sub-cellarer, who was told to be kind and to possess polished manners. Besides taking the chief's place when occasion required, in most well-regulated religious establishments certain ordinary duties were assigned to the sub-cellarer. They were mainly concerned with the important matters of bread and beer. He kept the keys of the cellar, and drew the necessary quantity of beer before each meal. When he took his place in the refectory he handed his keys to the cellarer, in case anything should be required during the meal. He was specially charged with seeing that the cellar was kept tidy, and that the jugs and other "*vasa ministerii*" were clean. When the barrels were filled with new beer, they were to be constantly watched by him for fear of an accident. In winter he was to see that straw or hay bands were to be placed round the vats to protect them from frost, and that, if need be, fires were lighted ; in summer he should have the windows closed with shutters, to keep the cellar cool. He was not to serve any beer till at least the fourth day after it had been made.

His special help, in seeing to the bakery and the bread, was the *granatorius*, or guardian of the grain. It was his duty to receive the grain when it came from the farms, and to note and check the amounts, to see to the grinding, and to superintend the bakery. He had to watch that the flour was of the proper quality, and on feast days he was supposed to give a better kind of bread and a different shape of loaf. At times the community might have hot bread—a special treat—and if it were not quite ready, the meal could be delayed for a short time on such occasions. The granator was supposed to visit the manors and farms several times in the year, to estimate the amount of flour that would be required, and to determine whence it was to be furnished, and when. Under the assistant-cellarer and the granator were several official servants, of

whom the miller, the baker, and the brewer were the chief.
It was the sub-cellarer's place to entertain any tenants of
the monastic farms who might come on business, or for
any other reason, to the monastery ; and from him any of
the monks could obtain what was necessary to entertain
their relatives or friends when they visited them, or the
small tokens of affectionate remembrance, called *exennia*,
which they were permitted to send them four times in the
year.

4. THE REFECTORIAN

The *refectorian* had charge of the refectory, or as it
is sometimes called, the *frater*, and had to see that all
things were in order for the meals of the brethren. He
should be "strong in bodily health," says one Custumal,
"unbending in his determination to have order and
method, a true religious, respected by all, determined to
prevent anything tending to disorder, and loving all the
brethren without favour." If the duties of his office required it, he might be absent from choir, and each day
after the Gospel of the High Mass he had to leave the
church and repair to the refectory, in order to see that
all was ready for the conventual dinner, which immediately
followed the Mass.

Out of the revenues attached to his office, the refectorian
had to find all tables and benches necessary, and to keep
them in repair ; to purchase what cloths and napkins,
jugs, dishes, and mats might be required. Three times
a year he received from the monastic farms five loads of
straw, to place under the feet of the brethren when they
were sitting at table, and the same quantity of hay to spread
over the floor of the refectory. Five times a year he had
to renew the rushes that were strewn about the hall ; and

on Holy Saturday, by custom, he was supposed to scatter bay leaves to scent the air, and to give a festal spring-like appearance to the place. In summer he might throw flowers about, with mint and fennel, to purify the air, and provide fans for changing and cooling it.

In preparation for any meal, the refectorian had to superintend the spreading of the table-cloths; to set the salt and see that it was dry; to see that in the place of each monk was set the usual loaf, that no wood-ash from the oven was on the underside of the bread, and that it was covered by the napkin. The drink had to be poured into jugs, and brought in, so as to be ready before the coming of the community; and on the table the cup of each monk was to be set at his place. In some houses the spoons also were distributed before the commencement of the meal; but in others, after the food had been brought in, the refectorian himself brought the spoons and distributed them, holding that of the abbot in his right hand a little raised, and the rest in his left hand. Both cups and spoons were to be examined and counted every day by the refectorian, and he had to repair them when necessary, and see that they were washed and cleaned every day.

Amongst the refectorian's other duties may be mentioned his care of the lavatory. He was to provide water—hot if necessary—for washing purposes, and was to have always a clean hanging-towel for general use, as well as two others always ready in the refectory. All towels of any kind were to be changed twice a week, on Sundays and Thursdays. The refectorian was to be blamed if the lavatory was not kept clean, or if grit or dirt was allowed to collect in the washing-trough. He had to keep in the lavatory a supply of sand and a whetstone for the brethren to use in scouring and sharpening their knives. When the abbot was present at meals, he had to see that the ewer and basin with clean towels were prepared for him to wash his hands. On Maundy Thursday the tables were to be set with clean white cloths, and a *caritas,* or extra glass of wine, was to be given to all the community. At the approach of the festival of All Saints the refectorian had to see that the candlesticks were ready for the candles to light the refectory ; one candlestick being provided for every three monks at the evening meal from November 1 to the Purification—February 2. Lastly, it was the refectorian's duty to sample the cheeses intended for the community. He could taste two or three in a batch, and if he did not like them reject the whole lot. At Abingdon a "weight of cheese" was equal to eighteen stone, and such a "weight" was supposed to last the community five days !

5. THE KITCHENER

The office of kitchener was one of great responsibility. He was appointed in Chapter by the abbot with the advice of the prior, and he should be one who was agreeable to the community. According to the Custumal of one great English abbey, the kitchener was to be almost a paragon of virtue. He ought to be "a truly religious man, just, upright, gentle, patient, and trustworthy. He should be ready to accept suggestions, humble in his demeanour, and kind to others. He should be known to be of good disposition and conversation ; always ready to return a mild answer to those who came to him." He was "not to be too lavish, nor too niggardly, but ever to keep the happy mean in satisfying the needs of his brethren, and in his gifts of food and other things to such as made application to him. And as the safeguard of all the rest, he should strive ever to keep his mind and heart in peace and patience."

The kitchener needed to be well instructed in the details of his office. He had to know, for example, how much food would be required for the allowances of the brethren, in order to know what and how much to buy, or to obtain from the other officials. He was to have what help he needed, and, besides the cooks, he had under him a trustworthy servant, sometimes called his *emptor*, or buyer, who was experienced in purchasing provisions, and knew how and at what seasons it were best to fill up the monastic store-houses. It was obviously of great importance, in order to prevent waste, that the kitchener should keep a strict account of what was expended in provisions and of what amounts were served out to the brethren. Each week he had to sum up the totals, and at the end of the month he had to present his accounts for examination to the superior, being prepared to explain why the cost of one week was greater than that of another, and in general to give an account of his administration.

As his name imported, the kitchener presided over the entire kitchen department. He was directed to see that all the utensils made use of were cleaned every day. He was to know the number of dishes required for each portion, and to furnish the cook with that number; he was to see that food was never served to the community in broken dishes, and was to be particular that the bottoms of the dishes were clean before allowing them to leave his charge, so that they might not soil the napery on the refectory tables. Whilst any meal was being dished, he was to be present to prevent unnecessary noise and clatter, and he was to see that the cooks got the food ready in time, so that the brethren might never be kept waiting. If the High Mass and Office, preceding the dinner, were for any reason protracted beyond the usual time, the kitchener was to warn the cooks of the delay. In the refectory his place was opposite to that of the prior on the left, but if there were need, he could move about during the supper to arrange or change the portions. In a special manner he was to see to the sick, and serve them with food that they might fancy or relish or that was good for them.

In some places the office of kitchener, like many of the others, was endowed with special revenues which had to be administered by the kitchener. At Abingdon, for example, the rents of many of the town tenements were assigned to it. From his separate revenue the abbot in the same place paid into the kitchener's account more than £100 a year, to meet the expenses of his table, chiefly in the entertainment of guests. Besides money receipts, in most monasteries there were many payments in kind. In the same abbey, to take that place as a sample, at the beginning of Lent various fisheries had to supply so many "sticks of eels." So, too, on the anniversary of Abbot Watchen, the kitchener had the fish taken from the fish-stew at one of the monastic manors; and during Lent, from every boat which passed up the Thames carrying herrings, except it were a royal barge, the kitchener took toll of a hundred of the fish, which had to be brought to him by the boat's boy, who for his personal service received five herrings and a jug of beer.

The character of the religious kitchener as sketched in one English Custumal is very charming.

"He should be humble at heart and not merely in word; he should possess a kindly disposition and be lavish of pity for others; he should have a sparing hand in supplying his own needs and a prodigal one where others are concerned; he must ever be a consoler of those in affliction, a refuge to those who are sick; he should be sober and retiring, and really love the needy, that he may assist them as a father and helper; he should be the hope and aid of all in the monastery, trying to imitate the Lord, who said, 'He who ministers to Me, let him follow Me.'"

The long list of duties for the kitchener to attend to set forth in the monastic Custumals, and the grave admonitions which accompany them, show how very important a place that official occupied in the monastery. He had to attend daily in the larder to receive and check the food. When the eggs were brought, for example, by the "vitelers," he had to note who brought them, and whence they came, and to settle how they were to be used. He was to see that the paid "larderer" had meat and fish, salt and fresh, and that the fowls and other birds were fed whilst they were under his charge, waiting for the time they would be wanted for the table. After having made his daily inspection of the outer larder, the kitchener was to visit the inner larder, in order to see that all the plates and dishes were properly scoured, that all the food ready for cooking was kept sweet and clean, and that all the fish was well covered with damp reeds to keep it fresh. Moreover, he was to inspect the fuel, to see that the supply was always kept up by the doorkeeper of the kitchen, with the help of the turnbroach.

The kitchener was warned, not without reason, no doubt, to be careful about his keys. They were to be kept in his room, and no one might touch them without having first obtained his leave. "And," says the Custumal, "he should prudently take heed not to put too much trust in the cooks and the servants, and on account of the danger of temptation" should not let them have his keys without going personally to see what they wanted them for. In this way only was it possible to guard against waste and alienation of the monastery goods.

In discharge of his duties, which were exercised for the common good, the kitchener might easily be excused from choir duties. During the morning Office he was permitted, for example, to say his Mass, and his first daily duty was to visit the sick to see if there were anything they would relish that he could get, and to cheer them with a few kindly words.

Among the many things that the kitchener might be called upon to provide at various times for the brethren, it may be mentioned that he had to furnish the cantor with some of the best beer when he desired to mix the ink for the writers.

6. THE WEEKLY SERVERS IN THE KITCHEN

Closely connected with the office of kitchener is that of the weekly servers, for they were among his chief, though constantly changing, assistants. They entered upon their weekly duties on the Sunday after Lauds, when those who were finishing their week and those who were beginning had to ask and receive the triple blessing. Immediately after receiving the benediction, the new officers went to their work. They drew water to wash with, and after their ablutions went to the kitchen to be ready to do whatever might be needful.

During their week of service, if there were two Masses, one server went to the first, the other to the second. Whilst the community were in the cloister at reading-time, both were to be at work in the kitchen. They had to be in the refectory ready to serve at meal times, and before all refections they were to see that the lavatory was prepared for the brethren. If there were a frost they had to provide basins of hot water and put them near the washing-place, and they were to make ready the water, towels, and other things requisite on shaving days. After each meal one of the weekly servers in an apron went to the kitchen to assist in washing up the dishes and plates.

On Saturdays they had to prepare hot and cold water, with towels, in the cloister, for the weekly feet-washing; to clean out the lavatory and scour the pot used for boiling water in the kitchen; to help to sweep up and tidy the kitchen, and to prepare wood for the fire next day. In the evening, as the last day of their weekly service, they performed the *mandatum*, or feet-washing : the first server washed the feet of the brethren, beginning with those of the abbot, and the second wiped them with the towels he had already dried and warmed. As a last act they returned and accounted for all the vessels and other things they had received when entering upon their duties on the previous Sunday.

CHAPTER V

THE OBEDIENTIARIES (*continued*)

7. THE INFIRMARIAN AND HIS WORK

THE official appointed to have the care of the infirm and sick should have the virtue of patience in a pre-eminent degree. "He must be gentle," says one Custumal, "and good-tempered, kind, compassionate to the sick, and willing as far as possible to gratify their needs with affectionate sympathy." When one of the brethren was seized with any sickness and came to the infirmary, it was the infirmarian's first duty to bring thither the sick man's plate, his spoon, and his bed, and to inform the cellarer and kitchener, so that the sick man's portion might be assigned to him in the infirmary refectory.

Whenever there were sick under his charge the infirmarian was to be excused, as far as was necessary, from regular duties. He said Mass for the sick, if he were a priest, or got some priest to do so, if he were not. If the sick were able to recite their Office, he said it with them, provided lights, if necessary, and procured the required books from the church. Whatever volumes they needed for reading he borrowed from the aumbry in the cloister; but he was warned always to take them back again before the cantor locked up the cupboard for the

night. If there were more than one monk sick at the
same time and they could help themselves, the infirmarian
was then to go to the regular meals in the refectory ; but
he was to return to his charges as soon as possible and
see that they had been properly served. He always slept
in the infirmary, even when there were no sick actually
there, and this because he had always to be ready for any
emergency. Out of the revenue assigned to his office he
had to find whatever might be necessary in the way of
medicine and comforts for the sick. He was charged to
keep the rooms in the infirmary clean, the floors sparsely
covered with fresh rushes, and to have a fire always
burning in the common-room when it was needed. According to one set of English directions, the infirmarian
was advised always to keep in his cupboard a good supply
of ginger, cinnamon, peony, etc., so as to be able at once
to minister some soothing mixture or cordial when it was
required, and to remember how much always depended
in sickness on some such slight act of thoughtful sympathy
and kindness.

The mediæval rules of the infirmary will probably
strike us, with our modern notions, as being strangely
strict upon the sick. The law of silence, for instance,
was hardly relaxed at all in the infirmary ; the sick man
could indeed talk about himself and his ailments and
necessities to the infirmarian at any time, and the latter
could give him every consolation and advice ; but there
was apparently no permission for general conversation,
even among the sick, except at the regular times for
recreation ; even at meal times the infirm ate in silence
and followed, as far as might be, the law of the convent
refectory.

BROTHER JOHN OF WALINGFORD

THE INFIRMARIAN OF ST. ALBAN'S

The brethren who were unwell were not all received in the infirmary for treatment. There were some monks sick, as one set of regulations points out, who were ailing merely from the effect of the very monotony and the necessarily irksome character of the life in the cloister; from the continued strain of silence; from the sheer fatigue of choral duties, or from sleeplessness and such-like causes. These did not need any special treatment under the infirmarian's care; they required rest, not medicine; and the best cure for them was gentle exercise in the open air, in the garden or elsewhere, with temporary freedom from the strain of their daily service. Those who had grown old in their monastic service were to find a place of rest in the infirmary, where they were to be specially honoured by all. They too, however, had to keep the Rule as far as they were able without difficulty, and were to remember, as one English Custumal reminds them, "that not even the pope could grant them a dispensation contrary to their vows." So they had to keep silence, for instance, if possible, and especially the great night silence after Compline.

The curious practice of periodical blood-letting, regarded according to mediæval medical knowledge as so salutary, formed part of the ordinary infirmarian's work. The operation was performed, or might be performed, on all, four times a year, if possible in February, April, September, and October. It was not to take place in the time of harvest, in Advent or Lent, or on the three days following the feasts of Christmas, Easter, or Pentecost. The community were operated upon in batches of from two to six at a time, and the special day was arranged for them by the superior in Chapter, who would announce at the proper time that "those who sat at this or that table were to be blooded." In settling the turns, consideration had, of course, to be paid to the needs of the community. The weekly server, for example, and the reader, and the hebdomadarian of the community Mass were not to be operated upon during the period of their service ; and when a feast day was to be kept within four days of the blood-letting, only those were to be practised on who could be spared from the singing and serving at the necessary ecclesiastical functions of the feast.

From first to last, the operation of blood-letting occupied four days, and the process was simple. At the time appointed, the infirmarian had a fire lighted in the calefactory, if it were needed, and thither, between Tierce and Sext, if the day was not a fast, or between Sext and None if it were, the operator and his victims repaired. If the latter desired to fortify themselves against the lancet, they might proceed beforehand to the refectory and take something to eat and drink. During the time of healing, after the styptic had been applied and the bandages fastened, the discipline of the cloister was somewhat mitigated. The patient, for instance, could always spend the hours of work and reading in repose, either lying on his bed or sitting in the chapter-room or cloister, as he felt disposed. Till his return to full choir work, he was not to be bound to any duty. If he were an obedientiary or official, he was to get someone to see to his necessary duties for him during the time of his convalescence. If he liked to go to the Hours in choir, he was to sit ; he was never to bend down or do penance of any kind, for fear of displacing the bandages, and he was to go out of the church before the others, for fear of having his arm rubbed if he were to walk in the ranks. During the three days of his convalescence he said his Compline at night in the chapter-room or elsewhere, and then went straight to bed before the community. Though he had still to rise for Matins with the others, after a brief visit to the church he was allowed to betake himself to the infirmary and there to say a much shortened form of the night Office with the infirmarian and others. When this was done he was to return at once to bed. In the refectory the monk who had been "blooded" received the same food as the rest, with the addition of a half-pound of white bread and an extra portion, if possible, of eggs. On the second and third days this was increased in amount, and other strengthening food was given to him. In some places these meals were served in the infirmary after the blood-letting; and it was directed that the infirmary servant should on the first day after the bleeding get ready for the patients sage and parsley, washed in salt and water, and a dish of soft eggs. Those who found it necessary to be cupped or scarified more frequently, adds one set of regulations, had to get leave, but were not to expect to stay away from regular duties on that account.

8. THE ALMONER

The conventual almoner was not necessarily a priest; and although, as his name imports, his chief duty was to distribute the alms of the monastery to the poor, there were generally many other functions in behalf of the brethren which he had to discharge.

"Every almoner must have his heart aglow with charity," says one writer. "His pity should know no bounds, and he should possess the love of others in a most marked degree ; he must show himself as the helper of orphans, the father of the needy, and as one who is ever ready to cheer the lot of the poor, and help them to bear their hard life."

In order to distribute the alms of the house the almoner might be absent from the morning Office, and although he should be discreet and careful in his charities, not wasting the substance of the monastery, he should at the same time be kind, gentle, and compassionate. He should often visit the aged poor and those who are blind or bedridden. If amongst his numerous clients for assistance he ever found some who, having been rich, had been brought to poverty, and were perchance ashamed to sit in the almonry with the other poor, he should respect their feelings, and should try and assist them privately. He should submit without manifesting any sign of impatience to the loud-voiced importunity of beggars, and must on no account abuse or upbraid them, "remembering always that they are made to the image of God and redeemed by the blood of Christ."

The general measures for the relief of poverty were in the hands of the almoner ; but he is told that should he find that his charity to any individual was likely to be continuous, he must consult the superior ; and in like manner, when anyone has been a pensioner of the house, the almoner must not stop the usual relief without permission. Whilst engaged with Christ's poor in the almonry, in ministering to the wants of the body, he should never forget those of the soul, and should, as a priest, when opportunity served, speak to them about spiritual matters, of the need of Confession and the like. He had charge of all the old clothes of the religious, and could distribute them as he thought fit, and before Christmas time he was enjoined not to omit to lay in a store of stockings, etc., so as to be able to give them as little presents to widows, orphans, and poor clerks.

To the office of almoner belonged the remnants of the meals in the refectory, the abbot's apartments, the guest-house and the infirmary. At the close of every meal one of the weekly servers took round a basket to collect the portions of bread, etc., which the monks had not con-sumed, and after the dinner the almoner could himself claim, as left for him, anything that was not guarded by being covered with a napkin. In many places, on the death of a monk, it was the almoner's duty to find the community an extra portion for the labour involved in the long Office for the dead, and to remind them to pray for the soul of the deceased. In some monasteries, on the other hand, the almoner daily received a loaf and one whole dish of food that the poor person who received it might pray for the founder of the monastery. In most houses, too, upon the death of any member of the establishment, a cross was put in the refectory upon the table in front of the place where the dead monk had been accustomed to sit, and for thirty days the full meal of a religious was served and given to the poor, that they might pray for the departed brother.

The almoner also superintended the daily maundy, or washing the feet of the poor selected for that purpose. At Abingdon, for example, every morning, after the Gospel of the morning Mass, the almoner went to the door of the abbey, and from the number of those waiting for an alms he chose three, who subsequently had their feet washed by the abbot, according to the approved custom. After this maundy they were fed and sent away with a small present of money. On the great maundy, on the Thursday before Easter, it was the almoner's duty to select the deserving poor to be entertained—sometimes they were to be equal in number to the number of the community—and after they had had their meal, the almoner furnished each religious with a penny to bestow upon the poor man he had served.

As an ordinary part of his office the almoner had also a good deal to do with any monastic school, other than the claustral school for young religious, which was connected with a monastery. There, young clerks were to have free quarters in the almonry, and the almoner was frequently to see them set to argue one against the other, to sharpen their wits. He was to keep them strictly, or, as it was called in those days of belief in corporal punishment, "well under the rod," and he had to find, out of the revenues of his office, all "discipline rods" both for the boys and for use in the monastic Chapter. On feast days, when there were no regular lessons, these young clerics were to be set to learn the Matins of the Office of the Blessed Virgin ; or to practise writing upon scraps of parchment. If they did not learn, and especially if they would not, the almoner was to get rid of them, and fill their places with those who would.

As before noted, to the almoner belonged, at least partially, the duty of attending to the mortuary-rolls or notices of deaths. That is to say, he had to supervise the "breviators," or letter-carriers, who were sent to announce the death of the brethren, or who came with such rolls. He received the rolls, and gave them into the hands of the cantor to copy and to notify to the community. If it were the mortuary-roll of a prelate, and especially if it announced the death of the head of any associated monastery, the superior was to be informed at once, in case he should desire to add to the roll something special about the dead ; that is, more than the mere name of the place, which was simply meant to testify that the notice had been seen and read in Chapter. Whilst the bearer of the roll was waiting to receive back his "brief," he was to be entertained liberally in the almonry. Sometimes the almoner was to get the cantor to multiply copies of the death-notice, and these he at once despatched far and wide by the hands of such poor people as were tramping the country and called at the monastery for assistance.

Amongst the miscellaneous duties of the office of almoner, in some places that official had to see that the mats under the feet of the monks in the choir were renewed each year for the Feast of All Saints. He had also to find the rushes for the dormitory floor. From St. Dunstan's Day, May 19th, till Michaelmas the cloister was kept strewn with green rushes, which the almoner had to find, as well as all the mats used in the cloister and on the stairs, and also in some houses the bay-leaves or "the herb-benet, or common hedge avens," to scatter in the refectory and cloister at Easter. At the time of the long processions also on the Rogation days, two of the almonry servants, standing at the church door, were wont to distribute boxwood walking-sticks to such of the community who through age or infirmity needed them to walk with.

The almoner, says one Custumal, should remember that from his office might be derived great spiritual gain.

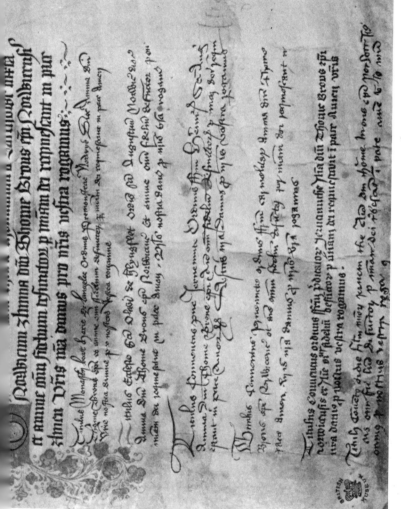

END OF MORTUARY ROLL

THOMAS BROWN, BISHOP OF NORWICH D. 1445

He should keep before his mind our Lord's words: "I was hungry, and you gave me to eat," etc. For this reason alone he should ever be gentle and kind to the poor, for in them he was really ministering to the Lord Jesus Christ Himself. He ought to endeavour to be seldom, if ever, without something to give away in charity, and he should try to keep a supply of socks, linen and woollen cloth, and other necessities of life, so that if by chance Christ Himself were at any time to appear in the guise of a poor, naked, and hungry man, "He might not have to depart from His own house unfed, or without some clothes to cover the rags of His poverty."

9. THE GUEST-MASTER

In mediæval days the hospitality extended to travellers by the monastic houses was traditional and necessary. The great abbeys, especially those situated along the main roads of the country, were the halting-places of rich and poor, whom business, pleasure, or necessity compelled to journey on "the King's highway." For this and many other causes, such as the coming to the monastery of people desiring to be present at church festivals and other celebrations, visits of the relatives of monks, and of those who were concerned in the business transactions of a large establishment, the coming and going of guests was probably of almost daily occurrence. The official appointed to attend to the wants of all these and to entertain them on behalf of the monastery was the *hospilarius* or guest-master.

The official guest-master had the reputation of the religious house in his hands. He required tact, prudence, and discretion in a full measure. Scribbled on the margin of a monastic chartulary as a piece of advice, good indeed for all, but most of all applicable to the official in the charge of the guests, are the following lines :—

"Si sapiens fore vis, sex serva quæ tibi mando
    Quid dicas, et ubi, de quo, cui, quomodo, quando."

Which may be Englished thus :—

"If thou wouldst be wise, observe these six things I com-
    mand you,
Before speaking think *what* you say and *where* you say it ;
    about and *to* whom you talk, as well as *how* and *when*
    you are conversing."

On the other hand, the guest-master is frequently warned that he must certainly be neither too stand-off, silent, or morose in his intercourse with strangers. And, as it is part of his duty to hold converse with guests of all sorts and conditions, with men as well as women, "it becomes him," says one Custumal, "to cultivate," not merely a facility of expression in his conversation, but pleasing manners and the gentle refinement which comes of and manifests a good education. All his words and doings should set the monastic life before the stranger "in a creditable light," since it becomes him to remember the proverb : "Friends are multiplied by agreeable words, enemies are made by harsh ones."

The guest-master's first office was to see that the guest-house was always ready for the arrival of any visitor. He was to make certain that there was a supply of straw sufficient for the beds ; that the basins and jugs were clean inside and out ; that the floors were well swept and spread with rushes ; that the furniture was properly dusted, and that, in a word, the whole house was kept

free from cobwebs and from every speck of dirt.   Before
the coming of an expected guest the master was personally
to inspect the chamber set apart for him ; to see that
there was a light prepared for him should he need it ;
that the fire did not smoke ; and that writing materials
were at hand in case they were required.   Moreover, he
was to ascertain that all things were ready in the common
rooms for his entertainment.   When it was necessary to
procure something that was needful, the master could
enter the kitchen, which was, of course, otherwise out of
the enclosure for the monks generally.   He was to get
coal and wood and straw from the cellarer ; the cups,
platters, and spoons that were required from the refectorian ; and the sub-cellarer was to arrange as to the food
itself.   At Abingdon the guest-master had a special
revenue to be spent upon what must have been a source
of very considerable expense in those days, the shoeing of
the horses of travellers generally who came to the abbey,
and especially of those belonging to religious and to poor
pilgrims.   People also at various times left small bequests
for this as for other monastic charities.   In the same
abbey, the guest-master had also a small yearly sum,
charged on a house in the town, which had been left by
"Thurstin the tailor," to help to entertain poor travellers,
as a memorial of the day when he and his wife had been
received into the fraternity of the monastery.

When word was brought to the guest-master of the
arrival of a guest, he was charged forthwith to leave
whatever he was about, and to go at once to receive him,
as he would Christ Himself.   He was to assure him—
especially if he were a stranger—of the monastic hospitality, and endeavour from the first to place him at his

ease. He was to remember what he would wish to be done in his own regard under similar circumstances, and what he would desire to be done to himself he was to do to all guests. "By showing this cheerful hospitality to guests," says one English Custumal, "the good name of the monastery is enhanced, friendships are multiplied, enmities are lessened, God is honoured, charity is increased, and a plenteous reward in heaven is secured." The whole principle of religious hospitality, as practised in a mediæval monastery, is really summed up in the words of St. Benedict's Rule : *Hospites tamquam Christus suscipiantur*—Guests are to be received as if they were Christ Himself.

Directly the guest-master had cordially received the new-comer at the monastery gate, he was to conduct him to the church. There he sprinkled him with holy water and knelt by him, whilst he offered up a short prayer of salutation to God, into whose house he was come safely after the perils of a journey. After this the master conducted his guest to the common parlour, and here, if he were a stranger, he begged to know his name, position, and country, sending to acquaint the abbot or superior if the guest was one who, in his opinion, ought to receive attention from the head of the house. When the guest was going to stay beyond a few hours, he was taken after this first and formal reception to the guest-house, where, when he had been made comfortable, according to the Rule, the master arranged for the reading of some passages from the Scriptures or some spiritual work. If the strangers were monks of some other monastery, and the length of their visit afforded sufficient time, he showed them over the church and house, and if they had servants and horses he sent to acquaint the cellarer, that they too might receive all needful care. If a conventual prior came on a visit he was to be given a position and portion of food, etc., similar to that of the prior of the house, and every abbot was to be treated in all things by the monks like their own abbot. For each monk-guest the master got from the sacrist four candles, and the chamberlain found the tallow for the cressets in the guest-house. It was the master's duty to see that the guests kept the rules, which were to be made known to them on their first coming. Strangers were entertained for two days and nights by the house without question. If any of them wished to speak with one of the monks, leave had to be first obtained from the superior.

When the guest desired to say the Office, books and a light were to be provided in the guest-hall, and the master was to recite it with him if he so desired. If on great feasts guests desired to be present in the church for Matins, the master called them in ample time, waited for them whilst they rose, and then with a lighted lantern accompanied them to the choir. There he was to find them a place and a book and leave them a light to read by. Before Lauds he came to them with his lantern to take them back to their chambers that they might again retire to bed till the morning Office.

Either the guest-master, or his servant, had to remain up at night till the fires were seen to be protected and the candles put out. If the guest was obliged to depart early in the morning, the master had to obtain the keys of the gate and of the parlour from the prior's bedplace. After having let the visitor out, he was charged to take care to relock the doors and to replace the keys. At all times when guests were leaving the master was bound to be present, and before wishing them Godspeed on their journey, he was instructed to go round the chambers, "in order," says one Custumal, "to see that nothing was left behind, such as a sword, or a knife ; and nothing was taken off by mistake which belonged to his charge by his Office, and for which he was responsible." With the departure of guests came the duty of seeing that everything in the guest-house was put in order again, and was ready for the advent of others.

10. THE CAMERARIUS, OR CHAMBERLAIN

The chief official duties of the chamberlain of a religious house were concerned with the wardrobe of the brethren. He consequently had to know what and how much clothing each religious ought to have by rule, and what in fact he had. For this purpose he was provided with an official list of what was lawful, or required, and from time to time with his servant he had to examine the clothing of the monks, removing what was past repair, and substituting new garments for the old, which were placed in the poor-cupboard to satisfy the charitable intentions of the almoner. In the distribution of these cast-off clothes, however, it was to be remembered that those who worked for the monastery had first claim, if they were in need, upon the old garments of the monks which had found their way to the poor-cupboard.

It is somewhat difficult to discover exactly the amount of underclothing considered sufficient for religious, especially as in most places there seems to have been little difficulty in furnishing more, if there was any particular reason shown for additional clothing. Three sets, however, of shirts, drawers, and socks, seem to have been an ordinary allowance for priests and deacons, and probably two sets for others ; with two tunics, scapulars, and hoods, and two pairs of boots. These last were over and besides the " night-boots," which were apparently made of thick cloth, with soles of some heavy noiseless material, such as our modern felt.

The chamberlain by virtue of his office had also to provide the laundresses and superintend their work. These necessary servants were to mend as well as wash all sheets, shirts, socks, etc., and all clothes that needed regular cleansing and reparation. All underclothing was to be washed, according to one set of rules, once a fortnight in summer, and once every three weeks in winter. Great care was to be taken that no losses should occur "in the wash," and all the clothes sent to the tub were to be entered on "tallies," or lists, and returned in the same way into the charge of the official.

The chamberlain, according to the amount of his work, could generally have a monk as assistant chamberlain either for a time, or continuously. Amongst the duties assigned to this assistant was that of looking to the repairs needed in the clothes, which in a large establishment were sometimes very heavy. In one of the Custumals, any monk who wanted a garment repaired, had to place it in the morning in one of the bays of the cloister leading to the chapter-house. Thither each day came the assistant chamberlain to see what had been placed there, and what was wanted. He then carried what he found to the tailor's shop and fetched it again when the repairs had been executed. This necessary establishment was generally well organised. For example, at Abingdon there were

four lay officials and five helpers in the tailor's department. The first had charge of the skins and furs ; the
second was the master tailor ; the third the master cutter ;
and the fourth was called the "proctor of the shop" ;
and his office was to see that all materials had been
supplied by the camerarius, that there was a store of cloth

GLOUCESTER CLOISTERS, THE LAVATORY

and skins, an abundance of needles, pins, and thread,
and a sufficiency of knives and scissors, and wax for the
thread. The proctor of the shop also had charge of the
lights and fire, and he himself slept in the shop and was
responsible for its safe custody.

The camerarius by his office had to provide all the cloth
and other material necessary for the house. For such

purposes he had to attend at the neighbouring fairs, whither merchants brought their goods, where he purchased what was necessary. For such matters he frequently had the use of a cart and horse, with its driver. When vendors of cloth came to the monastery the chamberlain had to interview them, and, if necessary, entertain them out of the revenue attached to his office.

In mediæval times, when patent methods of heating were unknown and windows were often unglazed or badly glazed, the cold of our northern climate required the general use of skins and furs as lining to the ordinary winter garments for protection from the weather and draughts. The cloister was no exception, especially when the monks had to spend some hours each night in their great unwarmed churches; and so we find in the Custumals that the camerarius was warned to prepare a store of lamb-skins and cat-skins before the cold set in, and he was granted a special supply of salt for the purpose of curing them. He had charge also of the boots of the community; and, at one place at least, three times in the year he had a right to a supply of pigs'-fat from the kitchener, in order that he might compound the grease with which the community liberally anointed the leather of their boots to keep it supple and to make it weather-proof.

On the chamberlain of every monastic house devolved also the duty of making preparation for the baths and for the shaving, etc., of the brethren. He had to purchase linen cloth for the towels in the cloister lavatory, for the monks' baths, and for the general feet-washing each Saturday. He was charged always to keep an eye upon the lavatory, and, when it was frozen in the winter, he was told to see that there were hot water and warm dry

towels for the monks' use. He had also to buy the wood
needful to warm the water for the baths, which were to be
taken by all, three or four times in the year; and he had
to keep by him a store of sweet hay to spread round about
the bathing tubs for the monks to stand on. From
November to Easter he was to provide hot water for the
general feet-washing on Saturdays, and on Christmas Eve
he was charged to see that a good fire was kept burning
in the calefactory, so that when the monks came out from
their midnight Mass and Office, they should find a warm
room and plenty of hot water to wash in after their long
cold vigil in the church. For all these occasions, too, the
camerarius had to provide a supply of soap, as well as for
the washing of heads and for shaving purposes.

In Cluniac monasteries, at least, the arrangements for
shaving had also to be made by the chamberlain. The
brother who undertook the office of barber kept his imple-
ments—razors, strop, soap, and brushes, etc.—in a small
movable chest, which usually stood near the dormitory
door. When necessary he carried it down to the cloister,
where, at any time that the community were at work or
sitting in the cloister, he could sharpen up his razors or
prepare his soaps. When the time of the general "*rasura*"
came, the community sat silently in two lines, one set along
the cloister wall, the other facing them with their backs to
the windows. The general shaving was made a religious
act, like almost every other incident of cloister life, by the
recitation of psalms. The brothers who shaved the others,
and those who carried the dishes and razors, were directed
to say the *Benedicite* together before beginning their
work; all the rest as they sat there during the ceremony,
except of course the individual actually being operated

upon, said the *Verba mea* and other psalms. The sick, and those who had leave, were shaved apart from the rest in the warmer calefactory. It would seem that the usual interval between the times of shaving the monks' tonsures was about three weeks; but there was always a special shaving on the eve of all great festivals. Sometimes in monasteries situated in towns the work of shaving was performed by a paid expert. In the Winchester chamberlain's account-roll, there are entries for such payments, as, for example, "for thirty-six shavings, 4^s. 6^d."

According to custom, the chamberlain had also to find, out of his revenues, various little sums for specified purposes. For example, from the same Winchester rolls it appears that he paid 20s. to each monk, in three portions of different amounts, apparently as pocket-money; he also year by year paid the money for wine on Holy Innocents' Day for the boy-bishop celebration; he kept several boys in the school, and also defrayed the cost of a student at Oxford University. At Abingdon, in the same way, from rents received by him, the chamberlain had to furnish each of the monks with threepence to give to the poor whose feet were washed on Maundy Thursday. The chief virtues which should characterise the true monastic chamberlain are stated to be, "wisdom and learning, a religious spirit, a mature judgment, and an upright honesty."

11. THE MASTER OF NOVICES

The master of novices was, of course, one of the most important officials in every religious house. So far we have spoken of the obedientiaries, who were immediately concerned with the management of the whole monastery; and the novice-master is placed here, not because his

was a less dignified or a less important office, but because
he was officially concerned merely with those who were
being proved for the religious life. The master of
novices, we are told, was to be a man of wide experience
and strength of character. "A person fitted for winning
souls," is St. Benedict's description of the ideal novice-
master. It is obvious that he should be able to discern
the spirits and prove them ; to see whether their call to
the higher life was really from God, or a mere passing
inclination or whim.

During the year of his probation the novice was in
complete subjection to his master. The postulant, who
came to beg for admission into religion, usually remained
in the guest-house for four days ; after that time, in some
houses, he came to the morning Chapter for three consecutive days, and, kneeling in the midst of the brethren,
urged his petition to be allowed to join their ranks and to
enter into holy religion in their monastery. After the
third morning, if his request was granted, he was clothed
in the habit of a monk, and was handed over to the
care of the novice-master, who was to train him, and to
teach him the practices of the religious life ; whose duty
it was to test him and to prove him ; and who, for a whole
year, was to be his guide, his master, and his friend.

One walk of the cloister, generally the eastern side,
was assigned to the use of the novices. In their work
and life they were to be separated, as much as possible,
from the rest of the community except in the church,
the refectory, and the dormitory. Even in these places
they were to be still under the immediate control and
constant watchful care of their master. From the day
of their reception the systematic teaching of the rules

and traditional practices of the religious life, which was imparted in the noviciate, was commenced. The first lesson given the novice was how he was to arrange the monk's habit and cowl, which were new to him; how to hold his hands and head; and how to walk with that modesty and gravity which become a religious man. These minutiæ were not always so easy to acquire; and to most, frequently presented some difficulty. The neophyte was next shown how he should bow, and when the various kinds of bows were to be made. If the bow was to be profound, it was pointed out to him how he could tell practically when it was correctly made, by allowing his crossed arms to touch his knees. Then he was instructed how to get into his bed in order to observe due modesty, and how to rise from it in the morning, in the common dormitory. In a word, he was exercised in all the usual monastic manners and customs.

After these first lessons in the external behaviour of a monk, the novice was taught the necessity and meaning of such regulations as custody of the eyes, silence, and respect for superiors and other brethren, both outward and inward. Step by step he was drilled in the exercises of the regular life, and taught to understand that they were not mere outward formalities, but were, or ought to be, signs of the inward change of soul indicated by the monk's cowl.

The cloister was the novice's schoolroom. His master assigned to him a definite place amongst his fellows, and after the morning Office he sat there in silence with the book given him, out of which to learn some one of the many things a novice had to acquire during the year of probation. The Rule: the prayers and psalms he had to

learn by heart : the correct method of singing and chanting and reading : and sometimes even the rudiments of
the Latin language, without a knowledge of which the
work of a choir brother was impossible, were some of his
daily studies; and hard work enough it was to get through
it all in twelve fleeting months. His master, however,
was ever at hand to help him and to encourage him to
persevere, if he only showed the real signs of a call to
the higher life.

Before beginning their work the novices always had
to recite a *De profundis* and a prayer, as an exercise in
decorum and deliberation. Not more than three of them
were to use the same book together. At times there
must have been a considerable amount of noise, for in
practising the reading, singing, and chanting they were
all directed to make use of the same tone, as they would
have to do in the church or refectory. The novice-master
began their exercises with them, but he could pass them
on for this kind of drilling to someone else, provided
he was competent and a staid and true religious.

Thrice during the year of probation, if the novice
persisted in his design, his master brought him to the
morning Chapter, where on his knees he renewed his
petition to be received as one of the brethren. At length,
as the end of the year approached, a more solemn demand
was made and, the novice having been dismissed from the
Chapter, the master gave his opinion, and the verdict of
the convent was taken. If the vote were favourable to the
petitioner, a day was appointed for him to make his vows,
and, having pronounced these with great solemnity, he
received the kiss of peace from all as a token of his
reception into the full charity of the brotherhood. In

some Orders, certainly amongst the Benedictines, the ceremony concluded with a formal and ceremonious fastening of the hood of the newly professed over his head. This he wore closed for three days, as a sign of the strict retreat from the world, with which he began his new life as a full religious; and just as our Lord was buried in the tomb for part of three days to rise again, so was he buried to the world to rise again to a new life. At the morning Mass of the third day the superior with some ceremony unfastened the hood, and the late novice joined the ranks of the junior monks, who for some years after their profession still remained under the eye and guidance of an immediate superior called the junior master.

12. THE WEEKLY OFFICIALS

To complete the account of the officers of a monastery some few words are necessary about the officials, whose duties lasted merely for the week. The first of these was known as the *hebdomadarian*, or the priest for the week. In most places, apparently, the hebdomadarian began his labours with the vespers on Saturday and continued them till the same time the following week. It was his chief duty to commence all the various canonical Hours during his week of office. He gave all the blessings that might be required; he blessed the holy water and, on the proper days, the candles and ashes. He gave even the blessings bestowed upon the weekly servers on the Sunday morning. Besides these duties it was his office to sing the High Mass on all days during the week, and in monasteries where there were two public Masses, during the week which followed his week of service, he took the early Mass and assisted at the second.

A second weekly official was the *antiphoner*, whose duty it was to read the Invitatory at Matins. He did so alone on ordinary days, and sang it with an assistant, or even with two or more, on greater feasts. He gave out, or intoned, the first Antiphon at the Psalms, the Versicles, the Responsoria after the Lessons, and the *Benedicamus Domino* at the conclusion of each Hour. He also read the "Capitulum," or Little Chapter, and whatever else had to be read at the morning Chapter.

Amongst the other weekly officials may be noted the servers and the reader at meals. These brethren could take something to eat and drink before the community came to the refectory, in order the better to be able to do their duty. The reader was charged very strictly always to prepare what he had to read beforehand and to find the places, so as to avoid all likelihood of mistakes. He was to take the directions of the cantor as to pronunciation, pitch of the voice, and the rate at which he was to read in public. If he were ill, or for any other reason was unable to perform his duty, the cantor had to find a substitute. The servers began their week of duty by asking a blessing in church on Sunday morning. They were at the disposal of the refectorian during their period of service, and followed his directions as to waiting on the brethren at meal times, preparing the tables, and clearing them after all had finished. With the reader, and other officials who could not be present at the conventual meals, they took theirs afterwards in the refectory.

CHAPTER VI

THE DAILY LIFE IN A MONASTERY

I. MATINS

THE night Office in most monasteries began at midnight, although in some places the time varied according to the seasons of the year, from that hour till half-past two or three o'clock. Midnight, however, was so generally the time, that, in considering the daily life of a monastery, it may be assumed that the night vigils began with the first hour of each day. At some short time before the hour appointed for the commencement of the night Office the signal for rising was given in the common dormitory. Sometimes the sub-sacrist was charged with the ringing of a small bell, as he passed rapidly down the passage between the monks' beds or cubicles. In other places it was the duty of the abbot himself, or his prior, to awaken the monks from their slumbers and invite them to come and keep their night watch in the church. In any case the sacrist and his assistant had to be up betimes and before the others, for, as has been already said, they had to see that the lights were lit on the stairs and in "le standards" in the church. It was the duty of one of the novices, however, to light candles for his fellows, and set them about the places they occupied in the choir, since they did not as yet know the psalmody by heart.

Meanwhile the monks when roused from their sleep were taught to begin the day by signing themselves with the cross and commending themselves to God's protection. As they rose from their beds they put on those parts of their monastic habit which had been laid aside during the hours of sleep, and shod themselves with their "night-boots." These were probably fur-lined, cloth protectors for the feet, which served the double purpose of keeping them warm during the winter nights spent in the cold church, and of rendering their footfall inaudible, during the hours of the greater silence which lasted from Compline till Prime. Each monk as he finished his simple preparation, seated himself in front of his bed and there waited in silence, with his hood drawn well over his head, till the bell began to toll. Then, preceded by a junior carrying a lighted lantern, the religious went out of the dormitory in companies of six at a time, and took their places in the choir. The juniors occupied as their normal position the stalls nearest to the altar, the youngest being next to the chancel step, the seniors being furthest away, and the superiors next to the entrance. The abbot or prior waited outside the church in the cloister, or at the entrance to the choir, until all had passed in before him and had taken their places, when he gave the signal for the tolling of the bell to cease, and then himself entered and took up his position in the stall next to the gate of the choir.

At the coming of the superior all rose from their knees, returned his salutation, and at once bowed down for what was known as the "Triple-prayer"—the Pater, Ave, and Creed—with which the night Office always commenced. Then the weekly antiphoner at a sign from the superior gave out the first of the " Fifteen," or "Gradual"

FRANCISCANS IN CHOIR

psalms. Great importance was always attached to the recitation of these psalms, and all the obedientiaries were bound to be present, except the guest-master when his duty to any stranger took him away, or the cantor on a day when any proper Lessons had to be read at Matins, and he was occupied officially in finding the places in the great chained book at the choir lectern. At the end of these psalms, by which, on all but the great feasts, the night Office was commenced, those officials who had duties to perform departed from the choir during the interval between the Psalms and the second ringing of the bells for the beginning of Matins proper.

When the second night-tolling ceased, at a sign from the superior, the hebdomadarian of the week, who had to sing the daily High Mass, began the Office with the usual *Deus in adjutorium*. This weekly official was bound always to be present at Matins during the time of his office when he sang the Mass; and so strict indeed was the law of connection between Matins and the Mass, that should the hebdomadarian be unable for any reason to be present at the former, he had to obtain the services of some priest who could assist at Matins, to sing the Mass for him.

After the Invitatory, which was said or sung by the weekly antiphoner, either alone or with a companion, or on the great feasts by the cantor and his assistant, the superior, or hebdomadarian priest, gave out the first antiphon, and the rest of the antiphons were taken in turns by the seniors on either side. At the conclusion of the psalms of each Nocturn, the reader appointed for the first Lesson fetched the lighted candle, bowed to either choir and to the abbot if he were present, and then ascending the steps of the reading - place, so held the candle that its light fell as he desired on the book which had been prepared by the cantor. Before beginning his reading he asked the usual blessing, bowing down from the place where he stood towards the abbot or superior, who gave it sitting in his stall. The Lesson was followed by the *Responsorium*, during which the reader of the Lesson made way for another, who had been appointed on the cantor's official list for the second Lesson, and so on, till after the last Lesson had been read, when the reader carried back the light to the place whence the first reader had brought it, that it might be found ready for the Lessons of the next Nocturn. In some places the readers of the fourth, eighth, and twelfth Lessons were told to extinguish the candle, taking care that it did not smoke so as to annoy the brethren. It was to be lighted again by one of the novices appointed for the purpose during the last psalm of each Nocturn.

If the abbot was to sing the twelfth Lesson, or to take part in a Responsory, or other portion of the service, as he did on the great festivals, the cantor had to come with the abbot's chaplain and others to his stall, bringing the necessary books with lights carried by servers, and the cantor in a low voice was to assist him in the singing. On feasts with twelve Lessons, whilst the *Te Deum* was being chanted, preparations were made for the solemn singing of the portion of the Gospel selected for the Office of the day. The church servants brought into the choir a portable reading-desk, which they placed at the steps leading to the presbytery. Others brought a cope of the colour of the day, with an amice, stole, and maniple. Meanwhile the sacrist had fetched the book of the Gospels with some solemnity from the altar, and had placed it on the desk, where the cantor was waiting to find the proper place. Having done so, at the indicated verse in the *Te Deum*, the cantor went to the stall of the hebdomadarian of the Mass, and bowing to him conducted him to the desk, assisted him to vest, and pointed out to him the place in the Holy Gospels that had to be sung or read. Meanwhile the servers had come into the choir from the sacristy with incense and lights, and when the *Te Deum* was concluded all turned towards the priest whilst he chanted the appointed Gospel, and finished Matins with the prayer of the day.

Immediately the bells began to ring for Lauds, and during the brief interval the priest unvested, and with the usual bow to each choir, which was slightly acknowledged by the monks on either side, he returned to his stall to wait till the cessation of the ringing gave the signal for the beginning of the next canonical Hour. Meantime the incense and lights had been taken back into the vestry, and the sacrist, having carried the Gospel-book back to the altar, the servants removed the desk out of the choir. The cantor busied himself during the interval at the great chained Antiphonary on the lectern, in order to see that all the places of Lauds were marked, and that the hanging lantern in front of the book was burning brightly enough to light up the great parchment page with its large square notes and big letters. In this interval the monks either remained sitting in their stalls with their hoods covering their heads, or they could take the opportunity of leaving the choir, to restore their circulation by a brisk turn in the cloister, or for any other purpose.

2. LAUDS

In ancient days the Office of Lauds was called *Matutinæ Laudes* — "the morning praises" — because they were supposed to be always celebrated at dawn of day. In mediæval monasteries, however, this canonical Hour was generally said or sung, with only a short interval between it and Matins. It would, therefore, have been probably somewhere about one o'clock in the morning that Lauds usually began.

If the feast was of sufficient rank for the hebdomadarian to be vested in a cope, he then occupied the stall next to the abbot; if not, he remained in his own place, and, when the tolling of the bell ceased and gave notice of the conclusion of the interval, he at once intoned the *Deus in adjutorium* for the beginning of Lauds. It was his place to give out the first antiphon, the second being taken by the abbot, or by the first religious in choir. The rest of the antiphons were given out as at Matins, by one on each side in turn. The Chapter— called the "Little Chapter"—was supposed to be known by heart, and no book or light was allowed to be used in saying it.

The hebdomadarian gave out the antiphon of the *Benedictus*, and if he were vested in cope he would have to incense the altar or altars during the singing of that canticle. For this purpose two thurifers, and acolytes bearing candles, came from the sacristy before the antiphon was begun, and the thurifers, after the incense had been blessed by the abbot, accompanied the hebdomadarian to the High Altar, returning whence they had come after the ceremony had been performed. On Sundays, at the con-

clusion of Lauds, the hebdomadarian gave the blessing to
the outgoing and incoming weekly servers.

Directly the Office was over the community retired once
more to the dormitory and to bed. The juniors led the
way with a lighted lantern, as when they had come down
to Matins. The prior, however, waited in his stall until
he had seen that all had passed out of the church except
the sacrist, who had to remain behind to see that the lights
were safely put out, and that the *Collectarium*, or book of
Collects, and other choir books were carefully replaced in
the aumbry. Then he too retired again to his bed in the
room near the church. It would have been probably some
time about half-past one or two in the morning before the
monks found themselves once more in bed for their second
period of repose.

3. PRIME AND THE EARLY MASS

It is somewhat difficult to say exactly at what time the
Hour of Prime was generally said in a mediæval monastery. It is possible, however, to assume that it was not
earlier than six or later than seven o'clock in the morning.
One Consuetudinary, that of St. Mary's, York, says that
the bell was to ring for that Hour at seven, "unless for
some reason the time was changed ; but that Prime must
never be said before daybreak."

At seven o'clock, then, or thereabouts, after the monks
had been allowed five hours for the term of their second
repose—making with the rest they had had previous
to the midnight Office, about eight hours in all—the
prior, or whoever was appointed for the duty, roused the
brethren. This was done by sounding a bell for the space
of a *Miserere* psalm, and before the ringing was finished

the religious were expected to be already out of bed. They were now, at their second rising, to dress themselves in their day clothes and shoes, and to betake themselves to the church, where they were to be in their places before the bell had ceased to toll. Prime with its hymn, three psalms, and the beautiful morning prayer: " O Lord God Almighty, Who hast brought us to the beginning of this day, so assist us by Thy grace, that we may not fall this day into sin, but that our words may be spoken and our thoughts and deeds directed according to Thy just commands," did not take very long, and concluded with the usual *Benedicamus Domino*. Immediately after this the great bell was rung for the *Missa familiaris*, or early Mass, chiefly intended for the servants and workpeople of the establishment. At this the community were not bound to be present; and so, whilst the bell was tolling, they passed into the cloister to begin their washing and complete their dressing, etc. The seniors and priests first occupied the lavatories, since they had now to say their own private Masses as soon as they were ready. Whilst the seniors were dressing, the juniors waited in their places reading or praying till their turn came. When the sign was made that the lavatories were free, the novice-master ceased his instructions, and the novices put down their psalters in their places in the cloister; the juniors returned their books to the shelves of the aumbry in the cloister, and then they went in turns to wash, going afterwards to the corner near the door of the refectory to smooth their hair.

It was during this hour after Prime that those who desired to approach the Sacrament of Penance could always be sure of finding a confessor in the chapter-room, where alone, be it remarked, the confessions of the brethren were heard. On all Sundays and feast days the early Mass was delayed until the washing was finished, when the religious who were not priests went in procession to the church to hear this Mass and to receive the Holy Eucharist. On these occasions they were sprinkled with holy water at the door of the church, and a crucifix was offered to them to kiss.

On other days during this time, except the priests who, as has already been pointed out, now said their private Masses, the monks either took their books and studied in the cloister ; or, if they were obedientiaries, busied themselves in the necessary duties of their various offices.

The early Mass had to be taken in turn by all the priests, except by the infirmarian, who always celebrated for the sick in the infirmary, and by some of the other officials whose duties prevented their celebrating at this time. The priest, whose name was on the *tabula* to take this Mass, had to see that the altar had been prepared, and that the places were marked in the missal beforehand, so as not to cause unnecessary delays. At the same time those about to celebrate their private Masses prepared their chalices and cruets in the sacristy ; and, assisted by the junior monks not in priest's orders, went to the altars assigned to them. When two priests had their names entered on the *tabula* for the same altar, the senior took the first turn and the junior followed. If the former did not come, the latter was to wait till the priest saying the early Mass had got to the Epistle, and then he could himself take the altar, presuming that his senior had for some reason been unable to come.

4. THE MIXTUM

Before the next public duty, which was the *morning Mass*—celebrated it would seem about half-past eight, or thereabouts—on all days but fasting days, the community were called to the refectory for what was variously called the *mixtum*, or breakfast. Three strokes of the bell at the church door was the signal for this slight refection which the young members, who were not priests, could take at an earlier hour, if the superior so wished or thought good. This meal—if meal it could be called—was very slight, and consisted, according to one set of directions, of a quarter of a pound of bread, and a third of a pint of wine or beer. There was, however, even in this slight refection a religious decorum and a certain amount of ceremony. The weekly reader asked a blessing, and the first religious present in the refectory gave it, saying: "May the Giver of all good gifts bless the food and drink of his servants." Then the small portion was served out and consumed by each in silence, and standing. At the end, each monk said to himself when he had finished : "Grant, we beseech Thee, O Lord, for Thy name's sake eternal life to all our benefactors. Amen."

In Lent the *mixtum* was not taken except on Sundays. It was also omitted on the three Rogation days, on the Ember days, and on certain vigils of feasts, which by ecclesiastical law were days of fasting.

5. THE MORNING OR CHAPTER MASS

Whilst the monks were at their morning refection the first bell was kept ringing for the morning Mass. This Mass was frequently called the " Ladye Mass," because it was usually celebrated at the altar of our Blessed Lady, and as a votive Mass in her honour, when the feast permitted it. In other places it was called the "Chapter Mass," because it was followed immediately by the daily Chapter. When the first bell had ceased to ring, the monks took up their position in that part of the cloister known as the *Statio*, that is, the place where all assembled when they had to go into the church in procession. This place naturally varied in different monasteries according to circumstances. In St. Mary's, York, it is described as being in the western walk of the cloister, before the common parlour.

On the second tolling of the bell the community proceeded in procession to the church. At the door they were presented with a crucifix to kiss, took holy water, and bowed to the representation of the Holy Trinity, or the crucifix, at the entrance. They then stood in their ranks in choir facing the altar, till, on the entrance of the superior, the bell ceased. Sometimes the Hour of Tierce was said before the morning Mass, but in any event the seniors were now in the stalls nearest to the altar.

At a sign from the cantor the novices took the graduals from the choir cupboard, or the psalters if the Mass was *de Requiem*, and distributed them. The priest came in at once and the Mass was said in a low but audible voice, with more or less solemnity according to the ecclesiastical rank of the day.

6. THE CHAPTER

Immediately after the conclusion of the morning Mass the great bell was set ringing for the daily Chapter. It would now have been somewhere about nine o'clock in the

day. As long as the tolling continued the religious as
a body remained sitting in their stalls in the church,
"thinking," as one Custumal says, "over any trans-
gressions against the Rule or good discipline of which
they may have been guilty." Meanwhile the chief
officials responsible for the order of the house, called
generally the *custodes ordinis*, repaired for a few minutes
to the private parlour to consult as to any matter which
might need correction, or to which public attention should
be called ; at the same time, on the sound of the bell, all
those who for any reason had not been present at the
Mass, hastened to the chapter-room. During this interval
one of the custodians of the cloister went round to see that
all the doors were so closed and fastened, that no one
could enter the monastery precincts during the time of the
Chapter.

When the brief talk of the custodians was over, the
junior among them went back to the door of the church
to stop the bell ringing, and its cessation was the signal
for the community to leave the choir and proceed to the
chapter-room, the juniors walking first. Here all stood
in their places till the entrance of the superior. If the
abbot were present all bowed as he passed through their
ranks, and as he reached his seat at the upper end of the
room, the prior and one of the seniors from the abbot's
side of the choir came forward to kiss his hand, bowing
to him both before and after this act of homage. By this
ceremony they publicly renewed their monastic obedience
on behalf of the community.

Whilst the community and superior were coming into
the Chapter, the junior appointed for the office of weekly
reader in the refectory, stood holding before his breast the

COMMUNITY IN CHAPTER HOUSE, WESTMINSTER

Martyrology, or book of the names of the saints daily
commemorated by the Church. When all had entered
and taken their seats, the reader came forward, and
placing the volume upon the lectern in the middle of the
room, asked the blessing of the president in the usual
form. This having been given, he read the portion of the
Martyrology which gave the brief notices of the lives of
the martyrs and other saints commemorated on the following day. When mention was made of any saint whose
relics were possessed by the house, or who was specially
connected with it as patron or otherwise, the community
removed their hoods and bowed down as a mark of special
reverence.

After the Martyrology all stood up and turned to the
crucifix, or *Majestas*, during the usual morning prayers,
which were said to call down God's blessing upon the
work of the day, and to ask His protection over all the
words and deeds to be uttered and done in His service.
With the blessing : " May the Lord Almighty regulate
our days and acts according to His peace " and the short
reading called the *Capitulum*, this portion of the daily
Chapter was concluded. Then, all again sitting, the abbot
or presiding superior said, *Loquamur de Ordine nostro :*
" Let us speak about the affairs of our house." At this
point the novices retired from the chapter-room, and also
any stranger religious, who was not professed for the
monastery, who happened to be present. About all
that was transacted in this part of the daily Chapter, the
strictest silence was enjoined. Some of the Custumals
even declare that they do not set forth the manner of
holding the Chapter, as the secrets of the religious family
are its own and all loyal sons would desire to keep them

inviolate. Other regulations, whilst permitting the infirmarian to convey to the sick monks who were not present
any order given, charged him on no account to relate anything else that happened in the Chapter, since no one was
ever allowed to speak about such matters, not even to
mention and discuss them with those who had been
present.

When the room had been cleared of all but the professed monks of the monastery, the Chapter devoted itself
to the correction of faults against good discipline. It was
lawful for any religious, except a novice, to speak in the
secrecy of Chapter about any matters that in his judgment
required to be corrected. These generally resolved themselves into one of three classes relating to regular life : (1)
negligences of all kinds, changes of customs, and mistakes in the divine service ; (2) want of due care in the
keeping of silence ; and (3) neglect of the proper almsgiving on behalf of the house. As to all things in the first
class it was the duty of the cantor and succentor to speak
first, and to call attention to anything they had noticed
amiss ; concerning shortcomings in the second class, the
superior and the guardians of the cloister, whose special
duty it was to watch over the monastic silence, were to
have the first say ; and as regards the third, naturally
the almoner and his assistant would have most information to give on all that regarded the monastic charities.

After the "proclamations" or "accusations," the superior pronounced the punishment. No one was allowed
to offer any defence or make any excuse, and the whole
process was summary and without noise or wrangling.
The penance was generally some corporal chastisement,
with rod or other discipline ; and this, which to our

modern ideas seems so curious, and indeed somewhat repellent a feature of mediæval monasticism, was evidently at the time regarded as quite a natural, and indeed a useful and healthy form of religious exercise ; for, besides being looked on as a punishment, this form of corporal chastisement was resorted to with permission of the superior as a common means of self-mortification. Such voluntary penances were chiefly sought for on days like the Fridays of Lent, and especially on Good Friday, and when some brother specially desired to offer up penitential works for the soul of some departed brother.

When the questions of discipline had been disposed of, which ordinarily would have taken only a very brief time, the superior, if he desired to say anything, made his short address or exhortation. He then, if there was any need, consulted his community about any temporal or other matter, or asked their consent, where such consent was required. In all such temporal matters many of the Custumals advise the junior members to defer to the age and experience of their elders, although they were of course free to give their own opinions, even if contrary to that of their elders.

It was at this time in the daily Chapter that any deed or charter to which the convent seal had to be affixed, and to which the convent had already assented, was sealed in presence of all by the precentor, whose duty it was to bring the common seal to the meeting when it was needed. When this part of the Chapter was finished, all matters such as the issuing of public letters of thanks or congratulation, etc., in the name of the community, were sanctioned, and the granting of the privilege of the

fraternity of the house to benefactors or people of distinction. When the actual ceremony of conferring this
favour, which was both lengthy and solemn, was to be
performed, it was at this point that the "confratres" and
"consorores" were introduced into the Chapter. After
the ceremony the "confratres" received the kiss of peace
from all the religious; the "consorores" kissed the hand
of each of the monks.

In the same way, on the day before a Clothing or
Profession, the candidate presented himself before the
abbot, at this point in the Chapter, and urged his petition. Also, before a monk was ordained priest he had
to come before the Chapter; and kneeling, to beg the
prayers of his brethren. The superior was charged to
explain to him again carefully at this time the respon-
sibilities of so high a calling, and to warn him of
the dangers and difficulties which he would have to
encounter in his sacred office. Then the superior pronounced over him a special blessing and offered up a
special prayer for God's assistance. When there were
many candidates for ordination who had to go elsewhere
to receive their Orders, it was at this time in the Chapter
that the schedule of their names was drawn up and
handed to the senior, who was to accompany them to the
bishop at whose hands they were to receive ordination.

Only on rare occasions, however, would there have been
any such matters of public business. Ordinarily speaking,
from the superior's address, if he made any, followed by
his blessing, the Chapter passed to the commemoration
of the departed. If the day was the anniversary of a
benefactor whose soul ought to be remembered in the
prayers of the community, the precentor, or the succentor

HENRY VI BEING RECEIVED AS A CONFRATER AT EDMUNDSBURY

in his absence, came forward immediately after the superior
had given his blessing, and standing in front of the
reading-place, said : " To-day, sir, we should have the
great bell rung "—or some other bell, according to the
solemnity of the anniversary. " For whom ? " asked
the superior. " For so-and-so," replied the precentor,
naming the special claim the person whose anniversary
it was, had upon the community. Then the superior,
bowing, said : " May his soul and the souls of all the
faithful, by the mercy of God, rest in peace." Whereupon
the precentor wrote the name of the benefactor upon the
" tabula " for the day, that no one might have the excuse
of absence for not knowing for whom the whole convent
had to offer up their prayers that day. Then from the lectern the reader announced the usual list of the anniversaries
of brethren entered in the necrology for the day ; and this
again was followed by the precentor reading any mortuary
roll, or notice of death of some religious of another house,
or of some personage of distinction, if any such had been
received. After reading such a roll, it was his duty to
explain to the community what were their obligations in
regard to the deceased. The Chapter was then concluded
with the *De profundis* and a prayer for the souls of all
departed brethren and benefactors.

On ordinary occasions, of course, the daily Chapter
would not occupy a very long time, possibly a quarter
of an hour or twenty minutes. At any rate, a full half-
hour of the morning would be left before the High Mass,
which began at ten o'clock. This time was generally
spent by the monks in conversation in the cloister. On
days when there was talking, the prior, or abbot if he
had been present, on coming into the cloister when the

Chapter was over, would sound three times the *tabula sonatila*, which was apparently a piece of hard wood, to which two other smaller pieces were loosely fastened, so that when shaken it gave forth a musical sound and served the purpose of our modern gong. This triple sounding of the *tabula* was always the signal for talking ; the superior, or whoever acted for him, pronouncing the word *Benedicite*, without which no conversation was to be permitted in the monastery. "By the three strokes," says one author who sees deep meanings in ordinary things, "is to be understood the signs of our mortality, representing our coming into the world, our passage through life, and our transit through the portals of death." The special significance of this thought in regard to conversation was apparently that in view of it, a bridle should be set upon the tongue and a guard upon the heart, which was so frequently disturbed by trifling images.

7. THE PARLIAMENT

After the Chapter the common business of the house was transacted. The discussion about all the many details of a great administration like that of a mediæval monastery necessitated regular consultations between the officials and the superior, and frequent debates upon matters of policy, or matters of business, or on points of the Rule or observance. These meetings were known as "the Parliament," or Discussions, and from them the word to signify our house of national representatives was taken.

One particular part of the cloister was selected where these monastic Parliaments were held, and thither all came who had any matter to suggest or business to transact with the officials. Here the abbot, or he who took his place, was ordered to be ever ready to hear what those had to say who sought him for guidance or direction. In another part of the cloister, during this time after Chapter, the senior monks met together to listen to devotional reading, and to discuss points that might strike them in their reading, or which had been suggested by the Divine Office. In the same way the juniors were to be in their places in the western walk of the cloister with their master, or one or more of the seniors, similarly engaged in asking questions as to observance, or seeking to know the meaning of any difficult passages in Holy Scripture. The novices, and the juniors who had been only recently professed, were together in the northern walk of the cloister, being taught the principles and practices of the monastic life. It was a precious time for the beginner, when the disciple was exhorted to question his instructor on all matters connected with the regular observance, but especially about the Rule and the Divine Office.

During this period of the Parliament the guardians of the cloister were directed to go about from group to group, to see that the laws of the regular life were observed as they should be. During this half-hour, except in the case of the officials who had to transact necessary business of the house, no conversations about worldly matters or vain tales were to be permitted. The Parliament time—between Chapter and High Mass—was devoted exclusively to spiritual matters or to the discussion of necessary business.

During this and all similar times of conversation the monks were warned to keep watch over their tongues.

When asked their opinion or advice, they were to give
it with modesty and moderation.   No signals were to be
permitted between various parts of the cloister ; the conversation was to be conducted in a low tone, and it was to
be considered a matter of first importance that at these
meetings all should be present.

CHAPTER VII

THE DAILY LIFE IN A MONASTERY—*continued*

8. THE HIGH MASS

THE daily "*Magna Missa*"—the Conventual, or High Mass—began at ten o'clock. The first signal was given by the ringing of a small bell some short time before the hour; and forthwith, on the first sound, the juniors and novices laid aside the tasks upon which they were engaged. All books were at once replaced on the shelves of the aumbry in the cloister, and then the monks waited in their places till the second signal. On this being given, talking at once ceased, and the religious made their way to the church. Meanwhile, on hearing the first signal, the hebdomadarian, or priest, who had to sing the Conventual Mass, and the other sacred ministers, after having again washed their hands "to be ready to fulfil their functions at the sacred altar with fitting purity" of body and mind, made their way to the sacristy to vest for the service.

The community having entered the choir and taken their places, the senior members nearest the altar, the prior, who was up to this time waiting outside the door of the church, gave the sign for the tolling of the bell to cease. As he did so, he himself entered the choir and took up his position in the stall nearest to the presbytery steps and opposite to that of the abbot when he was present. If Tierce had not already been said at the time of the morning Mass, after the usual silent Pater and Ave, the superior made a signal for that Hour " by rapping with his hand upon the wood of his stall." Whilst the community were engaged in the recitation of the Office, the ministers were completing their preparation in the sacristy, and when it was over, if the day were a Sunday, the priest came into the choir for the solemn blessing of the holy water. He was preceded by the thurifer bearing the processional cross between two candle-bearers, and was accompanied by the deacon and sub-deacon in albs. Two vases of water had been prepared on the first step of the presbytery by the church servers, and thither the procession went for the weekly blessing of the holy water. The cross-bearer mounted the steps and then turning somewhat to the north, stood with his face towards the priest; the deacon assisted upon the right hand of the celebrant and the sub-deacon on his left. The solemn blessings of the salt and water were then chanted by the priest, the whole community answering and taking part in the service. When the exorcism and blessing of the salt was finished, the sub-deacon, coming forward, took a little of it on a smaller dish and handed it to the priest to mix with the water. The rest of the blessed salt was then taken by one of the church servants to the refectorian, whose duty it was to see that a small portion was every Sunday placed in every salt-cellar in the refectory.

After the blessing of the holy water came the *Asperges*. The priest, having given the book of the blessings to one of the servers, received the *aspersorium*, or sprinkler, and dipping it into the vat of water, went to the altar, and after having sprinkled the front of it thrice, passed round it, doing the same at the back. Meanwhile the vat-bearer with the holy water awaited his return and then accompanied him as he gave the *Asperges* to all the religious in the choir. At the abbot's stall the priest paused, bowed, and presented the sprinkler, so that the superior might touch it and sign himself with the newly-blessed water. When the abbot had finished the sign of the cross, the priest passed down the ranks of the brethren, sprinkling them with the water, first on one side and then on the other. If a bishop were present in the choir, he was treated with the same special reverence shown to the abbot, and to him the blessed water was to be taken first. When all the brethren had received the *Asperges*, the priest accompanied by his ministers went to the choir gates and sprinkled those of the faithful who were in the body of the church.

After this two priests, accompanied by two of the brethren, proceeded to take the holy water round the house. One pair went through the public rooms and offices of the monastery sprinkling them and saying appropriate prayers in each. The other mounted to the dormitory and did the same for each bed and cubicle, and returning through the infirmary, gave to each of the sick brethren the same privilege of receiving the holy water, which their brethren in the church had had.

Whilst this was being done by the two priests and their associates, the community, under the direction of the pre-centor, passed out of the choir into the cloister for the Sunday procession. First walked the bearer of the holy water which had just been blessed. He was followed by the cross-bearer walking between two acolytes carrying

lighted candles. Then came the sub-deacon by himself
with the book of the Holy Gospels, and behind him the
priest who was to celebrate the Mass accompanied by
his deacon. These were succeeded by the community,
two and two, with the abbot by himself at the close
of the double line. Ordinarily the procession passed
once round the cloister, the monks singing the Responsories appointed for the special Sunday. On greater
feasts there was more solemnity, for then the community
were all vested in copes, which had been brought into
the choir by the church servers and distributed to the
monks after the *Asperges*. On these occasions, as also
on the Sundays, the Hour of Tierce followed, instead of
being said before the blessing of the holy water. On
the Wednesdays and Fridays of Lent also, and on the
Rogation days, there were processions ; but these were
penitential exercises, and on such occasions the community
walked barefooted round the cloister.

If the day was one of the solemn feasts, upon which
the abbot celebrated in pontificals, he was vested by the
sacred ministers before the altar in the sacristy, whilst
Tierce was being sung in the choir. At the conclusion
of the Hour he entered with due solemnity, being met at
the door of the choir by the prior and others, and he took
his seat upon a throne erected before his stall in the upper
part of the choir until the procession was formed. The
abbot only celebrated at the High Altar on these great
feasts ; and never except with full pontifical ceremonies, if
he had the right to use pontificalia at all.

In most monasteries several times a year—four or more,
according to custom and circumstances—there were exceptionally solemn processions with relics and banners.

On these occasions every care was taken to make the religious pageants worthy of the best traditions of the monastery. Such processions would be preceded by the vergers of the church with their maces of office; and the community, all vested in copes, walked in couples with some four feet between them and between the next couple. Every here and there a single individual walked in the middle carrying an appropriate banner; and at intervals the great shrines, which were the special pride of the house, or the chief notable relics, were borne by the requisite number of religious clad in sacred vestments. At the close of the procession came the abbot in full pontificalia, assisted by his sacred ministers. Finally, following the church servers, walked the *janitor* of the church, or "door-keeper," "who," according to one Custumal, "was to raise his rod well above his head, to warn the people who pressed on after the procession, to stand farther away."

These were the ceremonies preliminary to the High Mass on Sundays and on the greater festivals. Ordinarily speaking, the conventual High Mass would begin either directly after Tierce, or if that Hour had been already recited at the time of the early Mass, immediately the community had entered the choir, and the cessation of the bell-ringing had given notice that the prior was in his place. The two juniors appointed by the cantor had meanwhile taken the graduals and psalters from the presses in the choir, and had distributed them to the seniors, juniors, and novices according to their needs. The cantor of the week, also, had by this time put on his cope, had chosen a book, and had taken his stand at the lectern to be ready to lead the singing. The High Mass

then commenced and went on as usual till after the Blessing. At the Offertory the prior or some of the seniors
brought the oblations to the altar and gave them to the
celebrant. On Sundays, after the Blessing, the hebdomadarian priest gave the usual benediction to the weekly
reader, who had come forward from his place in choir to
the steps of the presbytery to receive it. The Gospel of
St. John was said after the priests and the ministers had
reached the sacristy and were standing before the altar
there, whilst the community were leaving the choir for
the next conventual duty, or were unvesting, if they had
that day worn copes or albs.

If the abbot celebrated, the ceremonial was somewhat
more elaborate. The prior made the oblation at the Offertory, and assisted the abbot to wash his hands after the
incensing of the altar, and before the Post-Communion at
the end of the Mass. If the abbot had been taking part
in the procession, at the end of it, when the religious
returned to the choir for Tierce, the abbot retired to the
sacristy, accompanied by the ministers, where he took off
his cope and put on the dalmatics and chasuble for the
Holy Sacrifice, waiting in the sacristy till the signal was
given for beginning the Mass.

9. THE DINNER

Dinner followed Mass directly, with only a brief interval
for the washing of hands. As a rule, the midday meal
would be served about eleven o'clock. The reader and
servers were permitted to take some slight refection
beforehand; and for this purpose could leave the church
before the conclusion of the service with the refectorian
and kitchener. On Sundays, however, the reader had to

wait till after he had received the usual weekly blessing, but he might then go straight from the altar to take his bread and wine.

Just before the close of the service in the church, the prior came out into the cloister and either himself began to sound the signal for the dinner, or caused someone else, appointed for the purpose, to do so. If through any accident the meal was not quite ready, or, as one Custumal says, "if the bread be still in the oven," it was the duty of the kitchener to wait for the coming of the prior and to inform him of the delay, so that the signal might not begin to sound before the cook was ready. In this case the community, upon coming out of the church, after they had performed their ablutions, sat as patiently as they could in the cloister till the signal was given. Ordinarily, however, the bell began to ring at their coming out of the choir, and continued to sound whilst they were preparing themselves for the meal, and, indeed, until all were in their places.

The prior, or the senior who was going to preside at the meal if he were absent, remained at the door of the refectory, and gave the sign for the bell to cease ringing when all was ready. Whilst waiting here, the various officials who had to make any communication to the prior about the meal, or ask any permission appertaining to their office, came to make their reports or proffer their requests. For example, the infirmarian had now to notify the names and number of the sick under his charge, or to ask permission for some one of the brethren to dine with them. The guest-master would do the same in regard to his guests, and, on the great feasts when the abbot had pontificated, he would frequently send his chaplain to the prior or presiding senior, when thus standing at the entrance to the refectory, to acquaint him that he had invited the sacred ministers who had assisted him in the function, to dine at his table. In some places also, on every fish-day, the cellarer acquainted the prior at this time what provision he had made for the community meal, in order that the superior presiding might judge whether there ought to be anything further supplied to the religious, by way of a *caritas*, or extraordinary dish.

The monks on entering the refectory were directed to pause in the middle and salute the *Majestas* over the high table with a profound bow. They then passed to their places to await the coming of the superior. If this was delayed they could sit down in their places till the bell, ceasing to ring, told them that the superior had given the sign for his entry. They then stood in their ranks and returned the bow he made to each side as he came into the hall. If the abbot dined in the refectory, each monk also individually saluted him as he passed up to his seat. The usual Grace was then chanted, and the prior, or whoever presided, gave the blessing to the reader, who came forward into the middle of the refectory to ask for it. Whilst the community were sitting down in their places at table, the reader mounted the pulpit and opened the book at the place he had already prepared. When all was quiet the superior sounded the small bell at his table as a sign that the reader might begin ; and, when the first sentence had been read, he sounded it a second time for the commencement of the meal. That the interval between the two bells might not be over long, the reader is warned in some monastic directions to make choice in all refectory reading of a short sentence as the first.

REFECTORY PULPIT, CHESTER

The monk who read one week had to serve the next, and during his week of reading he was never to be absent from his duty except with grave cause. For example, if he were to be invited during his week of office to dine at the abbot's table, he was to excuse himself and say that he was the conventual reader. The reason assigned is obvious : the reading had to be carefully prepared, and was besides a labour ; so that to ask anyone to take the duty unexpectedly would mean not only that he would have a burden placed upon him, but that the community would not have proper respect paid to it, in having to listen to reading that had not been prepared previously. One common and useful direction given to the refectory reader is, that he was not to hurry. The quantity he got through was immaterial compared with distinct pronunciation and careful rendering. Any specially noteworthy passage should be repeated so as to impress its meaning upon the hearers.

When the second signal had been sounded by the president's bell, the brethren uncovered their loaves, which had been placed under their napkins, arranged the latter, and broke their portion of bread. At the second signal, too, the servers began their ministrations. In some of the greater houses, at the beginning of the meal, two juniors, one from each side, took their goblets and spoons and came to the table of the presiding superior. Here they took up their places, standing at either end of the table, unless the superior should invite them to sit. These junior monks were to act as the special servers of the religious presiding in the refectory. They were to assist him in his wants, to anticipate them if possible, and to act as his messengers should he require them to do

so. On first taking up their position, the senior of the
two was directed to cut the superior's loaf in two for him,
the other was to fill his goblet with the beer or wine served
to the community. These two assistants at the president's
table had to eat their meals as they stood or sat, as the
case might be, at the ends of the high table, and were to
be helped immediately after the president himself.

When the sign for beginning the meal had been given,
two other juniors, one on each side of the refectory, rose
from their places, and, receiving the jugs of beer or wine
from the cellarer or his assistant, proceeded to fill the
goblets set before each of the religious. When this was
done they asked permission from the superior, by a sign,
to fill the measure of drink intended as the convent's
charity to the poor. Meanwhile the servers had gone to
the kitchen-hatch to bring in the dishes. These were
taken usually first to the superior, and from this dish the
two juniors serving at his table were helped ; then, should
there have been any one of the brethren lately dead, his
portion, to be given to the poor, was served out into a
special dish. Finally, in many places, two dishes were
taken by the servers to the tables on each side of the
refectory ; one to the top and the other to the bottom and
so passed along the tables, the monk who passed the dish,
and he to whom it was passed, bowing to each other with
ceremonial courtesy.

In some houses the method of serving was somewhat
different : the portions were served separately, having
been previously divided under the direction of the
kitchener or refectorian. When the first dish was pottage,
the serving always began with the youngest member
of the community, the superior receiving his last ; in

other cases the first dish was always taken to the superior's table. The servers were exhorted always to attend to their work, not to keep standing about the kitchen-hatch, and much less to stop gossiping there; but to watch carefully and even anxiously for any sign that might be made to them by the brethren.

In some Custumals there were minute directions for the serving. Those who served the brethren were not to rush about, nor stand aimlessly in one place, nor gossip with the kitchen-servers even about the dishes they received. They were to watch to supply what was wanted; they were to serve with decorum and with patience, as if, indeed, they were waiting upon our Lord Himself; and they should not attempt too much at a time, as, for example, to try to carry in more dishes, etc., than they were well able to do. As a rule, they were to be contented to use both hands to carry one dish.

During the service of the first course, the reading was to proceed uninterruptedly; but when the community had finished eating it, a pause was made until the second course had been set on the table. Meanwhile, at some religious houses at this point in the dinner, the poor man selected that day to receive the alms of the community, or as the recipient of the portion of a deceased brother during the thirty days after his death, was brought into the refectory by the almoner. His share was given to him, and one of the juniors helped him to carry his food to the door. At this point, too, that is, after the first course, if there were not many to serve, permission from the superior was to be asked by a sign for one of the two servers to sit down and begin his meal.

The second course was served in a way similar to the
first. Many and curious are the directions given as to
what the monks might or might not do according to the
code of mediæval monastic manners. The regular food,
for example, was not to be shared with anyone, as, indeed, all had received their own portion ; but if anything
special or extra was given to an individual, except for
sickness, then he might, and indeed would be considered
wanting in courtesy if he did not, offer to share it with
his two neighbours. These neighbours, however, were
not to pass it on. If the superior in his discretion sent
a brother some extra dish, the recipient was directed to
rise and bow his thanks. If the dish came from the table
of the abbot, when out of the refectory, he who received
it was still to bow towards the abbot's place as if he were
present. If it came from anyone else than the superior,
the recipient had to send it by the server to the senior
presiding in the refectory, that he might, if he so pleased,
partake of it, or even dispose of it altogether according
to his pleasure. If any mistake was made in serving, or
if by any accident something was dropped or spilt on the
tables or ground, the delinquent had to do penance in the
middle, until the prior gave a sign to him to rise, by
rapping on the table with the handle of his knife.

Some of the hints as to proper decorum at table seem
curious in these days. No one was to clean his cup with
his fingers, nor wipe his hands, or mouth, or knife upon
the tablecloths. If he had first cleaned the knife with
a piece of bread, however, he might then wipe it on his
own napkin. The brethren were exhorted to try and
keep the tablecloths clean. Stained cloths were to be
washed without delay ; and to avoid stains, all soft and

cooked fruit was to be served in a deep plate or bowl. Every care was to be taken not to drop crumbs upon the floor ; salt was to be taken with a knife, and the drinking-cup was to be held always in both hands.

When the prior, or the senior presiding at the table in his place, saw that the monks had finished their repast, he knocked upon the table with the handle of his knife, as a sign for the collection of remnants intended for the poor. The two juniors appointed for this purpose then came forward, each carrying a basket, and bowing in the middle to the superior, passed down each side of the refectory, collecting the pieces of bread and anything else that the religious had placed in front of them as their individual alms. Whatever portion of bread any monk desired to keep for the evening meal, he guarded by covering it with his napkin. Any loaf, or part of a loaf, left uncovered after the dinner was over, was claimed by the almoner, as belonging to "the portion of the poor" at his disposal.

When the two juniors had finished their task, the prior rapping the table a second time, gave the sign for the servers to collect the spoons and knives, and take them to the kitchen hatchway to be removed for washing in the place set aside for that purpose. Meanwhile the monks folded their napkins and waited silently for a third signal, upon which they rose from their places and took up their position for Grace, facing each other on the inner sides of the tables. When they were ready in their ranks, the reader who was waiting in the pulpit, at a sign from the prior, sang the usual conclusion of all public reading: "*Tu autem Domine, miserere nobis,*" the community answering "*Deo gratias.*" Then followed the chanted

Grace, which was concluded in the church, to which the community went in procession, during the singing of the *Miserere* or other psalm.

The officials and religious who had been occupied with serving, stood on one side at the end of the meal, and as the brethren went out from the refectory they bowed to them, to show their reverence for the community in its corporate capacity. The servers then went to the lavatory and washed their hands in preparation for their own meal. The refectorian remained behind when the community went out of the refectory, so as to see that all was ready for the second table. At this second meal the cellarer generally presided; and one of the junior monks was appointed to read whilst it was being eaten by the servers and by all those who for any reason had been prevented from dining at the first table.

10. AFTER DINNER

The community dinner would probably have taken about half an hour; and by the time the monks came from the church after finishing their Grace, it would have been about 11.30 in the morning. The first duty of the monks on coming into the cloister was to proceed to the lavatory to wash their hands again—a not wholly unnecessary proceeding in the days when forks were unknown, and fingers supplied their place at table. At Durham a peculiar custom was observed by the monks each day after dinner on coming from the church. They betook themselves to the cemetery garth "where all the monks were buried; and they did stand all bareheaded, a certain long space, praying among the tombs and graves for their brethren's souls being buried there." If None had already been said in choir, the community had now several hours to devote to reading or work, or both. If that canonical Hour had yet to be said, then the religious, after their ablutions, took their books and sat in the cloister till the monks at the second table had finished their meal, when the signal was given, and all went to the church and recited None together, returning to their occupations immediately afterwards, by which time it would have been about midday.

After washing his hands on coming out from Grace, the prior, or the senior who had presided in the refectory in his place, was directed in some houses to go and satisfy himself that all was well at the second table, and that those who had served others were themselves well served. From the refectory he had to go to the infirmary to visit the sick, and to see for himself that their needs had been properly supplied. When these two duties had been fulfilled, it was the custom in some places for the prior on occasions to invite some of the seniors to his room for a glass of wine, to warm themselves in winter, and for what is called in one Custumal "the consolations of a talk." When the prior was not present, the presiding senior was allowed to invite some of the brethren to the *domus recreationis*—the recreation-room. At certain times and on certain feasts the whole community joined in these innocent and harmless meetings.

At this same time the juniors and novices with their masters were permitted with leave to go out into the garden and other places to unbend in games and such-like exercises proper to their age. In this way they were assisted when young to stand the severe strain of cloister discipline. Without the rational relaxation intended by

such amusements, to use the simile constantly applied to
these circumstances, "as bows always bent" they would
soon lose the power of "aiming straight at perfection."

The monk, it must be remembered, was in no sense "a
gloomy person." There is hardly anything that would
have interfered more with the purpose of his life than any
disposition to become a misanthrope. His calling was no
bar to reasonable recreation. In fact, the true religious
was told to try and possess *angelica hilaritas cum mon-
astica simplicitas*. Thus at Durham we read of the green-
sward "at the back of the house towards the water" where
the younger members of the community played their
games of bowls, with the novice-master as umpire. On
the stone benches, too, in the cloisters at Canterbury,
Westminster, Gloucester, and elsewhere, traces of the
games played centuries ago by the young religious may
still be seen in the holes and squares set out symmetri-
cally, and oblongs divided by carefully-drawn cross-lines.
Sometimes we read of hunting, contests of ball, and other
games of chance. Archbishop Peckham was apparently
somewhat shocked to find that the prior of Cokesford, in
Norfolk, at times indulged in a game of chess with some
of his canons. In other houses he found that dogs were
kept and even stranger pets like apes, cranes, and falcons
were retained in captivity by the religious. It is difficult
to draw the exact line by passing which monastic gravity
is supposed to be injured, and so there was, no doubt,
constant need for regulation on all these matters. But
some such amusements were necessary, and by them,
the tension of long-continued conventual exercises was
relieved. The monastic granges to which from time to
time the religious went for a change of scene and life

were most useful in this regard and enabled them to recreate their strength for another period of service.

In the disposition of the early part of the afternoon, some slight changes had to be made between the winter and summer observance. In summer, immediately after the dinner, the community retired to the dormitory for a sleep, or rest, of an hour's duration. This was the rule from Easter till the feast of the Exaltation of the Holy Cross in September, and all the community were bound to observe the hour for repose if not for sleep. The period of rest, thus allowed at midday, was taken in reality from the night. During the summer the times for vespers, and supper, and bed were each an hour later than they were in the winter months, when the light failed earlier. This hour, by which in summer the sleep before Matins was shortened, was made up by the rest after dinner. During the same period, except on vigils and such-like days when None was said before the dinner, that canonical Hour was recited after the midday sleep. On the signal for the termination of the hour of repose the religious came from the dormitory and, having washed, sat in the cloister till the notice was given to proceed to the church for None, which at this time of the year would have been finished some time between 12.30 and one o'clock.

II. THE DAILY WORK

The chief working hours in a mediæval monastery, including a period for recreation and outdoor exercise, were between twelve o'clock and five in winter, and one o'clock and six in summer. It was during these five hours that the chief business and work of the house was transacted. The officials then attended to the duties of their offices; the writers and rubricators made progress in their literary and artistic compositions in the cloister or scriptorium ; the juniors and novices studied with their masters, or practised public reading and singing under the precentor or his assistant; those who had work in the kitchen, or the bakehouse, or the cellar, etc., addressed themselves to their allotted tasks. In a word, whilst the morning of each monastic day was devoted mainly to prayer and the church services, the afternoon was fully occupied in many and various labours and in the general administration of the monastery. Of course manual labour, that is the working in the gardens, or fields, or workshops of the establishment, always occupied at least a part of the working hours of every monastery, and frequently a large part. This manual labour was necessary for health and exercise, and it was insisted upon in all monastic codes, not so much as an end in itself, as a means to avoid idleness, and to strengthen the constitution of individuals by regular and systematic corporal exercises. The work of a labourer in the fields and gardens was never looked upon as derogatory to the monastic profession ; and St. Benedict expressly tells his followers that they are to look upon themselves "as true monks, when they have to live by the labour of their hands."

This manual labour was generally a conventual work, that is, undertaken in common ; and the permission of the superior was always required to stay away from it. In some Orders, such as the Cistercian and Cluniac, it was performed with a certain amount of ceremonial usage. The prior, for example, rang the bell, or struck the *tabula*

CARMELITE IN HIS STUDY

to call the brethren together, distributed the necessary tools amongst them, and then led the way to the place where they were to dig, or weed, or plant, etc. In the Cluniac houses, the abbot went with the community. When they were assembled at the door of the cloister he was to be informed, and he then came into their midst saying, "*Eamus ad opus manuum*"—"Let us go to our manual labour." Upon this, the youngest leading the way, the monks went in procession to where they had to work, saying the *Miserere* or other psalm. Arrived at the place, they stood round the abbot till the psalm was ended, then the abbot said the *Deus in adjutorium*—"O God, come to my aid," etc., with the "Our Father" and the versicle of Prime to obtain God's blessing on the labours of the day: "Look down, O Lord, upon Thy servants and upon Thy works, and guide Thou Thy sons." To which the community replied: "And may the glory of the Lord our God be upon us, and may He guide us in the works of our hands and direct us in our manual labour." Then bowing to the abbot and to each other, they began the task allotted to them.

At the conclusion of their period of labour the religious returned to the cloister as they had come; the tools were gathered up and put away; and after a short time allowed for washing, they went to the refectory for an afternoon drink of some kind. After this they returned to their places in the cloister: the novices and juniors to their studies, the seniors to their reading or writing.

12. THE VESPERS

At five o'clock in winter and at six in summer the bell rang for Vespers. In some houses, however, as for instance at Durham, the Vespers were always sung at the fixed hour of three in the afternoon, which would divide the working hours of the day into two portions. This would probably have been the rule in all cathedral monastic churches, where, as being public places of worship, regularity of hours would have been aimed at. At the first signal for the Vesper hour the books were all replaced in the aumbry in the cloister, and the community then waited until the commencement of the tolling of the great bell, when they betook themselves to their places in choir. The Vespers were sung with varying pomp and ceremony, according to the rank of the feast celebrated, and the monks were vested for the service in cowls, albs, or copes, according to the solemnity of the occasion.

13. THE SUPPER

Immediately after the Vespers, at the beginning of the "Suffrages of the Saints," or later if Vespers of the "Office of the Dead" were to be said, the cellarer and refectorian left the choir to see that all was prepared for the evening meal, should there be one. At Durham the hour of supper was always five o'clock, after which the doors of the cloister and public rooms were locked and the keys given to the sub-prior until seven o'clock the following morning. In English monasteries the general rule as to supper apparently was that during the summer half of the year—that is from Easter to the 14th September —the second meal was served on all days, except on vigils and fast days. From the feast of All Saints to Advent, supper was only granted on the great feast days, when the community were vested in copes in the choir. During

Advent, and in fact till Easter, except during the short
time between Christmas and the Epiphany, there was but
one meal a day in most religious houses.   The infirm and
those who through weakness needed more food had to
receive special dispensation from the superior.

On supper days the prior, or whoever was presiding in
the choir, left the church at the same time as the cellarer
and refectorian, and began to ring the bell or gong for
the meal.   The community then came out of the church
and, as at dinner, went to wash their hands at the lavatory, and thence to their places in the refectory.   In many
monasteries it was the custom for the seniors to serve and
read during this meal, which was short, consisting of one
good and full dish (*generale*), and one pittance or light
additional plate, consisting of cheese, fruit, nuts, or the
like.   The prior was served, as at dinner, by two juniors,
who took their places at the ends of his table and had
their meal there.   There was a special "pittance" for this
table, and from it the prior, or whoever was acting for
him, was supposed to reserve something for the senior
who was reading.   One dish with the "pittance," and
sufficient to serve those who sat thereat, was placed at the
head of each table and passed down.

The conclusion of the supper was like that of the dinner.
The religious went to finish their Grace in the church,
and thence passed up to the dormitory to change their
day habits, girdles, and boots for those better adapted for
the night.   When this was done they went again into the
cloister to wait there till the signal should be given for
the evening Collation or reading.   At Durham there was
no interval between the supper and the Collation ; but
"Grace being said," we are told, "the monks all departed

to the chapter-house to meet the prior, every night, there
to remain in prayer and devotion till six of the clock,
at which time upon the ringing of a bell they went to
the *Salve*."

14. THE COLLATION AND COMPLINE

About half-past six in winter, and half-past seven in
summer, a small bell was rung in the cloister to call all
together for the evening reading, called the *Collation*,
which took place in the chapter-room.   Whilst the bell
was ringing any of the community who desired, on days
when there was no supper, could go to the refectory and
obtain some kind of drink, called the *potum caritatis,*
with which possibly was also given a small portion
of bread, to sustain them till their dinner the following
day.   When they had finished this very modest refection,
the brethren at once betook themselves to their places in
the chapter-hall, where the reader was already waiting in
the pulpit with the book open at the place where he left
off the night before.

Meanwhile the abbot, or prior in the absence of the
abbot, waited for a time in the private parlour ready to
hear any petitions for exemption from rule, and grant
any leave that might be necessary.   When this business
had been transacted he came to the Collation, at which
all were bound to be present.   The reading apparently
only occupied a short time, and in the brief interval
between this and the Hour of Compline the community
could in the summer pass into the cloister, or in winter
time could go to warm themselves at the fire in the
common recreation-room.

15. COMPLINE AND BED

At seven o'clock in the winter, and eight in the summer, the tolling of the bell called the community to Compline—the last conventual act of the monastic day. This Hour was not necessarily said in the choir of the church. At St. Mary's, York, for example, the brethren recited their Compline standing in the Galilee, the juniors nearest to the door. The Office began with the *Confiteor*, as the Collation had already taken the place of the *Capitulum*, with which otherwise the Hour of Compline commenced. When the anthem to the Virgin Mother of God, with which Compline always concluded, was being said or sung, all turned to the Crucifix or *Majestas*.

Immediately the triple-prayer of the Pater, Ave, and Creed, said at the end, was finished, the superior gave a signal, and the community rose and passed to the door of the church. Here either the superior or the junior priest who had said the prayers at Compline was ready to sprinkle each with holy water as he passed in solemn silence to the dormitory. Before half-past seven, then, in winter, and an hour later than this in summer, all would have been in bed, and the busy round of duties, which so completely filled the working day of every mediæval monastery, would have come to an end.

CHAPTER VIII

THE NUNS OF MEDIÆVAL ENGLAND

NO account of English monastic life would be complete without some special reference to the nuns and nunneries. It is, it may be first observed in passing, altogether wrong to apply the word "convent" exclusively to houses of nuns, as is so frequently done in these days. The title "convent" as well as that of "monastery" and "abbey" was applicable to any house of either monks or nuns, and the exclusive use of the word for a religious house of women is, indeed, of quite modern origin.

It is unfortunate that our information in regard to the inner life of the nuns in pre-Reformation England is so scanty. Beyond the delightful picture we get of the social life of the nuns of Kington in Old Jacques' recollections, as recorded by John Aubrey, and the charming portrait of the prioress who

> " Was so charitable and so pitous . . .
> and al was conscience and tendre herte,"

in Chaucer's tales, there is but little information to be obtained about the nuns of England ; of the simple, hard, yet happy lives they led in their cloistered homes, and of the ample charity they dispensed to all in their immediate neighbourhood.

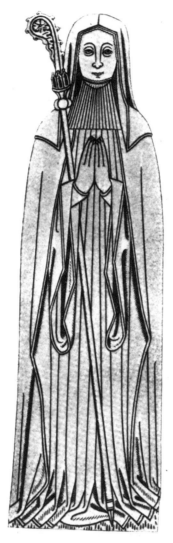

ELIZABETH HARVEY
ABBESS OF ELSTOW

Of course, so far as the usual forms, manners, and customs of cloister life are concerned, what has been already said of the monastic method of life generally, applies to nuns, with certain necessary reservations, as well as to monks and canons. It will be useful, however, to furnish the reader with some account of certain special features of female religious life. One of the most charming mediæval pictures of that life is given in an account of the abbesses of the Benedictine nunnery of Wherwell, in Hampshire. It records the unblemished life and good deeds of the abbess Euphemia, who ruled the house from A.D. 1226 to 1257, and is translated from the chartulary of the abbey by the Rev. Dr. Cox in the second volume of the *Victoria History of the County of Hampshire.* The account is too delightful not to be given in full.

"On the 6th of the Kalends of May, in the year of grace 1257, died the blessed mother abbess, Euphemia, most worthy to be remembered, who, by our affection and good fellowship, and with divine sanction, succeeded the late abbess Maud of sweet memory. It is, therefore, most fitting that we should always perpetuate the memory, in our special prayers and suffrages, of one who ever worked for the glory of God, and for the weal of both our souls and bodies. For she increased the number of the Lord's handmaids in this monastery from forty to eighty, to the exaltation of the worship of God. To her sisters, both in health and sickness, she administered the necessaries of life with piety, prudence, care, and honesty. She also increased the sum allowed for garments by 12d. each. The example of her holy conversation and charity, in conjunction with her pious exhortations and regular discipline, caused each one to know how, in the words of the Apostle, to possess her vessel in sanctification and honour. She also, with maternal piety and careful forethought, built, for the use of both sick and sound, a new and large infirmary away from

the main buildings, and in conjunction with it a dormitory
with the necessary offices.   Beneath the infirmary she constructed a watercourse, through which a stream flowed with
sufficient force to carry off all refuse that might corrupt
the air.

"Moreover she built there a place set apart for the refresh-
ment of the soul, namely a chapel of the Blessed Virgin, which
was erected outside the cloister behind the infirmary.   With
the chapel she enclosed a large space, which was adorned
on the north side with pleasant vines and trees.   On the other
side, by the river-bank, she built offices for various uses, a
space being left in the centre where the nuns are able from
time to time to enjoy the pure air.   In these and in other
numberless ways, the blessed mother Euphemia provided for
the worship of God and the welfare of the sisters.   But notwithstanding all this, she also so conducted herself with regard
to exterior affairs, that she seemed to have the spirit of a man
rather than of a woman.   The court of the abbey-manor, owing
to the useless mass of squalid outbuildings, and the propinquity
of the kitchen to the granary and old hall, was in much danger
of fire ; whilst the confined area and the amount of animal
refuse was a cause of offence to both the feet and nostrils of
those who had occasion to pass through.   The mother Euphemia,
realising that the Lord had called her to the rule of the abbey
at Wherwell, not that she might live there at ease, but that
she might, with due care and despatch, uproot and destroy
and dissipate all that was noxious, and establish and erect
that which would be useful, demolished the whole of these
buildings, levelled the court, and erected a new hall of suitable
size and height.   She also built a new mill, some distance from
the hall, and constructed it with great care in order that more
work than formerly might be done therein for the service of the
house.   She surrounded the court with a wall and the necessary
buildings, and round it she made gardens and vineyards and
shrubberies in places that were formerly useless and barren,
and which now became both serviceable and pleasant.   The
manor-house of Middleton, which occupied a dry situation and

was close to a public thoroughfare, and was further disfigured by old and crumbling buildings, she moved to another site, where she erected permanent buildings, new and strong, on the bank of the river, together with farmhouses. She also set to work in the same way at Tufton, in order that the buildings of both the manor-houses in that neighbourhood might be of greater service, and safer against the danger of fire. These and other innumerable works, our good superior Euphemia performed for the advantage of the house, but she was none the less zealous in works of charity, gladly and freely exercising hospitality, so that she and her daughters might find favour with One Whom Lot and Abraham and others have pleased by the grace of hospitality. Moreover, because she greatly loved to honour duly the House of God and the place where His glory dwells, she adorned the church with crosses, reliquaries, precious stones, vestments, and books. And because the bell-tower above the dormitory fell down through decay one night, about the hour of Matins, when by an obvious miracle from heaven, though the nuns were at that moment in the dormitory, some in bed and some in prayer before their beds, all escaped not only death but even any bodily injury, she caused another bell-tower of worked stone to be erected, conformable to the fair appearance of the church and the rest of the buildings, of commanding height, and of exquisite workmanship. But as she advanced in years, towards the end of her life, there was imminent danger of the complete collapse of the presbytery of the church ; by the advice of skilled builders, she caused the presbytery to be taken down to the last stones of the foundations ; and because the ground was found to be undermined and unsafe, she caused the damp soil to be dug out to a depth of twelve feet till firm and dry ground was found ; when, having invoked the grace of the Holy Spirit, with prayers and tears she laid with her own hands the first stone of the foundations. Moreover she rejoiced to have found favour with God, so that before her last days were ended she saw this work that she had begun brought to its desired end. Thus she, who had devoted herself when amongst us to the service of His house and the habitation of His glory, found the due reward for her merits with our Lord Jesus Christ, through the prayers and merits of the Blessed Virgin Mary and of the blessed apostles SS. Peter and Paul, in whose honour, at the instigation of the abbess Euphemia, this church was dedicated, who with the Father and the Holy Ghost, ever liveth and reigneth God through all the ages of eternity. Amen."

Of the life, social and religious, led by the nuns of England, something may be learnt from the few scattered account-books that have survived the general destruction of documents in the sixteenth century. The following sketch is founded upon one such paper-book of accounts now in the public Record Office. It was printed privately some few years ago, and is here reproduced as affording, in the judgment of some, a not uninteresting glimpse into the cloister life and work led in the nunneries in the early days of the fifteenth century. The accounts were kept in a small book by a nun called Dame Petronilla.

Her family name (or was it that of her birthplace?) was Dunwich, and in keeping her accounts she had as assistant and auditor another nun, Dame Katherine Midelton. Their convent was Grace Dieu in Leicestershire — the only religious house of Augustinian nuns in England. The scanty but picturesque ruins of their old convent may still be seen not far from the present Cistercian Abbey of Mount St. Bernard, and quite near to Grace Dieu Manor-house, the home of Ambrose Phillipps de Lisle. The convent was founded in Charnwood Forest by Lady Rohesia de Verdon in the middle of the thirteenth century, and it is said that the boundary of the garden, made by the sisters to resemble that of Gethsemane, may yet be traced with a little trouble. Wordsworth wrote several

BENEDICTINE NUNS IN CHOIR

of his poems in the immediate neighbourhood, and thus
describes the situation of the old nunnery as seen, or
rather *not* seen, from Cole Orton some few miles away:—

> " Beneath yon eastern ridge, the craggy bound
> Rugged and high of Charnwood's forest ground
> Stand yet, but, stranger, hidden from thy view,
> The ivied ruins of forlorn Grace Dieu."

Our guide-books, of course, ascribe the destruction of the
convent in 1539 to the fact of serious complaints having
been made of certain irregularities on the part of the
inmates. Most people nowadays know how to estimate
these "complaints" at their right value, proceeding as
they did from the Visitors of Henry VIII., who having
been sent for the purpose of finding evidence of irregularities to justify the intended spoliation, of course found
them. In the special case of this convent of Grace Dieu
we have subsequently the direct testimony of the country
gentlemen of Leicestershire, that the fifteen nuns following the rule of St. Austin then inmates of the establishment, and whose good name had been so vilely traduced
by the king's emissaries, were all "of good and virtuous
conversation and living," and that their presence in the
wilds of Charnwood Forest was a blessing to the neighbourhood.

We are, however, concerned with the convent of Grace
Dieu in much earlier days: very nearly a century and
a half before its final destruction in 1539. Dame Petronilla and Dame Katherine kept their accounts of the
establishment in this old paper-book "from the Feast
of the Purification of the Blessed Virgin Mary, in the
first year of King Henry V.," for four years: that is, from
1414 to 1418. The volume in question, though simple

enough in its style of book-keeping, presents in reality the general accounts of the house. Probably Dame Petronilla would have opened her eyes very wide indeed at the present system of elaborate checks and counter-checks devised to exercise the brains and possibly the patience of modern cellarers, and "double entry" and such-like mysteries would probably have seemed to her a useless expenditure of time and nerve-power, and hardly consistent with the religious simplicity which ascetic writers had taught her to cultivate. Her system is simplicity itself: so much received for such a thing, ordinary or extraordinary: so much spent, and on what; that is all.

In one point, however, this careful nun does not hesitate to take a considerable amount of trouble. What would a cellarer say to-day, were he or she asked to give the ages of all the live stock under their care! Dame Petronilla would have been quite able to do so at any moment, for from time to time she enters, not indeed the birth-days of the cattle and pigs, but their ages. In 1415, for example, which by the way was the ever-memorable year of Agincourt, this is her "tally" of all the pigs in the keeping of the herd, Nicholas Swon (or should it be Swine?)

" 5 boars, *i.e.*—two aged three years, two aged two, and one aged one ; ten sows, *i.e.*—nine at three years, and one aged one ; forty-one small pigs of a year, and thirty of six months old ; ten full grown pigs, and ten *porcelli lactantes sub matribus* or sucking pigs."

Pork, it is clear, must have been one of the chief articles of food for the nuns and their retainers, since there are frequent notices of pigs transferred from the farm to the larder ; on two occasions during the four years, Dame Petronilla chronicles the death of a good many of the convent pigs from disease. Their stock of cattle appears somewhat large at first sight, till it is realised that with one thing and another there were a good many mouths to feed in this establishment. Thus in one year we find a list of 32 cows, "three of which had not calved; three bulls, 16 steers, 22 heifers and eight bull calves." Besides this there were 27 yoke-oxen under the care of their driver, and 29 calves, one of which on the account-day is noted as having, since the making of the list, gone to the cook to furnish forth the conventual dinner. At this same time Henry Smyth, the outdoor bailiff, gives in the account of Henry, the shepherd, which shows that he had 103 ewes and 52 lambs under his pastoral charge.

The revenue of the convent consisted chiefly of the rent of lands and buildings and the sale of produce, timber and such-like. Thus we have the rent of a farm at Belton put down as £21 17s. 9d., this being the largest item in the receipts, and indeed a very large item in those days from any farm rent. From another parcel of land, besides the rent, one year Dame Petronilla and her assistant, Dame Katherine Midelton, account for the price of sixteen quarters of lime at 9¾d. the quarter. Roger Dan, the miller, pays a rent of £5 13s. 4d. for the mill at Belton, and at the same time there is another receipt for "half a hundred merkefish and twelve stone of cheese." Besides these and other similar sums which are entered under the heading of "ordinary," we find such "extra-ordinary" receipts as £3 for twenty-four ash trees, and a few shillings for the skins of lambs that had been used in the kitchen. Another year we see that 100 kids were

sold at 2s. each, and that there was a sale of hurdles and
faggots about Shrovetide. Thirty stone of wool was purchased at one time by one Thomas Hunte, a neighbour,
who, by the way, had his two daughters evidently at
school in the convent ; once there was a sale of fish from
the mill down at Belton, and it brought into the nuns'
exchequer over £6.

The mention of Thomas Hunte's daughters may be
supplemented by evidence in these accounts of other
children being under the care of the " White Ladies " of
Grace Dieu. Thomas Hunte appears to have paid at the
rate of 17s. 4d. for each of his two children, but as it is
expressly stated that it was for their food only, probably
their education was thrown in without consideration.
Lady Beaumont also had a daughter in the convent, for
whom she and her lord undertook to pay £2 13s. 4d. a
year; but when Dame Petronilla last made up her accounts,
or rather in the last account we have from her pen, the
good nuns had only got £2.   Lord Beaumont, however,
was evidently too great a personage to be reminded of the
missing 13s. 4d., and the convent authorities evidently
desired to stand well in his favour.   They fed him well,
for instance, when he came to see his child ; for on one
occasion Dame Petronilla gives some of the expenses of
his entertainment.   These included, besides 1½d. for " 1
shoulder le molton," and 8d. for two lambs, an almost
unique payment for two fowls for the nobleman's table.
This slight glimpse of the relations between the convent
and the neighbouring gentry, in regard to the education
of their children, affords a corroboration of one of the
laments made at the general dissolution, that their destruction was a terrible thing for those who had hitherto made

use of them for this purpose. According to Robert Aske, the leader of the Pilgrimage of Grace, one of the reasons why the Yorkshire people strongly resented their over-throw, was because "in nunneries their daughters were brought up in virtue."

Another practice revealed by these old accounts was that of people coming to stop at the convent for the celebration of some of the greater feasts. Thus for one "All Saints' Day," Mary de Ecton, Joan Villiers, and the two daughters of Robert Neville were lodged and entertained by the nuns. These visitors eventually made an offering for the hospitality shown them; as, for instance, on this very occasion each of the Neville ladies paid 5s. and Joan Villiers 6s. 8d. The last-named lady was at Grace Dieu no less than four several times in the year 1418, and each time left behind a similar offering. At another time Giles Jurdon paid 7s. for the board of his daughter during the week of Pentecost, when she prob-ably came to visit her sister, who, known as Dame Eliza-beth, was a nun in the convent. Roger Roby also, who was apparently the father of Dame Alice, was entertained by the nuns twice in the year 1416, and gave an alms of 6s. 8d. at one visit and 13s. 4d. at the other.

It may be of interest to give a list of the nuns at this time living in Grace Dieu. They were fourteen in num-ber, exclusive of the prioress, and their names were:—

> Dame Margaret Kempston, prioress.
> Dame Alice Mortimer, sub-prioress.
> Dame Margaret Twyford.
> Dame Philippa Jake.
> Dame Alice Dunwich.
> Dame Katherine Midelton.

Dame Anne de Norton.
Dame Alice Roby.
Dame Margery Witham.
Dame Katherine Pounce.
Dame Alice Prestwold.
Dame Elizabeth Jurdon (originally put 3rd).
Dame Petronilla Dunwich (originally put 5th).
Dame Elizabeth Hakulthorp.
Dame Alice Powtrell or Pouncstrell.

The spiritual needs of this community were, of course, ministered to by a chaplain. He is generally called "Sir William," but on one occasion he appears as "Sir William Granger, or Norwich." He was paid 38s. 4d. a year as his stipend, and this was to include 6d. as the price of a pair of gloves. On certain occasions, as on the greater feasts, Sir William had other clerical help, such as that of "Henry the Chaplain," and the "Parson of Hatherun." It is not uninteresting to notice that the nuns' little present for the services of these reverend gentlemen was, it would seem, delicately handed to them in purses purchased for the purpose. They had also the ministration of an "extraordinary" confessor, a certain Friar William Young, and to him was given 1s. 8d. for the expenses of his journey each time he came to the convent. Something additional was, of course, bestowed on him when, as in 1418, he remained to help in the Holy-Week services. At times, not very frequently, "my Lady," the prioress, entertained the clergy at a little simple banquet; she did not merely provide for them, for that, of course, the convent always did with true hospitality; but she dined with them. Dame Petronilla does not say, when they "dined with my Lady," but

when "my Lady dined with them," as, for example, when
she notes on the Sunday within the octave of our Lady's
Assumption in the year 1416: "a sucking-pig for the
table of my Lady, because to-day she dined with the
Vicar."

It may be mentioned that Dame Petronilla and her
assistant Dame Katherine made up their accounts from
Sunday to Sunday, as far as expenses are concerned, so
that in running through the pages it is possible to form some
idea of how these good mediæval nuns lived. I do not think
that the most captious critic could charge them with feast-
ing on the "fat of the land," or with much indulgence in
the luxuries even of those primitive days. There is one
peculiarity, however, in these otherwise excellent accounts,
which rather interferes with a full knowledge of the
commissariat at Grace Dieu. The sisters did not think
it necessary to enter among the payments the value of
the farm and garden produce they consumed, beyond the
cost of sowing and gathering into their barns. However, we know that they must have eaten bread and made
use of the exceedingly few vegetables and pot-herbs that
were then grown in the gardens of England, so we may
take these as additional to the "food stuffs" shown
in the accounts as paid for. A few examples will be
sufficient to give the reader an insight into the general
catering at Grace Dieu early in the fifteenth century.
These are the first entries among the expenses written by
Dame Petronilla when she commenced her duties as
"Treasurer," as she calls herself in one place, after the
Feast of the Purification, 1414.

"For two Sundays after the Purification purchased two small
pigs price 6*d*. For house food during the time of Lent, £3 6*s*. 8*d*.

For seventy hard dried fish for the same time, 11s. 6d.   A calf bought for the convent for Quinquagesima Sunday (Shrovetide), 9d.   Four small pigs for the same day, 9d.   Beef bought for the same day, 20d.   Mustard bought at Ashby, 1d.   Cheese bought on Friday in Sexagesima week, 5d.   Thomas Fene for 2 quarters of red-herrings for Lent, 12d.   Nicholas Swon (the swineherd, as the reader may remember), 2d. for catching two small pike at the sluice."

The Lenten arrangements for feeding the natural man and woman from Ash Wednesday to Easter Sunday in those hardy and robust days are, even to think of, enough to turn our refined and educated stomachs.   Eggs, to a certain limited extent, no doubt these good religious had ; although, on the principle before explained, we do not find them mentioned, except as included in their natural producer, the domestic hen.   But beyond this, during all this penitential time, the staple food, here as everywhere throughout England, was salted and dried fish.   Conger, green fish, ling, and codling stockfish, wealing or whiting, and mackerel are among those named 1 Russell's *Book of Nurture* as the usual Lenten food. How tired the mouth of even the most ascetic religious must have got of the taste of salt fish, however much it was disguised with mustard sauce, or, as on great festivals, "baken, dressed, and dished with white sugar"!   No wonder the rising generation in those primitive times were warned by Russell to look carefully upon what they ate for fear they might light on some unsavoury morsel ; and "of all manner salt fish," he says, "look ye pare away the pele (skin) before beginning upon it."   No wonder that after six weeks of salt herring, stockfish, and such-like, our ancestors in the cloisters could look forward to the time-honoured Easter-day joke of "the devil on horseback," or a split red-herring riding as a jockey on the back of a duck, perpetrated by the convent cook.

Lent, however, is naturally not a fair sample of the food supplied to the Grace Dieu nuns, so let us take the page of expenses for Easter week. Here it is :—

"A stall-fed ox, 16s. 1 pig from the farm. 3 small pigs, price 14d. 1 calf, price 2s. Almonds and rais (raisins), 12d., and for Friday 150 fresh herrings and a stockfish (*i.e.* cod), 2s."

The almonds and raisins were a great luxury to the good sisters, and only on a few other occasions during the four years of Dame Petronilla's housekeeping does this extraordinary expense occur ! We cannot help thinking, too, with what pleasure the nuns must have welcomed the change of fish diet on the Friday in Easter week. Two shillings was in those days a great sum to pay for any article of food, but the fresh sea fish must have been scarce enough in Charnwood Forest before the days of railroads. "White herring fresh, if it be seaward and newly caught, with the roe white and tender," says an old authority, "is toothsome food"; and the *Book of Nurture* tells "the cook" how best to prepare it for his master's eating.

" The white herring by the bak a brode ye splat him sure,
    Both roe and bones voyded, then may your lord endure to
        eat merily with mustard."

We need not linger further over the food supplied to the sisters. One week was very much like another, and the changes were few and far between. It is not often that the accounts show such expenses as " paid to the wife of James the miller for twelve chickens for the table, 12d."— spring chickens, too, they must have been, for they were eaten on Low Sunday. One All Saints' Day, by the way, the nuns had four geese, for which the price paid was 3*d*. each; and one Christmas Day their table was supplied from the farm with nine fowls, and we are told they had seven at their dinner, the other two being reserved to furnish forth their supper. Pork, beef, veal, and fish : these were the ordinary dishes supplied. Mutton, curiously, though not altogether rare, does not appear very frequently in their *menu*, and lamb is named as a dish at only one of my lady prioress's little banquets ; although the receipt for "lamb-skins sold from the kitchen" shows that it was not altogether unknown to the common table. Probably these nuns were "good housewives," in the best sense, and preferred to get all they could out of their flocks in the shape of wool, etc., rather than eat tender, but tasteless and immature mutton.

It should be remembered that in the commissariat of Grace Dieu was evidently included the feeding of the retainers of the convent, as well as that of the nuns. These domestics were many, and were fed certainly as well, and sometimes apparently better than were the ladies themselves. The names of two-and-twenty men-servants and eight women who were retainers of the convent, and their wages, or "rewards" as they are called, are preserved in the account-book. They vary very considerably, from 26*s*. 8*d*. paid to one Henry Smith, to 2*s*. 6*d*. bestowed on "Hirdeman"; and among the women the difference ranges from 22*s*. 6*d*. paid to Isabel Botelor, to 1*s*. 8*d*. to Matilda Gerrard. Henry Smith, named above, seems to have been a sort of factotum, a real treasure and excellent servant. He is called bailiff in one place, and was no doubt of a higher standing than most

of the others. Whatever there was to be done, inside
or outside the house, it is evident that no one but Henry
Smith could see to it properly.

Besides their wages, these retainers of the Augustinian
dames had their cottages and clothes looked to for them
by the convent bursar. Thus before the autumn work
of cleaning the land and sowing the winter corn com-
mences, we find a record of "twenty-four pairs of shoes"
given out, which are charged to the convent account at
2s. 8½d.—not the pair, but the two dozen. This sum
would appear, perhaps, ridiculously small, even for those
days, had we not some reason to think that the leather
for making them was provided to the local cobbler from
the convent store; for on one occasion Dame Petronilla
notes that she paid 8d. for tanning (*pro albacione*) the
skin of a horse, bought of Robert Harston. Another
present from the nuns to their workpeople in view of
these autumn works, the cost of which appears in these
accounts, was a pair of gloves to each of the thirty men
and women about to be engaged in the weeding and
ditching and hedging; as for their clothes, these were
all made on the premises from the raw material. Thus
in one year we read :—

"Paid for the spinning of six score (bundles) of linen flax,
5s.; paid for weaving the three score ells of linen cloth from the
same, 3s. 4d.; paid for woofing and warping three-and-twenty
ells of woollen cloth, 6s. 2d.; paid for spinning twenty lbs. of
wool at 1¼d. the pound, 2s. 6d.; paid for dyeing twenty-seven
ells of cloth blood red, at 4d. the ell, 7s. 8d. ; paid for spinning
woollen cloth for ordinary livery, 11d."; and so on.

All this evidently was for the clothes of the entire establishment, including the men and women who worked on the

farm, and in the laundry, the kitchen, and the bakehouse, etc.

Curiously, as it seems to us perhaps now, each of the nuns had a maximum allowance of 6*s*. 8*d*. a year for clothes. It taught them, no doubt, to look after the articles of their dress with care and thrift, better than if the white woollen tunic, scapular and veil, woven from the produce of their own flock of sheep, and the still whiter linen wimple spun from the flax and made into good sound cloth by their own hands, or at least under their own direction, were to appear to drop from the hand of Providence without reference to cost. One or two curious entries seem to show that friends sometimes gave the annual sum allowed for the clothing of some of the nuns. Thus one year William Roby paid "for the clothes of his relation, Dame Agnes Roby"; and at another time Margaret Roby brought the 6*s*. 8*d*. for the same purpose when she came on a visit. One interesting item of knowledge about the work of the nuns is conveyed in a brief entry of receipt. It is clear that these ladies were good needlewomen, and their work must have been exceptionally excellent, seeing that a cope was purchased from them by a neighbouring rector for £10.

The indication that these accounts give us of the farming operations of the Grace Dieu nuns is sufficient to make us wish that Dame Petronilla had been a little more explicit; still we are grateful for what we learn about the crops, and their sowing, and weeding, and gathering, the stacking of the wheat, and oats, and peas, and the threshing out of the grain. Thus the wages of Adam Baxter and his wife, and the wife of Robert Harston for weeding thirty acres of barley are set down. Each of these, by the way,

had a pair of gloves given them before they were set to
the task, and the entire work cost the convent 10s. 3d.
Three men beyond the usual farm staff were ordinarily
employed in cutting the grass, and in making and stacking the hay.   In the general harvesting, men and women
were employed in the fields ; and, be it remarked, their
labour was paid for at the same rate.   What are called
the autumn works—the harvesting and the subsequent
cleaning of the ground—seem to have lasted about seven
or eight weeks, and were begun soon after the feast of
the Assumption of our Blessed Lady.   It is curious, and
not uninteresting, to find that the Irish came over for the
harvesting in Leicestershire in the fifteenth century as
they do now ; thus we have Mathew Irishman and Isabel
Irish named, together with Edward Welshman, as engaged in the fields of Grace Dieu in 1415.   Altogether,
the cost of the extra labour in the autumn works amounted
to nearly £10, a large sum indeed in those days.

Besides payments of extra money for the harvesting and
regular work, some indication of the kindly way in which
the good nuns recognised the services of their dependents
on special occasions appears in these accounts.   In the
lambing season, for instance, Henry, the shepherd, was
given 2d. "for his good service and care of the sheep,"
and John Stapulford received the same sum "for looking
after the lambs before their weaning," whilst John Warren
for "fold-hurdling" was rewarded with 1s. ; and to take
another instance of a somewhat different kind, the convent bailiff at Kirby, one Richard Marston, was given a
purse, as a sign that the nuns appreciated his care of their
property.   One chance entry shows that when the sheep
were being sheared, the labourers were given extra meat for

their meals, since Dame Petronilla gives 16*d.* for a calf to feed them specially, on a day when evidently she and her sisters in religion were eating fish in the convent refectory.

A word must now be said about that necessary item in the accounts of every well-regulated religious house, "repairs." These seem to have exercised the two bursars of Grace Dieu very considerably. The special trouble evidently began with the roof of the house. In the first year of their stewardship they had in, of course, Robert the Slater, and for some reason his bill was only partly met in that twelvemonth. All during Lent, he and his mate were at work mending holes, and making others. From the house his ministrations extended to the cloister. Then came the gutters all over the establishment, which stood in urgent need of attention, as gutters always appear to do, even in our more civilised days. Next it was found that the church must be looked to ; and before this was over, the dependants had come to the conclusion that whilst all this repairing was being done at the convent and Robert the Slater was about with his mate and his material upon the ground, it would be a pity not to renovate their cottages. Poor Dame Petronilla must have been well-nigh distracted at the thought that Robert the Slater—who, by the way, did more than roofing, and seems to have been a jack-of-all-trades, though loose tiles were his forte—having once secured a foothold in the establishment, had come to stay. But she gave in with exemplary resignation, and the dependants had their cottages repaired, or what was the same thing, received money to pay for them. Taking one thing with another, more than £10 went in this way during the first year of the procuratorial reign of Dames Petronilla and Katherine.

Among the workmen that haunted Grace Dieu in these days, and who, if there is any fitness in things so far as ghosts are concerned, ought to be found haunting the ruins to-day, was one called Richard Hyrenmonger. He came, we learn, from Donington, and the accounts prove that he must have had a good store of all kinds of nails, and keys, and bolts, judging by the variety he was able to produce. Under him worked John the Plumber, or rather two Johns the Plumber, senior and junior; and, like modern plumbers are wont to do, they appear to have plagued Dame Petronilla and her assistant with their constant tinkering at the pipes and drains of the establishment. "John the senior" and "John the junior," for example, were six days mending "le pype," for which they were paid 3s. 4d. ; but apparently it was not properly done, for just after this, "le pype" misbehaved itself again, and Dame Petronilla had to purchase a new *brass* pipe to bring the water to the door of the refectory, and the two Johns were at work again. Of course Richard the Ironmonger always found a lot of work for himself on the farm, so that what with one thing and another, Grace Dieu must have been a very comfortable inheritance for him.

Among the miscellaneous manners and customs of the good nuns of Grace Dieu which are recalled to us in these faded papers of accounts, very few of course can find place here. One such is the yearly visit of the candle-maker to prepare the tallow dips for the dark winter evenings. The preparation made for his coming appears in the purchase of tallow and mutton fat to be used for rush-lights and cresset-lights, which must have done hardly more than make visible the darkness of a winter evening and an early winter morning at Grace Dieu. My lady prioress apparently had an oil lamp of some kind, and we read of special candles for the wash-place and at the door of the refectory, etc.   It is to be supposed that the nuns had some means of warming themselves during the cold winter months, for we read of a travelling tinker employed upon mending a chimney to the hall fireplace, and probably they were burning logs from out of Charnwood somewhere or other ; but in these accounts there is no mention of fuel except on one occasion, when Richard the Ironmonger had some coal purchased for him ; but this was only that he might heat a ploughshare that had got out of shape.

Another most important matter in mediæval times was the annual salting of the winter provisions which took place in every establishment.   On St. Martin's Day, November 11th, the mediæval farmer considered seriously what was the number of his live stock, what was his store of hay, and how long the one could be kept by the other.   The residue of the stock had to go into the salting-tub for the winter food of the family and dependants.   So at Grace Dieu the purchase of the salt for the great operation is entered in the accounts.   On one occasion also Dame Petronilla, "when a boar was killed"—whether by accident or not does not appear—had it spiced as well as salted, and it was no doubt served up on great occasions as a special delicacy in the common refectory.

The picture of the Grace Dieu nuns afforded by these accounts is that of charming, peace-loving ladies ; good practical Christian women, as all nuns should be ; taking a personal interest in the welfare of their tenants and dependants ; occupied, over and besides their conventual and religious duties, in works of genuine charity.   They taught the daughters of the neighbouring gentry, and

were not too exacting in requiring even what had been
promised as the annual pension. They encouraged ladies
to come and join them in celebrating the festivals of the
church, and out of their small means they set aside a not
insignificant portion for the care and clothing of sick in
their infirmary; whilst out of their income they found not
less than eight corrodies—or pensions—which cost them
£7 7s. 4d., or more than five per cent. of their annual
revenue. Of their work mention has already been made.
They grew the wool and spun it and wove it into cloth,
not only for their own garments, but also for those of their
retainers; whilst a chance entry of receipt reveals that
they were indeed skilled in a high degree in ecclesiastical
embroidery. That they were not guilty of "dilapidation"
of their house their extensive repairs prove; and that
they cared for their lands and farm buildings must be
obvious from the purchases made, and the items of expense in connection with every kind of agricultural im-
plement. They took their burden in common ecclesiastical
expenses, even contributing their quota of 3d. towards
the expenses of the *Procurator cleri* of the district to Convocation. They were peace-loving, if we may judge from
the absence of all law expenses, save and except one small
item for an appearance at the local marshal's court, and
whether even this was for themselves or for one of their
tenants, and what it was about, does not appear. As it
was only 2d., it could not have been much to interfere
with the general harmony which apparently existed in the
neighbourhood. They lived, too, within their income,
which was, more or less, £103 13s. 6d. a year. It is true
that in the first year, owing probably to the exceptional
repairs which the nuns undertook, they went somewhat

beyond their means.   The sum was only slight, being but
£7 11s. 10½d., and it is pleasant to observe that "out of
love of the nuns," and "to relieve the house of anxiety,"
a lady paid the deficit, making her gift £7 12s.

Dame Petronilla and Dame Margaret! how little they
could have thought when they penned their simple accounts that they would have given such pleasurable
information five hundred years after their time!   How
little they could ever have dreamed of the pleasant light
their jottings would have thrown on so many of their
doings and their little ways!   They were kind, prudent,
charitable souls, without a doubt, and if they might at
times have used better ink than they did, that fault was a
point of holy parsimony.   And if they might have given
here and there just a little more information on certain
points, they are willingly forgiven and more than forgiven, for what they have left to posterity.   Their souls,
oft so troubled and vexed by the many cares incidental to
the office of a conventual Martha, have long doubtless
been in peace, and their spirits no longer vexed by
Richard the "Hyrenmonger" and the two Johns, the
senior and junior plumbers.   What would they think,
could they to-day revisit the scene of their former labours
and cares?   The old home they evidently loved so well is
past repairing now, and not even the kindly help of that
old servant and friend of the convent, Henry Smith,
could avail to suggest the best way of setting about
reparation.

All the larger nunneries and probably most of the
smaller ones, to whatever Order they belonged, opened
their doors for the education of young girls, who were
frequently boarders.   In fact the female portion of the

FRANCISCAN NUNS IN CHOIR

population, the poor as well as the rich, had in the convents their only schools, nuns their only teachers, in pre-
Reformation times. Chaucer, in describing the well-to-do
miller of Trompington, says—

> "A wyf he hadde, come of noble kyn ;
> Sche was i-fostryd in a nonnery . . .
> Ther durste no wight clepe hir but *Madame*
> What for hir kindred and hir nortelry
> That sche had lerned in the nonnerye."

John Aubrey, too, writes almost as an eye-witness of the
Wiltshire convents that "the young maids were brought
up . . . at nunneries, where they had examples of piety,
and humility, and modesty, and obedience to imitate and
to practise. Here they learned needlework, the art of
confectionery, surgery (for anciently there were no apothe-
caries or surgeons—the gentlewomen did cure their poor
neighbours : their hands are now too fine), physic, writing,
drawing, etc. Old Jacques could see from his house the
nuns of the priory (St. Mary's, near Kington St. Michael)
come forth into the nymph-hay with their rocks and
wheels to spin : and with their sewing work. He would
say that he had told threescore and ten : but of nuns
there were not so many, but in all, with lay sisters and
widows, old maids and young girls, there might be such a
number. This," he concludes, "was a fine way of breed-
ing up young women, who are led more by example than
precept ; and a good retirement for widows and grave
single women to a civil, virtuous, and holy life."

In the well-known case of Nunnaminster, Winchester,
there were, at the time of the suppression, twenty-six girl
boarders who were reported by the local commissioners to
be daughters of "lords, knights, and gentlemen." The

list that is set forth begins with a Plantagenet and includes
Tichbornes, Poles, and Tyrrells. So, too, in the case of the
Benedictines of Barking, of Kingsmead, Derby, and of
Polesworth and Nuneaton, Warwickshire ; of the Cluniacs
of Delapré, Northampton ; of the Cistercians of Wintney,
Hants ; and of the Gilbertines of Shouldham, Norfolk,
it can be established that not only were many of the nuns
of good birth, but that their pupils were in the main drawn
from the same class.

The Episcopal Visitations of the Diocese of Norwich for
1492 to 1532, edited by Dr. Jessop, throw some interesting
light on the inner life and social working of the nunneries
of East Anglia. From the names of the inmates it
becomes evident that some of these houses were in the
main occupied by ladies of gentle birth, such as Wil-
loughbys, Everards, Wingfields, Jerninghams, and the
like. This was especially the case with the Austin
house of Campsey and the Benedictine houses of Bungay
and Thetford. When Bishop Nicke visited the last of
these houses in 1514, complaint was made to him by one
of the ladies that the prioress was intending to admit an
ignorant (*indocta*) novice, and particularly one Dorothy
Sturges, who was deaf and deformed. Apparently the
arguments of the objector prevailed, but poor Dorothy
was, not long after, admitted to the smaller nunnery of
Blackborough.

When the priory of Carrow, a favourite retreat for the
religious daughters of the citizens of Norwich, was visited
in 1526, several of the ladies were advanced in years.
The sub-prioress, Dame Anna Marten, had been in the
convent for sixty years, and two others, Dames Margaret
and Katherine, had been thirty-eight years in religion. It

is a little touching to note that almost the only complaints
that reached the bishop's ears were those of the aged
sub-prioress and Dame Margaret that the pace of chanting the Office by the sisters was too rapid, and lacking
the proper pauses, and that of Dame Katherine who found
the beer too small. At the next recorded visitation, six
years later, all these good old ladies were still at Carrow,
though Dame Anna's age did not allow her to discharge
the duties of sub-prioress ; but she was then (1532) in
charge of the infirmary. At this time the bishop interfered, probably at the suggestion of the aged dames, to
stop an accustomed Christmas game (on Holy Innocents'
Day), when the youngest of the novices assumed the
functions of a lady abbess, after the same fashion as a
boy-bishop amongst the choir boys. The nuns of Carrow
maintained a school for some of the better-class girls of
the city and district, and doubtless this Christmas-tide
sport was intended in the main for their delectation.

NUN ASKING PARDON OF AN ABBESS

CHAPTER IX

EXTERNAL RELATIONS OF THE MONASTIC ORDERS

I. THE BISHOP

NORMALLY, the bishop of the diocese in which a religious house was situated, was its Visitor and ultimate authority, except in so far as an appeal lay from him to the pope. In process of time exemptions from the regular jurisdiction of the diocesan tended to multiply; whole Orders, like the Cistercian and the Cluniacs among the Benedictines, and the Premonstratensians among the Canons Regular, and even individual houses, like St. Alban's and Bury St. Edmunds, on one ground or another obtained their freedom from the jurisdiction of the Ordinary. In the case of great bodies, like those of Citeaux, Cluny, Prémontré, and later the Gilbertines, the privilege of exemption was in the first instance obtained from the pope, on the ground that the individual houses were parts of a great corporation with its centre at the mother-house. Such monasteries were all subject to the authority of a central government, and regular Visitors were appointed by it. In the thirteenth century, on the same principle, the mendicant Orders, whose members were attached to the general body and not to the locality in which they might happen to be, were freed from the immediate control of the bishops of the various dioceses in which their convents were situated.

In the case of individual houses, the exemption was granted by the Holy See as a favour and a privilege.   It is hard to understand in what the privilege really consisted, except that it was certainly considered an honourable thing to be immediately subject only to the head of the Christian Church. Such privileges were, on the whole, few ; only five Benedictine houses in England possessed them, and even such great and important abbeys as Glastonbury, in the South of England, and St. Mary's, York, in the North, were subject to the regular jurisdiction of the diocesan. In the case of the few Benedictine houses which, by the intercession of the king or other powerful friends, had obtained exemption in this matter, regular fees had to be paid to the Roman chancery for the privilege. St. Alban's, for example, at the beginning of the sixteenth century, made an annual payment of £14 to the papal collector in lieu of the large fees previously paid on the election of every new abbot, and as an acknowledgment of the various privileges granted to him, such as, for example, the right to rank first in dignity among the abbots, and for the abbot to be able "even outside his own churches to use pontificalia and solemnly bless the people."   Edmundsbury, in the same way, paid an annual sum for its exemption and privileges, as also did Westminster, St. Augustine's (Canterbury), Waltham Holy Cross, and a few others.   By this time, too, some of the Cluniac houses, such as Lewes Priory and Lenton, had obtained their exemption and right of election.

In regard to the non-exempt monasteries and convents —that is ordinarily—the relation between the bishops and the religious houses was constant; and, apparently, with exceptions of course, cordial. The episcopal registers show that the bishops did not shirk the duty of visiting, and correcting what they found amiss in the houses under their control; and whilst there is evidence of a natural desire on their part to bring the regular life up to a high standard, there is little or none of any narrow spirit in the exercise of this part of the episcopal office, or of any determination to worry the religious, to misunderstand the purpose of their high vocation, or to make regular life unworkable in practice by any over-strict interpretation of the letter of the law. It is, of course, after all, only natural that these good relations should exist between the bishop and the regulars of his diocese. The unexempt houses were not extra-diocesan so far as episcopal authority went, like those of the exempt Orders; but they were for the most part the most important and the most useful centres of spiritual life in each diocese. It was therefore to the bishop's interest as head of the diocese to see that in these establishments the lamp of fervour should not be allowed to grow dim, and that the good work should not be permitted to suffer through any lessening of the cordial relations which had traditionally existed between the bishops and the religious houses within the pale of his jurisdiction.

The bishop's duties to the religious houses in his diocese were various. In the first place, in regard to the election of the superior: here much depended upon the actual position of the monastery in regard to the king, to the patron, or even to the Order. If the king was the founder of the house or had come to be regarded as such, which may roughly be said to have been the case in most of the greater monastic establishments, and especially in those which held lands immediately from the Crown, then the bishop had nothing to say to the matter till the royal assent had been given. The process has been already briefly explained ; but the main features may again be set out. On the death of the superior, the religious would have to make choice of some of their number to proceed to the court to inform the king of the demise and to obtain the *congé d'élire,* or permission to elect. The first action of the king would be the appointment of officials to administer the property in his name during the vacancy, having due regard to the needs of the community. He would then issue his licence for the religious to choose a new superior. All this, especially if the king were abroad or in some far-off part of the country, would take time, sometimes measured by weeks. On the reception of the *congé d'élire,* the convent proceeded to the formal election, the result of which had to be reported to the king ; and if he assented to the choice made, this was signified to the bishop, whose office it was to inquire concerning the validity of the election and the fitness of the person chosen—that is, he was bound to see whether the canonical forms had all been adhered to in the process and the election legal, and whether the elect had the qualities necessary to make a fitting superior and a ruler in temporals and in spirituals. If after inquiry all proved to be satisfactory, the bishop formally confirmed the choice of the monks and signified the confirmation to the king, asking for the restitution of temporalities to the new superior. If the election was that of an abbot, the bishop then bestowed the solemn blessing upon the elect thus confirmed, generally in some place other than his own monastic church, and wrote a formal letter to the community, charging them to receive their new superior and show him all obedience. Finally, the bishop appointed a commission to proceed to the house and install the abbot or prior in his office.

In the case of houses which acknowledged founders or patrons other than the king, the deaths of superiors were communicated to them, and permission to proceed to the choice of successors was asked more as a form than as a reality. The rest was in the hands of the bishops. In ordinary circumstances where there was no such lay patron, a community, on the death of a superior, merely assembled and at once made choice of a successor. This election had then to be communicated at once to the bishop, whose duty it was to inquire into the circumstances of the election and to determine whether the canonical formalities had been complied with. If this inquiry proved satisfactory, the bishop proceeded to the canonical examination of the elect before confirming the choice. This kind of election was completed by the issue of the episcopal letters claiming the obedience of the monks for their new superior. It was frequently the custom for the bishop to appoint custodians of the temporalities during the vacancy at such of these religious houses as were immediately subject to him. The frequency of the adoption by religious of the form of election by which they requested the bishop to make choice of their superior is at least evidence of the more than cordial relations which existed between the diocesan and the regulars, and of their confidence in his desire to serve their house to the best of his power in the choice of the most fitting superior.

Sometimes, of course, the episcopal examination of the process, or of the elect, would lead to the quashing of the election. This took place generally when some canonical form had not been adhered to, as on this matter the law was rightly most strict. Less frequently, the elect on inquiry was found to lack some quality essential in a good ruler, and it then became the duty of the bishop to declare the choice void. Sometimes this led to the convent being deprived of its voice in the election, and in such a case the choice devolved upon the bishop. Numerous instances, however, make it clear that although legally the bishop was bound to declare such an election void, he would always, if possible, himself appoint the religious who had been the choice of the community.

In other instances again, the bishop's part in the appointment of a new superior was confined to the blessing of the abbot after the confirmation of the election by the pope, or by the superior of the religious body. This was the case in the Cistercian and Cluniac bodies, and in such of the great abbeys as were exempt from episcopal jurisdiction. Sometimes, as in the case of St. Alban's, even the solemn blessing of the new abbot could by special privilege be given by any bishop the elect might choose for the purpose.

Outside the time of the elections and visitations, the bishops exercised generally a paternal and watchful care over the religious houses of their diocese. Before the suppression of the alien priories, for example, these foreign settlements were supervised by the Ordinary quite as strictly as were the English religious houses under his jurisdiction. These priories were mostly established in the first instance to look after estates which had been bestowed upon foreign abbeys, and the number in each house was supposed to be strictly limited, and was, in fact, small.   It was not uncommon, however, to find that more than the stipulated number of religious were quartered upon the small community by the foreign superior, or that an annual payment greater than the revenue of the English estate would allow was demanded by the authorities of the foreign mother-house. Against both of these abuses the bishop of the diocese had officially to guard.   We find, for instance, Bishop Grandisson of Exeter giving his licence for a monk of Bec to live for some months only at Cowick Priory, and for another to leave Cowick on a visit to Bec.   Also in regard to Tywardreath, a cell of the Abbey of St. Sergius, near Ghent, the same bishop on examination found that the revenue was so diminished that it could not support the six monks it was supposed to maintain, and he therefore sent back three of their number to their mother-house on the Continent.   This conclusion, be it remarked, was arrived at only after careful inquiry, and after the bishop had for a time appointed a monk from another religious house to assist the foreign superior in the administration of the temporals of his priory.   Upon the report of this assistant he deprived the superior for negligence, and appointed custodians of the temporalities of the house.   From the episcopal registers generally it appears, too, that once the foreign religious were settled in any alien priory, they came under the jurisdiction of the bishop of the locality, in the same way as the English religious.   The alien prior's appointment had to be confirmed by him, and no religious could come to the house or go from it, even to return to the foreign mother-house, without his permission.

In regard to all non-exempt monastic establishments of men and convents of women, the episcopal powers were very great and were freely exercised. Thus to take some examples: the Benedictine abbey of Tavistock in the fourteenth century was seriously troubled by debt, partly, at least, caused by an incapable and unworthy superior. This abbot, by the way, had been provided by the pope; and apparently the bishop did not consider that his functions extended beyond issuing a commission to induct him into his office. In a short time matters came to a crisis, and reports as to the bad state of the house came to the ears of Bishop Grandisson. He forthwith prohibited the house from admitting more members to the habit until he had had time to examine into matters. The abbot replied by claiming exemption from episcopal jurisdiction, apparently on the ground that he had been appointed by the Holy See. The bishop, as he said, "out of reverence for the lord Pope who had created the both of us," waived this as a right and came to the house as a friend, to see what remedy could be found to allay the rumours that were rife in the country as to gross mismanagement at the abbey. How far the bishop succeeded does not transpire; but a couple of years later the abbot was suspended and deposed, and the bishop appointed the Cistercian abbot of Buckland and a monk of Tavistock to administer the goods of the abbey pending another election. How thoroughly the religious approved of the action of the bishop may be gauged by the fact that they asked him to appoint their abbot for them.

In the ordinary and extraordinary visitations made by the bishop, the interests of the religious houses were apparently the only considerations which weighed with

him. Sometimes the injunctions and monitions given at
a visitation appertained to the most minute points of
regular life, and sometimes the visitatorial powers were
continued in force for considerable periods in order to
secure that certain points that needed correction might be
seen to. One curious right possessed and exercised by
the bishop of any diocese on first coming to his see, was
that of appointing one person in each monastery and
convent to be received as a religious without payment
or pension. It is proper, however, to say that this right
was always exercised with fatherly discretion. Again and
again the records of visitations in the episcopal registers
show that the bishop did not hesitate to appoint a co-
adjutor to any superior whom he might find deficient
in the power of governing, either in spirituals or temporals. Officials who were shown to be incapable in
the course of such inquiries were removed, and others
were either appointed by the bishop, or their appointment sanctioned by him. Religious who had proved
themselves undesirable or impossible in one house were
not unfrequently translated by the bishop to another.
Thus in A.D. 1338-9 great storms had wrought destruction at Bodmin. The priory buildings were in ruins,
and a sum of money had to be raised for the necessary
repairs which were urgently required. Bishop Grandisson
gave his permission for the monks to sell a corrody—or
undertaking to give board and lodging for life at the
priory—for a payment of ready money. A few years
later, in 1347, on his visitation the bishop found things
financially in a bad way. He removed the almoner from
his office, regulated the number of servants and the
amount of food ; and having appointed an administrator,

sent the prior to live for a time in one of the priory granges, in order to see whether the house could be recovered from its state of bankruptcy by careful administration.

One proof of the friendly relations which as a rule existed between the bishop and the regular clergy of his diocese may be seen in the fact that the abbots and superiors were frequently, if not generally, found in the lists of those appointed as diocesan collectors on any given occasion. The superiors of religious houses contributed to the loans and grants raised in common with the rest of the diocesan clergy, either for the needs of the sovereign, the Holy See, or the bishop. That there were at times difficulty and friction in the working out of these well-understood principles of subordination need not be denied; but that as a whole the system, which may be described as normal, brought about harmonious relations between the bishop and the regulars must be conceded by all who will study its workings in the records of pre-Reformation episcopal government.

2. THE CHURCH IN ENGLAND GENERALLY

The monastic Orders were called upon to take their share in the common burdens imposed upon the Church in England. These included contributions to the sums levied upon ecclesiastics by Convocation for the pope and for the king in times of need; and they contributed, albeit, perhaps, like the rest of the English Church, unwillingly, their share to the "procurations" of papal legates and questors. Sometimes the call thus made upon their revenues was very considerable, especially as the king did not hesitate on occasions to make particular demands upon the wealthier religious houses. At Convocation, and in the Provincial Synods the regular clergy were well represented. Thus, from the diocese of Exeter in the year 1328–9 there were summoned to the Synod of London seven abbots to be present *personaliter*, whilst five Augustinian and seven Benedictine priories also chose and sent proctors to the meeting. As a rule, apparently, at all such meetings the abbots, and priors who were canonically elected to rule their houses with full jurisdiction, had the right, and were indeed bound to be present, unless prevented by a canonical reason. The archbishop, as such, had no more to say to the regulars than to any other ecclesiastic of his province, except that during a vacancy in any diocese he might, and indeed frequently did, visit the religious houses in that diocese personally or by commission.

3. THE ORDER

Besides the supervision and help of the bishop, almost every religious house had some connection with and assistance from the Order to which it belonged. In the case of the great united corporations like the Cluniacs, the Cistercians, the Premonstratensians, and later the Carthusians, the dependence of the individual monastery upon the centre of government was very real both in theory and in practice. The abbots or superiors had to attend at General Chapters, held, for instance, at Cluny, Citeaux, or Prémontré, and were subject to regular visitations made by or in behalf of the general superior. In the case of a vacancy the election was

supervised and the elect examined and confirmed either
by, or by order of, the chief authority, or, in the case
of daughter-houses, by the superior of the parent abbey.
Even in the case of the Benedictines, who did not form
an Order in the modern sense of the word, after the
Council of Lateran in 1215, the monasteries were united
into Congregations, for common purposes and mutual
help and encouragement. In England there were two
such unions, corresponding to the two Provinces of
Canterbury and York, and the superiors met at regular
intervals in General Chapters. Little is known of the
meetings of the Northern Province; but in the South
the records show that they were regularly held to the
last. The first and ordinary business of these General
Chapters was to secure a proper standard of regular
observance; and whatever, after discussion, was agreed
upon, provided that it met with the approval of the
president of the meeting, was to be observed without
any appeal. Moreover, at each of these Chapters two
or more prudent and religious men were chosen to visit
every Benedictine house of the Province in the pope's
name, with full power to correct where any correction
might be considered necessary. In case these papal
Visitors found abuses existing in any monastery which
might render the deposition of the abbot necessary or
desirable, they had to denounce him to the bishop of
the diocese, who was to take the necessary steps for
his canonical removal. If the bishop did not, or would
not act, the Visitors were bound to refer the case to
the Holy See. By the provisions of the Lateran Council
in A.D. 1215, the bishops were warned to see that the
religious houses in their dioceses were in good order,

"so that when the aforesaid Visitors come there, they may find them worthy of commendation rather than of correction." They were, however, warned to be careful "not to make their visitations a burden or expense, and to see that the rights of superiors were maintained, without injury to those of their subjects."

In this system a double security was provided for the well-being of the monasteries. The bishops were maintained in their old position as Visitors, and were constituted judges where the conduct of the superior might necessitate the gravest censures. At the same time, by providing that all the monasteries should be visited every three years by monks chosen by the General Chapter and acting in the name of the pope, any failure of the bishop to fulfil his duty as diocesan, or any incapacity on his part to understand the due working of the monastic system, received the needful corrective.

One other useful result to the monasteries may be attributed to the regular meetings of General Chapter. It was by the wise provision of these Chapters that members of the monastic Orders received the advantage of a University training. Common colleges were established by their decrees at Oxford and Cambridge, and all superiors were charged to send their most promising students to study and take their degrees in the national Universities. Strangely enough as it may appear to us in these days, even in these colleges the autonomy of the individual Benedictine houses seems to have been scrupulously safeguarded; and the common college consisted of small houses, in which the students of various monasteries dwelt apart, though attending a common hall and chapel.

4. THE IMPROPRIATED CHURCHES

In regard to the external relations of the monastic houses, a word must be said about their dealings with the parochial churches appropriated to their use. Either by the gift of the king or that of some lay patron, many churches to which they had the right of presentation became united with monasteries, and a considerable portion of the parish revenues was applied to the support of the religious, to keeping up adequate charity, or "hospitality" as it was called in the neighbourhood, or other such objects. The practice of impropriation has been regarded by most writers as a manifest abuse, and there is no call to attempt to defend it. The practice was not confined, however, to the monks, or to the action of lay people who found therein an easy way to become benefactors of some religious house. Bishops and other ecclesiastics, as founders of colleges and hospitals, were quite as ready to increase the revenues of these establishments in the same way.

In order that a church might be legally appropriated to a religious establishment the approval of the bishop had to be obtained, and the special reasons for the donation by the lay patron set forth. If these were considered satisfactory, the formal permission of the Holy See was, at any rate after the twelfth century, necessary for the completion of the transaction. The monastery became the patron of the benefice thus attached to it, and had to secure that the spiritual needs of the parish were properly attended to by the vicars whom they presented to the cure. These vicars were paid an adequate stipend, usually settled by episcopal authority.

Roughly speaking, the present distinction between a vicarage and a rectory shows where churches had been appropriated to a religious house or other public body, and where they remained merely parochial. The vicar was the priest appointed at a fixed stipend by the corporation which took the rectorial tithes. It has been calculated that at least a third part of the tithes of the richest benefices in England were appropriated either in part or wholly to religious and secular bodies, such as colleges, military orders, lay hospitals, guilds, convents; even deans, cantors, treasurers, and chancellors of cathedral bodies were also largely endowed with rectorial tithes. In this way, at the dissolution of the religious houses under Henry VIII., the greater tithes of an immense number of parish churches, now known as vicarages, passed into the hands of the noblemen and others who obtained grants of the property of the suppressed monasteries.

Whilst the impropriation of churches to monastic establishments undoubtedly took money out of the locality for the benefit of the religious, it is but fair to recognise that in many ways the benefit thus obtained was returned with interest. Not only did the monks furnish the ranks of the secular priesthood with youths who had received their early education in the cloister school or at the almonry; but the churches and vicarages of places impropriated were the special care of the religious. An examination of these churches frequently reveals the fact that the religious bodies did not hesitate to spend large sums of money upon the rebuilding and adornment of structures which belonged to them in this way.

HENRY VII GIVING CHARTER TO MONKS AT WESTMINSTER HALL

5. KING AND PARLIAMENT

Of many of the religious houses, especially of the greater abbeys, the king either was, or came to be considered, the founder. It has already been pointed out what this relation to the Crown implied on the part of the monks. Besides this the Crown could, and in spite of the protests of those chiefly concerned, frequently, if not ordinarily did, appoint abbots and other superiors of religious houses members of the commissions of peace for the counties in which their establishments were situated. They were likewise made collectors for grants and loans to the Crown, especially when the tax was to be levied on ecclesiastical property; and according to the extent of their lands and possessions, like the lay-holders from the Crown, they had to furnish soldiers to fight under the royal standard. In the same way the abbot and other superiors could be summoned by the king to Parliament as barons. The number of religious thus called to the House of Peers at first appears to have depended somewhat upon the fancy of the sovereign; it certainly varied considerably. In 1216, for example, from the North Province of England eleven abbots and eight priors, and from the South seventy-one abbots and priors—in all ninety religious—were summoned to Parliament by Henry III. In 1272 Edward I. called only fifty-seven, mostly abbots, a few, however, being cathedral priors; and in later times the number of monastic superiors in the House of Peers generally included only the twenty-five abbots of the greater houses and the prior of Coventry, and these were accounted as barons of the kingdom.

6. THE MONASTIC TENANTS

The division of the monastic revenues between the various obedientiaries for the support of the burdens of their special offices was fairly general, at least in the great religious houses. It was for the benefit of the house, inasmuch as it left a much smaller revenue to be dealt with by the royal exchequer at every vacancy. It served, also, at least one other good purpose. It brought many of the religious into contact with the tenants of the monastic estates and gave them more knowledge of their condition and mode of life; whilst the personal contact, which was possible in a small administration, was certainly for the mutual benefit of master and tenant. Since the prior, sacrist, almoner and other officials all had to look after the administration of the manors and farms assigned to their care, they had to have separate granges and manor-halls. In these they had to carry out their various duties, and meet their tenants on occasions, as was the case, for example, at Glastonbury, where the sacrist had all the tithes of Glastonbury, including West Pennard, to collect, and had his special tithe-barn, etc., for the purpose.

Two books, amongst others, *The Rentalia et Custumaria* of Glastonbury, published by the Somerset Record Society, and the *Halmote Rolls* of Durham, issued by the Surtees Society, enable any student who may desire to do so, to obtain a knowledge of the relations which existed between the monastic landlords and their tenants. At the great monastery of the West Country the tenure of the land was of all kinds, from the estates held under the obligation of so many knights' fees, to the poor cottier with an acre or two. Some of the tenants had to find part of their rent in service, part in kind, part in payment. Thus, one had to find thirty salmon, "each as thick as a man's fist at the tail," for the use of the monastery ; some had to find thousands of eels from Sedgemoor ; others, again, so many measures of honey. Some of those who worked for the monastery or its estates had fixed wages, as, for example, the gardeners ; others had to be content with what was given them.

Mr. Elton, in an appendix to the Glastonbury volume, has analysed the information to be found in its pages, and from this some items of interest may be given here. A cottier with five acres of arable land paid 4*d*. less one farthing for rent, and five hens as "kirkset" if he were married. From Michaelmas to Midsummer he was bound to do three days' labour a week of farm work on the monastic lands, such as toiling on the fallows, winnowing corn, hedging, ditching, and fencing. During the rest of the year, that is, in the harvest time, he had to do five days' work on the farm, and could be called upon to lend a hand in any kind of occupation, except loading and carting. Like the farmers, he had his allowance of one sheaf of corn for each acre he reaped, and a "laveroc," or as much grass as he could gather on his hook, for every acre he mowed. Besides this general work he had to bear his share in looking after the vineyard at Glastonbury.

Take another example of tenure : one "Golliva of the lake," held a three-acre tenement. It consisted of a croft of two acres and one acre in the common field. She made a small payment for this ; and for extra work she had three sheaves, measured by a strap kept for the purpose. When she went haymaking she brought her own rake ;

she took her share in all harvest work, had to winnow a specified quantity of corn before Christmas, and did odd jobs of all kinds, such as carrying a writ for the abbot and driving cattle to Glastonbury.

The smaller cottagers were apparently well treated. A certain Alice, for example, had half an acre field for which she had to bring water to the reapers at the harvest and sharpen their sickles for them. On the whole, though work was plenty and the life no doubt hard, the lot of the Somerset labourer on the Glastonbury estate was not too unpleasant. Of amusements the only one named is the institution of *Scot-ales*, an entertainment which lasted two, or even three days. The lord of the manor might hold three in the year. On the first day, Saturday, the married men and youths came with their pennies and were served three times with ale. On the Sunday the husbands and their wives came ; but if the youths came they had to pay another penny. On the Monday any of them could come if they had paid on the other days.

On the whole, the manors of the monastery may be said to have been worked as a co-operative farm. The reader of the accounts in this volume may learn of common meals, of breakfasts and luncheons and dinners being prepared ready for those who were at work on the common lands or on the masters' farming operations. It appears that they met together in the great hall for a common Christmas entertainment. They furnished the great yule-log to burn at the dinner, and each one brought his dish and mug, with a napkin "if he wanted to eat off a cloth"; and still more curiously, his own contribution of firewood, that his portion of food might be properly cooked.

Of even greater interest is the picture of village life led

by monastic tenants which is afforded by the *Durham Halmote Rolls*.

"It is hardly a figure of speech," writes Mr. Booth in the preface of this volume, "to say we have (in these Rolls) village life photographed. The dry record of tenures is peopled by men and women who occupy them, whose acquaintance we make in these records under the various phases of village life. We see them in their tofts surrounded by their crofts, with their gardens of pot-herbs. We see how they ordered the affairs of the village when summoned by the bailiff to the vill to consider matters which affected the common weal of the community. We hear of their trespasses and wrong doings, and how they were remedied or punished, of their strifes and contentions and how they were repressed, of their attempts, not always ineffective, to grasp the principle of co-operation, as shown by their by-laws ; of their relations with the Prior, who represented the Convent and alone stood in relation of lord. He appears always to have dealt with his tenants, either in person or through his officers, with much consideration ; and in the imposition of fines we find them invariably tempering justice with mercy."

In fact, as the picture of mediæval village life among the tenants of the Durham monastery is displayed in the pages of these *Halmote* accounts, it would seem almost as if the reader were transported to some Utopia of Dreamland. Many of the points that in these days advanced politicians would desire to see introduced into the village communities of modern England in the way of improved sanitary and social conditions, and to relieve the deadly dulness of country life, were seen in full working order in Durham and Cumberland in pre-Reformation days. Local provisions for public health and general convenience are evidenced by the watchful vigilance of the village officials over the water supplies, the stringent measures taken in regard to springs and wells, to prevent the fouling of useful streams, as to the common places for washing clothes, and the regular times for emptying and cleansing ponds and milldams.

Labour, too, was lightened and the burdens of life eased by co-operation on an extensive scale. A common mill ground the corn of the tenants, and their flour was baked into bread at a common oven. A smith employed by the community worked at their will in a common forge, and common shepherds and herdsmen watched the sheep and cattle of the various tenants, when pastured on the fields common to the whole community. The pages of the volume, too, contain numerous instances of the kindly consideration extended to their tenants by the monastic proprietors, and the relation which existed between them was in reality rather that of rent-chargers than of absolute owners. In fact, as the editor of this interesting volume says : " Notwithstanding the rents, duties, and services and the fine paid on entering, the inferior tenants of the Prior had a beneficial interest in their holdings, which gave rise to a recognised system of tenant-right, which we may see growing into a customary right ; the only limitation of the tenant's right being inability, from poverty or other cause, to pay rent or perform the accustomed services." And, it may be added, even when it was necessary for a tenant on these accounts to leave, provision was made with the new tenant to give the late owner shelter and a livelihood.

SENESCHAL JOHN WHITEWELL
AND MOTHER

ILLUMINATOR OF ST. ALBANS

CHAPTER X

THE PAID SERVANTS OF THE MONASTERY

NO account of the officials of a mediæval monastery would be complete without some notice of the assistants, other than the monks, who took so large a part in the administration. Incidentally something has already been said about the paid lay officers and servants; but their position requires that their place and work should be discussed somewhat more fully. They were all of them salaried servants; and frequently, if not generally, faithful, lifelong friends of the monks, whose interest in the well-being of the establishment with which they were connected was almost as keen and real as that of the brethren themselves. In some of the greater houses their number was very considerable, and even in small monasteries the records of the dissolution make it clear that there were, at least in most of them, a great number of such retainers. In many places the higher lay offices, such as steward, cook, etc., became in process of time, hereditary, and were much prized by the family in whose possession they were. It was also possible, of course, that by default of male heirs, the position might pass to the female line. Thus in one case the office of cook in a great Benedictine monastery was held by a woman in respect to her inheritance of the last holder. She became the ward of the superior, and he had thus a good deal to say to her marriage, by which she transmitted the office to her husband as her dower. Among the various paid officials the following were the most important.

1. THE CATERER, OR BUYER FOR THE COMMUNITY

The caterer, says one Custumal, " ought to be a broadminded and strong-minded man : one who acts with decision, and is wise, just and upright in things belonging to his office ; one who is prudent, knowing, discreet and careful when purchasing meat and fish in the market or from the salesman." Under the kitchener, the caterer had to look after the cook and his assistants, and every day to see that the expenses were properly and faithfully set down. He had to watch that the right things were given out to those who had to prepare them, and at the daily meals of the community it was his duty to stand at the kitchen hatchway and see that they were served up in a fitting manner. In the market, the buyer for the superior always gave way to the caterer for the community. In the case of Edmundsbury at least, it was settled by Abbot Sampson that this was always to be so. Under the conventual caterer were two servants always ready at his call to carry the provisions he purchased in the market to the monastery. The stipend of the caterer was whatever had been agreed as just, and he usually had clothes " according to his station," and certain provisions at his disposal.

2. THE ABBOT'S COOK

This official held more the position of a steward, or valet to the superior, than that of a cook. He had to go each morning to the abbot or prior for orders, and to find out what would be required for the superior's table for the day, and he had then to proceed to the kitchener to inform him what had to be provided. He helped in the kitchen on occasions such as great feasts, when he was asked to do so by the kitchener ; and as a matter of course, when there were many strangers or other persons to be entertained and the work was consequently heavy. For this and such-like services he received a stipend from the kitchener; but his ordinary payment came from the superior, who also furnished him with his livery. He was told by the Custumals to remember that, although he was the abbot's cook, he had, nevertheless, to obey the kitchener in all things, and to look conscientiously to try and prevent waste and superfluity in spices and such other things as passed through his hands.

If he needed help, the abbot's valet could have a boy to run on errands and generally assist ; and they were both warned that in the season for pig-killing and bacon-curing they, like all other servants, were to be ready to help in the important work of salting. He had, as part of his duty, to keep a careful list of all the spoons, mugs, dishes, and other table necessaries, and after meals to see that they were clean ; and, if not, to clean them before the close of the day. Once each year the inventory had to be shown to, and checked by, the kitchener.

3. THE LARDERER

The larderer should be "as perfect, just, and faithful a servant" as could be found. He had charge of the keys of all the outhouses attached to the great larder of the monastery, which in one Custumal are specified as "the hay-house, the stockfish-house, and the pudding-

house." These keys, together with that of the outer
larder itself, he had always to carry with him on his
girdle, as he alone might be responsible for their safety.
In all matters he, too, was to be under the kitchener, and
not to absent himself without his permission. Amongst
his various duties a few may be mentioned here. He had
to grind and deliver in powder to the cook all the pepper,
mustard, and spices required for the cooking of the conventual meals. When the convent were to have "bake-
meats," such as venison, turbot, eels, etc., the larderer
had to prepare the dish for the cook, and to sprinkle it
over with saffron. All the live animals intended for the
kitchen, such as sheep, bullocks, calves, pigs, etc., had
to pass through his hands. He had to see to the killing,
skinning, and preparing them for the spit; the tallow he
kept in order to provide the treasurer with material for
the winter candles. The larderer also had to see that
the live birds, such as pheasants, partridges, capons,
hens, chickens, pigeons, etc., were fed properly, and
were ready for the table when the kitchener should need
them. In the same way the store of fish, both in the
stews, and salted in the fish-house, were under his charge,
as were also the peas and beans for the convent pottage.

4. THE COOK

For the infirmary, and especially for the use of those
who had been subjected to the periodical blood-letting,
there was a special cook skilled in the preparation of
strengthening broths and soups. He was the chief or
meat-cook of the establishment, and had under him two
boys, one as a general helper, the other to act as his
"turnbroach." He was appointed to his office by the

abbot, and at least in the case of some of the greater houses it was secured to him for life by a formal grant. It was his duty to provide those who had been " blooded " with a plate of meat broth on the second and third day, and also to give them, and the sick generally, any particular dish they might fancy. Moreover, he had to furnish the whole community with soup, meat, and vegetables on all days when meat was eaten by the whole convent.

He had also to see to the process of salting any meat in the proper seasons, or whenever it might be necessary. He also prepared the various soups or pottages for the community; for instance, " Frumenty " on all Sundays, Tuesdays, and Thursdays, from August 1st to September 29th; or " Letborry," made with milk, eggs, and saffron on fish days, from July till October; or " Charlet," the same composition with the addition of pork, for other days during the same time; or " Jussel," from Easter to July; or " Mortrews," in which the quantity of meat was increased, and which was served on all days, except those of abstinence, during the winter months, from All Saints' day to Lent.

One English Custumal warns the cook to reflect often that his work in the kitchen is necessarily heavy and tedious; and that he should endeavour to keep up a goodly feeling between himself and his assistants, for " without this mutual assistance it is difficult " to do what his office requires of him for the good of others. For his trouble he had a fixed wage and a house; and many recognised perquisites, the choppings of joints, and two joints from every other chine of pork, as well as half the dripping that came from the joints roasted for the community.

5. THE GUEST-HALL COOK

The cook to attend to the needs of visitors was appointed by the cellarer, and had under him a boy to help in any way he might direct. His office was frequently for life, and certainly, once appointed, he could be removed only with difficulty. He had to get everything ready for the entertainment of strangers and of the parents of the religious, whenever they came to the monastery and at whatsoever hour of the day or night. Besides this ordinary work he had to assist, when disengaged, in preparing the meals for the monks, and in the season for salting the pork and mutton, to help in that work with the chief cook and the larderer. He was to be in all things obedient to the kitchener in the matters of his office, and in the times of his service was not to absent himself except with the permission of that official. His wages were paid by the cellarer according to agreement; and he had the usual kitchen perquisites of choppings and dripping.

6. THE FISH-COOKS

In the large monasteries, such as, for example, Edmundsbury, there were two cooks for the fish-dishes: the first was properly called the "fish-cook," the other the "pittance-cook." Their appointment was made for life, and by letters-patent signed by the abbot in Chapter, with the prior and the community as witnesses. Though called the "fish-cooks" these servants had also to attend to the general work of the kitchen, even on days when meat was eaten, and to cook the meat and make the gravy required; whilst the "pittance-cook" was specially detailed to fry or poach the eggs required for the extra portions, or to prepare whatever else took their place in the dishes served as pittances to the community, or to individuals such as the president of the refectory, and the priest who had sung the High Mass. These two cooks also had to help in the salting time, and in other common work of the kitchen.

7. INFIRMARY COOK

To serve the sick a prudent, skilful cook was to be chosen by the infirmarian, who, besides the knowledge of his art, should have compassion and feel pity for the sufferings and afflictions of the sick. Like the officers previously named, the appointment of the infirmary cook was for life; but though he could not be moved at the whim of a superior, he was not formally appointed in Chapter, but by a letter from the infirmarian. Day and night he was to show himself solicitous for the welfare of those in the infirmary, and be ready at all times to make for them what they needed or might fancy. He, too, had to help in the general kitchen, and he had to obtain thence all the requisite food for those who were having their meals in the infirmary. Like the rest of the above-named officials, he had to give what help he could in the kitchen in the seasons of great pressure, and in particular at the time for the winter salting, about St. Martin's Day.

When the infirmary cook or servant came to die, for his faithful service he was borne to the grave, like all the other servants of the monastery, by the whole convent. His body was met at the great door of the church by the community in procession, and after Mass had been celebrated for the repose of his soul by the sub-sacrist, the monks carried his remains, as that of a good and faithful servant gone to his reward, to his last resting-place. In

some houses there was even a special portion of the
consecrated ground dedicated to the burial of monastic
servants : at Bury, for example, it was called "Sergeant's
hill," and the Custumal says that in that "venerable
monastery" such old friends "shall never be forgotten in
the prayers and devout supplications of the community."

8. THE SALTER

The salter, who was also called the *mustardarius*, was
appointed by a letter of the kitchener ; and like the rest he
was irremovable after his appointment, except for grave
reasons, and then only with difficulty.   By his office he
had to see to the supply and preparation of all the mustard
used in seasoning the dishes and by the brethren in the
various places where food was partaken, such as the refectory, guest-hall, infirmary, etc.   This was by no means
the unimportant office we might in these days be inclined
to consider it, as it was then considered useful if not
necessary to take mustard with all salted food, flesh or
fish.   The quantity thus required in a large establishment
was very considerable.   The salter was also expected to
make some, if not all, the sauces required for certain dishes.
At Easter, for instance, he was to prepare "vertsauce"
with vinegar for the lamb, if the herb could be found for it;
by which it may be supposed that "mint-sauce" is meant,
except that this particular concoction was supposed also
to go with mackerel as well as lamb !

9. BELL-RINGERS AND CHURCH-SERVERS

On all days when the great bells were rung and the
services of the church were more elaborate than at ordinary
times, the ringers and servers had their rations and some

extra portion from the conventual refectory. In a great place like Bury St. Edmunds these days amounted to some two-and-forty in the year.

10. THE GARDENER

The gardener was appointed by the cellarer at his pleasure. His chief duty was to keep the convent supplied with herbs on four days a week in winter and spring, and with other vegetables in their season. He was frequently to visit the kitchen in order to learn what was required from him, and he was always to bring his vegetables and herbs cleaned and prepared ready for cooking.

11. THE CARRIERS

The carriers were servants who were continually occupied in the work of provisioning the establishment. They had to be at hand to carry to the monastic stores whatever the caterer bought in the market. Also in the time of the great fairs, they attended the cellarer to take charge of his purchases of spices, almonds and raisins, ling and stockfish, and salted herrings, red and white, and to convey them to the monastery. On ordinary days they were occupied in bringing to the cook the food he required from the various officials; in carrying in the fuel and keeping up the fires, and in carting away the refuse to the waste-heap. These carriers had a money wage and numerous perquisites; amongst other things, they could claim all the little barrels in which salmon, sturgeon, and salt eels had come to the monastic larder, and they might take and use what they could for their own meals of every pig that was brought to the salting-tub and found to be "measly."

12. DOOR-KEEPERS

In most great monastic houses there were naturally several porters or door-keepers. The *kitchen-porter* was in some ways the most important, as so much of the traffic from the outer world to the cloister came this way. He was set there for the purpose of preventing any un-authorised person gaining access to the kitchen so as to disturb the cook ; and at all times he had to check the coming in of seculars, or of begging clerks, or of the neighbours, unless they could show leave or business. He had to receive and distribute all the daily alms of food to those waiting at the gate. The *porter of the great cloister gate* had to watch over the main entrance of the house, to open the door to visitors, and at once to acquaint the guest-master of their arrival.

13. THE BRIEF-BEARER—BREVIATOR

The *brief-bearer*, by his office, was intended to carry the notice of the death of any of the brethren in the monastery round to other monasteries and religious houses in England. The abbot appointed this official, and the office was held for life. In Benedictine abbeys, according to a provision of the General Chapter of Northampton, the bearer of the mortuary roll was to be received with honour and entertained until he had obtained his roll again and could pass on to the next house on his list. Besides his regular wage and portion of food from the monastic kitchen, on the death of any monk he could claim as his right the mattress of the deceased brother, or in lieu of it a sum of six shillings and eightpence.

Besides the above-named officers there were, at least in

the greater houses, many minor paid officials and retainers. For example, the *discarius*, or server of dishes
in the refectory, was bound always to be at the kitchen-
hatch whenever conventual meals were in progress,
and it was his place to wait upon those who took their
meals at the second table. He was a kind of lower
servant in the kichen ; he had to help in bringing in the
fuel, and to see that the wheelbarrow for the waste was in
its place, and was emptied when it was necessary. After
the meals, the discarius washed the plates and dishes, and
saw that when dry, they were stacked in their proper cupboards ready for the next occasion.

Another minor official was the "turnbroach"—a boy
chosen by the cellarer for his activity. He had to be
always ready when required to turn the spits on which
meat or fish was cooking. He helped in carrying fuel for
the kitchen and elsewhere ; and when ordered, he had to
go to the ponds and stews to help to catch fish for the
conventual meal.

In some places, for example at Edmundsbury, there
were certain women employed at times by the monastery
for the making of pastry, etc., called *pudding-wives*.
They had a house or chamber near at hand to the kitchen,
called the " Pudding-house." These women were chosen
by the larderer with the assent of the chief cook ; they
lived in the neighbourhood and came up to the outer
kitchen offices when their services were required. Great
care was taken in the selection of these servants, and it
was directed that they " be always married, sober, of
good repute and honest, that all danger of detraction
from evil tongues be avoided." At all times when animals
were slaughtered, in particular about St. Martin's Day,

and when pigs were being killed, the services of these women were required to make black puddings. At other times, if the cook desired, they were to be ready to make pasties and other things which seemed to require the gentler touch of a female hand. Among the women servants there were, of course, also laundresses for the washing of the clothes of the community, and others for the infirmary, the guest-hall, and the church linen. All these were selected with care and upon the same principles which guided the selection of the above-mentioned pudding-wives.

CHAPTER XI

THE VARIOUS RELIGIOUS ORDERS

THE various Orders existing in England in pre-Reformation days may be classified under four headings: (1) Monks, (2) Canons Regular, (3) Military Orders, and (4) Friars. As regards the nuns, most of the houses were affiliated to one or other of the above-named Orders.

I. Monks

i. *Benedictines*

St. Benedict, justly called the Patriarch of Western Monachism, established his rule of life in Italy; first at Subiaco and subsequently at Monte Cassino about A.D. 529. The design of his code was, like every other rule of regular life, to enable men to reach the higher Christian ideals by the helps afforded them in a well-regulated monastery. According to the saint's original conception, the houses were to be separate families independent of each other. It was no part of his scheme to establish a corporation with branches in various localities and countries, or to found an "Order" in its modern sense. By its own inherent excellence and because of the sound common-sense which pervades it, the Rule of St. Benedict at once began to take root in the monasteries of the West, till it quickly superseded any others then in existence. Owing to its broad and elastic character, and hardly less, probably, to the fact that adopting it did not imply the joining of any stereotyped form of Order, monasteries could, and in fact did, embrace this code without entirely breaking with their past traditions.   Thus, side by side in the same religious house, we find that the rule of St. Columba was observed with that of St. Benedict until the greater practical sense of the latter code superseded the more rigid legislation of the former.   Within a comparatively short time from the death of St. Benedict in A.D. 543, the Benedictine became the recognised form of Western regular life.   To this end the action of Pope St. Gregory the Great and his high approval of St. Benedict's Rule greatly conduced.   In his opinion it manifested no common wisdom in its provisions, which were dictated by a marvellous insight into human nature and by a knowledge of the best possible conditions for attaining the end of all monastic life, the perfect love of God and of man.   Whilst not in any way lax in its provisions, it did not prescribe an asceticism which could be practised only by the few ; whilst the most ample powers were given to the superior to adapt the regulations to all circumstances of times and places ; thus making it applicable to every form of the higher Christian life, from the secluded cloister to that for which St. Gregory specially used those trained under it : the evangelisation of far-distant countries.

The connection between the Benedictines and England began with the mission of St. Augustine in A.D. 597. The monastery of Monte Cassino having been destroyed by the Lombards, towards the end of the sixth century,

BENEDICTINE MONK

BENEDICTINE NUN

the monks took refuge in Rome, and were placed in the Lateran, and by St. Gregory in the church he founded in honour of St. Andrew, in his ancestral home on the Cœlian Hill. It was the prior of St. Andrew's whom he chose to be the head of the other missionary monks he sent to convert England. With the advent of the Scottish monks from Iona the system of St. Columba was for a time introduced into the North of England; but here, as in the rest of Europe, it quickly gave place to the Benedictine code; and practically during the whole Saxon period this was the only form of monastic life in England.

ii. *Cluniacs*

The Cluniac adaptation of the Benedictine Rule took its rise in A.D. 912 with Berno, abbot of Gigny. With the assistance of the Duke of Aquitaine he built and endowed a monastery at Cluny, near Macon-sur-Saone. The Cluniac was a new departure in monastic government. Hitherto the monastery was practically self-centred; any connection with other religious houses was at most voluntary, and any bond of union that may have existed, was of the most loose description. The ideal upon which Cluny was established was the existence of a great central monastery with dependencies spread over many lands, and forming a vast feudal hierarchy of subordinate establishments with the closest dependence on the mother-house. Moreover, the superior of each of the dependent monasteries, no matter how large and important, was not the elect of the community, but the nominee of the abbot of Cluny; and in the same way the profession of every member of the congregation was made in his name and with his sanction. It was a great ideal; and for two centuries the abbots of Cluny form a dynasty worthy of so lofty a position. The first Cluniac house founded in England was that of Barnstaple. This was speedily followed by that of Lewes, a priory set up by William, earl of Warren, in A.D. 1077, eleven years only after the Conquest. The last was that of Stonesgate, in Essex, made almost exactly a century later. On account of their dependence upon the abbot of Cluny, several of the lesser houses were suppressed as "alien priories" towards the close of the fourteenth century, and those that remained gradually freed themselves from their obedience to the foreign superior. At the time of the general suppression in the sixteenth century there were thirty-two Cluniac houses; one only, Bermondsey, was an abbey; the rest were priories, of which the most important was that which had been nearly the first in order of time, Lewes.

iii. *Cistercians*

The congregation of Citeaux was at one time the most flourishing of the offshoots of the great Benedictine body. The monastery of Citeaux was established by St. Robert of Molesme in A.D. 1092. The saint was a Benedictine, and felt himself called to something different to what he had found in the monasteries of France. The peculiar system of the Cistercians, however, was the work of St. Stephen Harding, an Englishman, who at an early age had left his own country and never returned thither. He struck out a new line, which was a still further departure from the ideal of St. Benedict than was the Cluniac system. The Cistercians, whilst strictly maintaining the notion that each monastery was a family endowed with the principles of fecundity, formed themselves into an Order,

BENEDICTINE MONK OF THE CLUNIAC CONGREGATION

CISTERCIAN MONK

in the sense of an organised corporation, under the perpetual pre-eminence of the abbot and house of Citeaux, and with yearly Chapters at which all superiors were bound to attend. It was the chief object of the administration to secure absolute uniformity in all things and everywhere. This was obtained by the Chapters, and by the visitations of the abbot of Citeaux, made anywhere and everywhere at will. The Order spread during the first century of its existence with great rapidity. It is said that, by the middle of the twelfth century, Citeaux had five hundred dependencies, and that fifty years later there were more than three times that number. In England the first abbey was founded by King Henry I. at Furness in A.D. 1127, and of the hundred houses existing at the general suppression three-fourths had been founded in the twelfth century. The rest, with the exception of St. Mary Grace, London, established in 1349 by Edward III., were founded in the early part of the thirteenth century.

iv. *Carthusians.*

The Carthusians were founded in the eleventh century by St. Bruno. With the help of the bishop of Grenoble he built for himself and six companions, in the mountains near the city, an oratory and small separate cells in imitation of the ancient Lauras of Egypt. This was in A.D. 1086; and the Order takes its designation from the name of the place—Chartreuse. Peter the Venerable, the celebrated abbot of Cluny, writing forty years after the foundation, thus describes their austere form of life. "Their dress," he says, "is meaner and poorer than that of other monks, so short and scanty and so rough that the very sight affrights one. They wear coarse hair-shirts next their skin ; fast almost perpetually ; eat only bean-bread ; whether sick or well never touch flesh ; never buy fish, but eat it if given them as an alms; eat eggs on Sundays and Thursdays ; on Tuesdays and Saturdays their fare is pulse or herbs boiled ; on Mondays, Wednes-days, and Fridays they take nothing but bread and water ; and they have only two meals a day, except within the octaves of Christmas, Easter, Whitsuntide, Epiphany, and other festivals. Their constant occupation is praying, reading and manual labour, which consists chiefly in transcribing books. They say the lesser Hours of the Divine Office in their cells at the time when the bell rings, but meet together at Vespers and Matins with wonderful recollection."

A manner of life of such great austerity naturally did not attract many votaries. It was a special vocation to the few, and it was not until A.D. 1222 that the first house of the Order was established in England, at Hinton, in Somersetshire, by William Langesper. The last founda-tion was the celebrated Charterhouse of Shene, in Surrey, made by King Henry V. At the time of the general dissolution, there were in all eight English monasteries and about a hundred members.

II. The Canons Regular

The clergy of every large church were in ancient times called *canonici*—canons—as being on the list of those who were devoted to the service of the Church. In the eighth century, Chrodegand, bishop of Metz, formed the clergy of his cathedral into a body, living in common under a rule and bound to the public recitation of the Divine

CARTHUSIAN MONK

CANON REGULAR OF ST. AUGUSTINE

Office. They were known still as canons, or those living under a rule of life like the monks, from the true meaning of κανών, a rule. This common life was in time abandoned in spite of the provisions of several Councils, and then institutions other than Cathedral Chapters became organised upon lines similar to those laid down by Chrodegand, and they became known as Canons Regular. They formed themselves generally on the so-called Rule of St. Augustine, and became known, in England at least, as Augustinian Canons, Premonstratensian Canons, and Gilbertine Canons.

i. *Augustinian Canons*

The early history of the Austin, or Black Canons, is involved in considerable obscurity, and it is only after the beginning of the twelfth century that these Regulars are to be found in Europe. The Order was conventual, or monastic, rather than congregational or provincial, like the Friars: that is, the members were professed for a special house and belonged by virtue of their vows to it, and not to the general body of their brethren in the country. In one point they were not so closely bound to their house as were the monks. The Regular Canons were allowed in individual cases to serve the parishes that were impropriated to their houses; the monks were always obliged to employ secular vicars in these cures. The Augustinians were very popular in England; most of their houses having been established in the thirteenth and fourteenth centuries. The earliest foundation was that of Christ Church, or Holy Trinity, Aldgate, made by Queen Maud in A.D. 1108; and at the time of the dissolution there were about 170 houses of Augustinian Canons in

England; two of the abbeys, Waltham Cross and Ciren-
cester, being governed by mitred abbots. In Ireland they
were even more popular and numerous, the number of the
houses of canons being put at 223, together with 33 nunneries. The Augustinian priors of Christ Church, and
All Hallows, Dublin, and seven other priors of the Order,
had seats in the Irish Parliament. The habit of the
Order was black, and hence they were frequently known
as BLACK CANONS.

ii. *The Premonstratensian Canons*

This branch of the Canons Regular was established by
St. Norbert in A.D. 1119 at a place called Prémontré, a
lonely and desolate valley near Laon in France. Their
founder gave them the Rule of St. Augustine, and they
became known either as Premonstratensians, from their
first foundation, or Norbertines, from their founder. The
habit of these canons was white, with a white rochet and
even a white cap, and for this reason they were frequently
known as WHITE CANONS. Besides following the ordinary Augustinian Rule, these Canons made Prémontré
into a "mother-house," and the abbot of Prémontré was
abbot-general of the entire Order: having the right to
visit, either by himself or deputy, every house of the congregation; to summon every superior to the yearly General
Chapter; and to impose a tax for the use of the Order
upon all the houses. This, so far as England is concerned, lasted in theory until A.D. 1512, when all the
English houses were placed under the abbot of Welbeck.
Previously they had been for more than thirty years supervised on behalf of the abbot of Prémontré, by Bishop
Redman, who also continued to hold the office of abbot

PREMONSTRATENSIAN CANON

GILBERTINE CANON

of Shap. In England, just before the dissolution, there
were some thirty-four houses of the Order.

iii. *The Gilbertines*

The Canons of St. Gilbert of Sempringham are said to
have been established in A.D. 1139, although the actual
date appears to be uncertain, some annals putting the
foundation as early as A.D. 1131, others as late as A.D.
1148. St. Gilbert, the founder, was Rector of Sempringham
and composed his rule from those of St. Austin and St.
Benedict. It was a dual Order, for both men and women;
the former followed St. Augustine's code with some
additions, whilst the women took the Cistercian recension
of the Benedictine Rule.

These canons, according to Dugdale, had a black
habit with a white cloak and a hood lined with lamb's
wool. The women were in black with a white cap. In
the double monasteries the canons and nuns lived in
separate houses having no communication. At first the
Order flourished greatly. St. Gilbert in his lifetime
founded thirteen houses, nine for men and women and
four for men only. In these there are said to have been
seven hundred canons and fifteen hundred sisters.

The Order was under the rule of a general superior,
called the master or prior-general. His leave was necessary
for the admission of members, and, in fact, to initiate
business or at least give validity to the proposals of any
house. There were, in all, some twenty-six of these establishments in England at the time of the general dissolution. Four only of these were considered as ranking
among the greater monasteries whose income was above
£200 a year.

III. The Military Orders

i. *Knights Hospitallers of St. John of Jerusalem*

The Hospitallers began in A.D. 1092 with the building of a hospital for pilgrims at Jerusalem. The original idea of the work of these knights was to provide for the needs of pilgrims visiting the Holy Land and to afford them protection on their way. They, too, followed a rule of life founded upon that of St. Augustine, and their dress was black with a white cross upon it. They came to England very shortly after their foundation, and had a house built for them in London in A.D. 1100. They rose in wealth and importance in the country ; and their head, or grand prior as he was called, became the first lay baron in England, and had a seat in the House of Peers.

Upon many of their manors and estates the Knights Hospitallers had small establishments named *commanderies*, which were under the government of one of their number, called the commander. These houses were sometimes known as *preceptories*, but this was a term more generally used for the establishments of the other great Military Order, the Templars. An offshoot of both these orders was known as "The Order of St. Lazarus of Jerusalem." There were a few houses of this branch in England, which was founded chiefly to assist and support lepers and indigent members of all the Military Orders. They are, however, usually regarded as hospitals. The Knights of St. John of Jerusalem had their headquarters at the Hospital of St. John, near Clerkenwell, to which were attached some fifty-three cells or commanderies.

GILBERTINE NUN

KNIGHT HOSPITALLER

ii. *The Templars*

The Military Order of the Templars was founded, according to Tanner, about the year A.D. 1118. They derived their name from the Temple of Jerusalem, and the original purpose of their institute was to secure the roads to Palestine, and protect the holy places. They must have come into England early in the reign of King Stephen, as they had several foundations at this time, the first being that in London which gave its name to the present Temple. They became too rich and powerful; and having been accused of great crimes, their Order was suppressed by Pope Clement V. in 1309 : an act which was confirmed in the Council of Vienne in 1312. The head of the Order in England was styled the " Master of the Temple," and was sometimes, as such, summoned to Parliament.

Upon their manors and estates the Templars, like the Hospitallers, frequently built churches and houses, in which some of the brethren lived. These were subordinate to the London house and were in reality cells, under the title of " Preceptories." On the final suppression of the Order, their lands and houses, to the number of eighteen, were handed over to the Knights of St. John of Jerusalem. One house, Ferriby, in Yorkshire, became a priory of Austin Canons, and four other estates appear to have been confiscated. In all there were some three-and-twenty preceptories connected with the London Temple.

IV. The Friars

The friars differed from the monks in certain ways. The brethren by their profession were bound, not to any locality or house, but to the province, which usually consisted of the entire number of houses in a country. They did not, consequently, form individual families in their various establishments, like the monks in their monasteries. They also, at first, professed the strictest poverty, not being allowed to possess even corporate property like the monastic Orders. They were by their profession mendicants, living on alms, and only holding the mere buildings in which they dwelt.

i. *The Dominicans, or Black Friars*

The founder of these friars was a Spaniard named Dominic, a canon of the diocese of Osma, in Old Castile, at the close of the twelfth century. They were known as Dominicans, from their founder; "Preaching Friars," from their mission to convert heretics; in England, "Black Friars," from the colour of their cloak; and in France "Jacobins," from having had their first house in the Rue St. Jacques, at Paris. Their rule was founded on that of St. Augustine, and it was verbally approved in the Council of Lateran in A.D. 1215, and the following year formally by Honorius III. Their founder, having been a secular canon of Osma in Spain, his friars at first adopted the ordinary dress of canons; but about A.D. 1219 they took a white tunic, scapular, and hood, over which, when in church or when they went abroad, they wore a black *cappa*, or cloak, with a hood of the same colour. They first came to England with Peter de Rupibus, bishop

KNIGHT TEMPLAR

DOMINICAN FRIAR

of Winchester, in A.D. 1221, and their Order quickly spread. In the first year of their arrival they obtained a foothold in the University of Oxford, and at the time of the general suppression of the religious Orders in the sixteenth century they had fifty-eight convents in the country.

ii. *The Franciscan, or Grey Friars*

St. Francis the founder of the Grey Friars was contemporary with St. Dominic, and was born at Assisi, in the province of Umbria in Italy, in A.D. 1182. These friars were called Franciscans from their founder; "Grey Friars" from the colour of their habit; and "Minorites" from their humble desire to be considered the least of the Orders. Their rule was approved by Innocent III. in A.D. 1210 and by the General Council of the Lateran in A.D. 1215. Their dress was made of a coarse brown cloth with a long pointed hood of the same material, and a short cloak. They girded themselves with a knotted cord and went barefooted. The Franciscan Friars first found their way to England in A.D. 1224, and at the general destruction of Regular life in England in the sixteenth century they had in all about sixty-six establishments. A reformation of the Order to primitive observance was made in the fifteenth century and confirmed by the Council of Constance in A.D. 1414. The branches of the Order which adopted it became known as "Observants" or "Recollects." This branch of the Order was represented in England by several houses built for them by King Henry VII., although they are supposed to have been brought into England in the time of Edward IV.

The whole Order in England was divided into seven "Custodies" or "Wardenships," the houses being grouped round convenient centres such as London, York, Cambridge, Bristol, Oxford, Newcastle, and Worcester. Harpsfield says that the "Recollects" or "Observants" had six friaries, at Canterbury, Greenwich, Richmond, Southampton, Newark, and Newcastle.

The Minoresses, or Nuns of St. Clare

The Minoresses were instituted by St. Clare, the sister of St. Francis of Assisi, about A.D. 1212, as the branch of the Franciscan Order for females. They followed the Rule of the Friars Minor and were thus called "Minoresses," or Nuns of St. Clare, after their foundress. They wore the same dress as the Franciscan Friars, and imitated them in their poverty, for which cause they were sometimes known as "Poor Clares." They were brought to England some-where about A.D. 1293, and established in London, with-out Aldgate, in the locality now known as the Minories. The Order had two other houses, one at Denney, in Cambridgeshire, in which at the time of the general dis-solution there were some twenty-five nuns; and the other at Brusyard in Suffolk, which was a much smaller establish-ment. The nuns at Denney had previously been located at Waterbeche for about fifty years, being removed to their new home by Mary, countess of Pembroke, in A.D. 1348.

iii. Carmelites

The Carmelite Friars were so called from the place of their origin. They were also named "White Friars" from the colour of the cloak of their habit, and Friars of the Blessed Virgin. These friars are first heard of in the twelfth century, on being driven out of Palestine by the persecution of the Saracens. Their Rule is chiefly founded

FRANCISCAN FRIAR

FRANCISCAN NUN, OR MINORESS

on that of St. Basil, and was confirmed by Pope Honorius III. in A.D. 1224, and finally approved by Innocent IV. in 1250. They were brought into England by John Vesey and Richard Grey, and established their first houses in the north at Alnwick, and in the south at Ailesford in Kent. At the latter place the first European Chapter of the Order was held in A.D. 1245. In the sixteenth century there were about forty houses in England and Wales.

iv. *Austin Friars, or Hermits*

The body of Austin Friars took its historical origin in the union of several existing bodies of friars effected in A.D. 1265 by Pope Clement IV. They were regarded as belonging to the ranks of the mendicant friars and not to the monastic Order. They were very widely spread, and in Europe in the sixteenth century they are said to have possessed three thousand convents, in which were thirty thousand friars; besides three hundred convents of nuns. In England at the time of the dissolution they had some thirty-two friaries.

V. THE LESSER FRIARS

i. *Friars of the Sack, or De Penitentia*

These brethren of penance were called "Friars of the Sack" because their dress was cut without other form than that of a simple bag or sack, and made of coarse cloth, like sackcloth. Most authorities, however, represent this as merely a familiar name, and say that their real title was that of Friars, or Brethren of Penance. They took their origin apparently in Italy, and came to England during the reign of Henry III., where, about A.D. 1257, they

opened a house in London. They had many settlements
in France, Spain, and Germany, but lost most of them
after the Council of Lyons in A.D. 1274, when Pope
Gregory X. suppressed all begging friars with the exception
of the four mendicant Orders of Dominicans, Franciscans,
Austin Friars, and Carmelites. This did not, however,
apply universally, and in England the *Fratres de Sacco*
remained in existence until the final suppression of the religious Orders in the sixteenth century. The dress of these
friars was apparently made of rough brown cloth, and was
not unlike that of the Franciscans ; they had their feet
bare and wore wooden sandals. Their mode of life was
very austere, and they never ate meat and drank only
water.

ii. *Pied Friars, or Fratres de Pica*

These religious were so called from the colours of their
habit, which was black and white, like a magpie. They
had but one house in England, at Norwich, and had only
a brief existence, as the Pied Friars were obliged, by the
Council of Lyons, to join one or other of the four great
mendicant Orders. Their house, which, according to
Blomfield, stood in the north-east corner of the churchyard
of St. Peter's Church, was given to the Hospital of Bek,
at Billingford in Norfolk.

iii. *Friars of St. Mary de Areno*

These friars had likewise but one house, at Westminster,
founded towards the end of the reign of Henry III. They,
too, were short-lived as a body, falling under the law of
suppression of the lesser mendicant Orders. They, however, continued for a few years longer, as Tanner quotes a

CARMELITE FRIAR

AUSTIN FRIAR

Close Roll of 11 Edward II., to show that they were only dissolved in that year, A.D. 1318.

iv. *Friars of Our Lady, or de Domina*

The Friars of Our Lady are said to have lived under the Rule of St. Austin.   They had a white habit, with a black cloak and hood.   They were instituted in the thirteenth century, and had a house at Cambridge, near the castle. Before A.D. 1290 they were also settled at Norwich, where they continued until the great Pestilence in 1349, of which they all died.

v. *Friars of the Holy Trinity, or Trinitarians*

These religious were founded by SS. John of Matha and Felix of Valois about A.D. 1197 for the redemption of captives.   They were called "*Trinitarians*," because by their rule all their churches were dedicated to the Holy Trinity, or "*Maturines*," from the fact that their original foundation in Paris was near St. Mathurine's Chapel. The Order was confirmed by Pope Innocent III., who gave the religious white robes, with a red and blue cross on their breasts, and a cloak with the same emblem on the left side.   Their revenues were to be divided into three parts ; one for their own support, one to relieve the poor, and the third to ransom Christians who had been taken captive by the infidels.   They were brought to England in A.D. 1244, and were given the lands and privileges of the Canons of the Holy Sepulchre on the extinction of that Order.   According to the *Monasticon,* they had, in all, eleven houses in this country ; but these establishments were small, the usual number of religious in each being three friars and three lay brothers.   The superior was named "minister," and included in his office the functions of superior and procurator ; and the houses were united into a congregation under a *Minister major*, who held a general Chapter annually for the regulation of defects and the discussion of common interests.

vi. *Crutched, or Crossed Friars*

The Crossed Friars are said by some to have taken their origin in the Low Countries, by others to have come from Italy in very early times, having been instituted or reformed by one Gerard, prior of St. Maria di Morella at Bologna. In 1169 Pope Alexander III. took them under his protection and gave them a fixed rule of life. These friars first came to England in the year 1244. Matthew Paris, writing of that time, says that they appeared before a synod held by the bishop of Rochester, each carrying a stick upon which was a cross. They presented documents from the pope and asked to be allowed to make foundations of their fraternity in England. Clement Reyner puts their first establishment in this country at Reigate, in 1245, and their second in London in 1249. This last is the better known, as it has given the name of Crutched Friars to a locality in the city of London. The friars had a third house at Oxford, and altogether there were six or seven English friaries. Besides the cross upon their staves, from which they originally took their name, the friars had a red cloth cross upon the breasts of their habits.

vii. *The Bethlemite Friars*

The origin of these friars is uncertain, and they were apparently only known in England, and so may perhaps

FRIAR OF THE SACK

TRINITARIAN

be considered to have had their beginning in this country. Matthew Paris says that in the year 1257 they were given a house at Cambridge, in Trumpington Street. He describes their dress as being very like that of the Dominicans, from which it was distinguished only by having a red star, of five points with a round blue centre, on the scapular. This badge recalled the meaning of their name, representing as it did the star which led the Magi to Bethlehem.

viii. *The Bonshommes*

These friars were apparently of English origin. Some have thought that they were the same as the "Friars of the Sack," but this is by no means clear. Polydore Vergil says that Edmund of Cornwall, the brother of Henry III., on his return from Germany in A.D. 1257, built and endowed a fine monastery at Ashridge. This he gave "to a new order of men, never before known in England, called *Boni Homines,* the Bonshommes. They followed the rule of St. Augustine, wearing a blue-coloured dress of a form similar to that of the Augustinian hermits." The only other house possessed by the Bonshommes was at Edingdon.

LIST OF ENGLISH RELIGIOUS HOUSES

An asterisk (*) prefixed to a religious house signifies that there are considerable remains extant. A dagger (†) prefixed signifies that there are sufficient remains to interest an archæologist. No attention is paid to mere mounds or grass-covered heaps.

For these marks as to remains the author is not responsible. They have kindly been contributed by Rev. Dr. Cox and Mr. W. H. St. John Hope, who desire it to be known that they do not in any way consider these marks exhaustive; they merely represent those remains with which one or other, or both, are personally acquainted.

The following abbreviations for the names of the religious Orders, etc., have been used in the list :—

A.	= Austin Canons.	Franc.	= Franciscan, or Grey Friars.
A. (fs.)	= Austin Friars, or Hermits.	Franc. (n.)	= Franciscan nuns.
A. (n.)	= Austin nuns.	G.	= Gilbertines (canons following the
A.P.	= Alien priories.		rule of St. Austin, and nuns
A. (sep.)	= Austin Canons of the Holy		that of St. Benedict).
	Sepulchre.	H.	= Hospitals.
A.H.	= Alien Hospitals.	H. (lep.)	= Leper Hospitals.
B.	= Benedictines, or Black monks.	H.-A. (fs.)	= Hospitals served by Austin Friars.
B (fs.)	= Bethlemite Friars.	H.-B (fs.)	= Hospitals served by Bethlemite
B. (n.)	= Benedictine nuns.		Friars.
Bridg.	= Bridgettines.	H.G.	= Hospitals served by Gilbertines.
C.	= Cistercian monks.	Hosp.	= Knights Hospitallers.
C. (n.)	= Cistercian nuns.	M.	= Maturins, or Friars of the Holy
Carm.	= Carmelite, or White Friars.		Trinity.
Carth.	= Carthusians.	P.	= Premonstratensian Canons.
Cl.	= Cluniac monks.	P. (n.)	= Premonstratensian nuns.
Cl. (n.)	= Cluniac nuns.	P.F.	= Pied Friars.
Cru.	= Crutched, or Crossed Friars.	S.	= Friars of the Sack, or De Peni-
Dom.	= Dominican, or Black Friars.		tentia.
Dom. (n.)	= Dominican nuns.	Temp.	= Knights Templars.
F.A.	= Friars de Areno.	A plus (+)	= Ancient religious houses.
F.D.	= Friars de Domina, or of Our Lady.	+ (n.)	= Ancient religious house of women.

ORDER.	HOUSE.	COUNTY.
	Abberbury (*see* Alberbury).	
	Abberforth, Tadcaster (*see* Calcaria).	
B.	† Abbotsbury, abb. . . .	Dorset.
C.	* Aberconway, abb. . .	Denbigh.
B.	* Abergavenny, pr. . .	Monmouth.

ORDER.	HOUSE.	COUNTY.
B.	† Abingdon, abb.	Berks.
	cell :—Edwardstow	Suffolk.
H.	Abingdon, St. Helen's	Berks.
	St. John's.	
A.P.	Acley, or Lyre Ocle (cell to St. Benoit sur Soire)	Hereford.
A. (n.)	Aconbury	Hereford.
P.	* Agatha's, St., abb.	Yorks.
A.	Ailesham, pr.	Lincoln.
C.	Albalanda (see Whiteland)	Carmarthen.
A.	Alborn (united to Woodbridge, 1466)	Suffolk.
B.	* Alban's, St., abb.	Herts.
B.	cells :—Belvoir	Lincoln.
B.	* Binham	Norfolk.
B.	† Hatfield Peverell	Essex.
B.	Hertford	Herts.
B.	Pembroke	Pembroke.
B.	Redburn	Herts.
B.	* Tynemouth	Northumberland.
B.	Wallingford	Berks.
B.	Cocket Island (cell of Tynemouth)	Northumberland.
H. (lep.)	Alban's, St., St. Julian's	Herts.
H. (lep. women)	Alban, St., St. Mary de Pratis	Herts.
A.P.	Alberbury, or Abberbury (cell of Grandmont in Limousin)	Salop.
B.	† Alcester (see Evesham).	
A.	† Aldbury, pr.	Surrey.
	Aldeby (see Norwich).	
A.	Alensborne	Suffolk.
H.	Alkmonton	Derby.
A.P.	Allerton Malleverer (cell of Marmoutiers, Tours)	Yorks, W.R.

ORDER.	HOUSE.	COUNTY.
Carm. .	Allerton, North . . .	Yorks, W.R.
A. (fs.) .	Allerton, North . . .	Yorks, W.R.
H. .	Allerton, North, St. James .	Yorks, W.R.
H. .	Maison Dieu.	
P. .	† Alnwick, abb. . . .	Northumberland.
Carm. .	Alnwick (*see* Holne) . .	Northumberland.
H. .	Alnwick, St. Leonard's . .	Northumberland.
G. .	† Alvingham . . .	Lincoln.
B. (n.) .	Amesbury . . .	Wilts.
A.P. .	† Andover (cell of St. Florent at Samur in Anjou) . .	Hants.
H. .	Andover	Hants.
A.P. .	† Andwell (cell of Tyronne) . .	Hants.
A. .	† Anglesey, pr. . . .	Cambridge.
B. (n.) .	Ankerwyke . . .	Bucks.
Carth. .	* Anne's, St. (*see* Coventry) .	Warwick.
Hosp. .	Anstey	Wilts.
	Antony, St. (*see* Plympton).	
Carm. .	Appleby	Westmoreland.
H. (lep.)	Appleby	Westmoreland.
	Appleton (*see* Nunappleton).	
A.P. .	Apuldercombe (cell to Montisburg, Normandy) . .	Hants, I. of W.
B (n.) .	Arden	Yorks.
H. .	Armston	Northants.
B. (n.) .	Armthwaite . . .	Cumberland.
Cl. (n.) .	Arthington . . .	Yorks.
Dom. .	Arundel	Sussex.
A.P. .	* Arundel (cell to Séez, afterwards a college) . . .	Sussex.
H. .	† Arundel	Sussex.
A. .	* Ashby Canons, pr. . .	Northants.
A. (fs.) .	Ashen (*see* Clare).	
Temp. & Hosp.	† Aslakeby . . .	Lincoln.

ORDER.	HOUSE.	COUNTY.
H. .	Astley	Warwick.
A.P. .	Astley (cell to Evreux) . .	Worcester.
H. .	Athelington . . .	Dorset.
B. .	† Athelney, abb. . . .	Somerset.
A.P. .	† Atherington (cell of Séez) .	Sussex.
A. (fs.) .	Atherstone . . .	Warwick.
A.P. .	† Avebury (cell to St. George de Bocherville, Norm.) . .	Wilts.
	† Avecote (*see* Malvern, Great) .	
	Axholme (*see* Epworth).	
A.P. .	Axmouth (cell to Montisburg, Norm.) . . .	Devon.
Franc. .	Aylesbury . . .	Bucks.
+ .	Aylesbury . . .	Bucks.
H. (lep.)	Aylesbury, St. John . . St. Leonard	Bucks.
Carm. .	* Aylesford . . .	Kent.
H. .	Aynho	Northants.
	Babington (*see* Bebington).	
	Babwell (*see* Bury).	
+ .	Bachaunis . . .	Carmarthen.
A. .	Bactanesford (given to Finchale, 1196)	Durham.
A. .	Badlesmere . . .	Kent.
Temp. & Hosp.	* Badersley (South) . . .	Hants.
H. .	Bagby	Yorks.
H. (lep.)	Baldock	Herts.
Temp. & Hosp.	* Balsall	Warwick.
	Bamburgh (*see* Nostell).	
Dom. .	Bamburgh . . .	Northumberland.
H. .	Bamburgh . . .	Northumberland.
H. (lep.)	Banbury . . .	Oxford.

ORDER.	HOUSE.	COUNTY.
+ .	Bancornaburg, or Banchor .	Flint.
Dom. .	Bangor	Carnarvon.
+ .	Banwell	Somerset.
B. .	† Bardney, abb. . . .	Lincoln.
A. .	Bardon (near Puckeridge) . .	Herts.
B. .	Bardsey, abb. . . .	Carnarvon.
Cru. .	Barham, or Bergham (in parish of Lynton) . . .	Cambridge.
B. (n.) .	† Barking	Essex.
P. .	† Barlings, abb. . . .	Lincoln.
A. .	Barlinch, pr. . . .	Somerset.
H. .	Barnard Castle . . .	Durham.
Cl. .	Barnstaple, pr. . . .	Devon.
A (fs.) .	Barnstaple . . .	Devon.
H. .	Barnstaple . . .	Devon.
A. .	† Barnwell, pr. . . .	Cambridge.
Hosp. .	Barrow	Derbyshire.
	Barrow (see Colchester).	
+ .	Barrowe, or at Barwe . .	Lincoln.
B. (n.) .	Barrow Gurney, or Mynchen Barwe	Somerset.
B. .	Barton	Hereford.
C. (n.) .	Basedale	Yorks.
	Basseleck, or Basil (see Glaston-bury).	
H. .	* Basingstoke . . .	Hants.
C. .	* Basingwerk, abb. . . .	Flint.
B. .	* Bath Cathedral, pr. . .	Somerset.
	* cell :—Dunster.	
H. .	Bath, St. John Baptist's . .	Somerset.
	St. Mary Magdalene's.	
Hosp. .	Battisford . . .	Suffolk.
B. .	* Battle, abb. . . .	Sussex.
B. .	* cell :—Brecknock . .	Brecon.

ORDER.	HOUSE.	COUNTY.
H.	Bawtry	Yorks.
P.	† Beauchief, abb. . . .	Derby.
C.	* Beaulieu, abb. . . .	Hants.
	cell :—Farendon . . .	Hants.
	Beaulieu-Moddry, or Millbrook	
Carth.	* Beauvale, or Gresley Park .	Notts.
H. (lep.)	Bebington . . .	Cheshire.
H.	Bec	Norfolk.
H. (lep.)	Beccles, St. Mary Magdalen's .	Suffolk.
A.P.	Beckford (cell to St. Barbe en Auge, Norm.) . . .	Gloucester.
Franc.	Becmachen, or Bermache . .	Isle of Man.
+	Bectanesford (see Bactenesford) .	Durham.
Franc.	† Bedford	Beds.
+	Bedford	Beds.
H.	Bedford, St. John's .	Beds.
	St. Leonard's.	
L	Bedingham, or Redingham .	Sussex.
	Beeleigh (see Bileigh).	
	Bees, St. (see York, St. Mary's).	
A.	† Beeston, pr. . . .	Norfolk.
A.P.	Begare, near Richmond (cell to St. Begare, Brit.) . .	Yorks.
P.	* Begham, or Bayham, abb. .	Sussex.
	Belvoir (see Alban's, St.).	
B.	† Benet's of Hulme, St., abb. .	Norfolk.
A.P.	Benington Longa (cell of Savigny) . . .	Lincoln.
	Bentley (see Alkmonton).	
+	Bentley	Middlesex.
A.	Berden, pr. . . .	Essex.
+	Berkeley	Gloucester.
H.	Berkeley, St. James' and St. John's Longbridge.	Gloucester.

ORDER.	HOUSE.	COUNTY.
H.	Berkhamstede, St. John Baptist's	Herts.
H. (lep.)	St. John the Evang.	
H.	St. Thomas the Martyr's.	
H.	St. James'.	
A.	Berleston	Devon.
Cl.	Bermondsey, abb.	Surrey.
B.	cell :—Derby, St. James'	Derby.
H.	Bermondsey, St. Saviour's	Surrey.
H.	St. Thomas'.	
H.	Berton	Salop.
M.	Berwick	Northumberland.
+ (n.)	Berwick, South	Northumberland.
H.	Berwick, Maison Dieu	Northumberland.
H.	St. Mary Magdalen's.	
A.	Bethgelert, pr.	Carnarvon.
Franc.	Beverley	Yorks, E.R.
Dom.	† Beverley	Yorks, E.R.
Hosp.	Beverley	Yorks, E.R.
H.	Beverley, St. Giles	Yorks, E.R.
H.	Trinity H.	
H.	St. Nicholas.	
A.	Bicknacre, or Woodham Ferrers	Essex.
H.	Bigging	Herts.
P.	* Bileigh by Maldon, abb.	Essex.
A.	† Bilsington, pr.	Kent.
C.	* Bindon, abb.	Dorset.
	* Binham (see Alban's, St.).	
B.	* Birkenhead, pr.	Cheshire.
H.	Birmingham	Warwick.
A.P.	Birstall (cell to St. Martin de Alceio, Albemarle, France)	Yorks, N.R.
A.	† Bisham, pr. (at first belonged to Temp.)	Berks.
	Bissemede (see Bushmead).	
C.	Bittlesden, abb.	Bucks.

ORDER.	HOUSE.	COUNTY.
+	Bitumæam, or ad Tunconsam .	Worcester.
B. (n.) .	Blackborough . . .	Norfolk.
A.P.	Blakenham (cell to Bec, Norm.)	Suffolk.
A.	† Blackmore, pr. . . .	Essex.
P.	Blackwase, or Blackhouse (cell of Lavendon and of Bradsole)	Kent.
Carm. .	Blakeney, or Sniterley . .	Norfolk.
P.	* Blanchland, abb. . . .	Northumberland.
+	Bleatham	Westmoreland.
A.	† Bliburgh, or Blythbury, pr. .	Suffolk.
B. (n.) .	Blithbury . . .	Stafford.
+	Blockley, or Bloccanlegh . .	Worcester.
B.	† Blyth, or Brida, pr. . .	Notts.
H. (lep.)	Blyth	Notts.
H.	Bocking, Maison Dieu . .	Essex.
A.	† Bodmin, pr. . . .	Cornwall.
Franc. .	† Bodmin	Cornwall.
H.	† Bodmin, St. Laurence's . .	Cornwall.
	St. Anthony's.	
	St. George's.	
G.	Bollington, or Bullington . .	Lincoln.
A.	* Bolton, pr. . . .	Yorks.
H. (lep.)	Bolton	Northumberland.
A.P.	Bonby (cell to Fromond, Norm.)	Lincoln.
C.	Bordesley, abb. . . .	Worcester.
+	Bosham	Sussex.
Dom. .	† Boston	Lincoln.
Franc. .	Boston	Lincoln.
Carm. .	Boston	Lincoln.
A. (fs.) .	Boston	Lincoln.
H.	Boston	Lincoln.
H.	Boughton . . .	Cheshire.
H.	Boughton (see Broughton) .	Essex.
A.	† Bourn, abb. . . .	Lincoln.

ORDER.	HOUSE.	COUNTY.
A.P.	Bourne, or Patricksbourne (cell to Beaulieu, Norm.)	Kent.
H.	Bowes	I. of Guernsey.
B.	* Boxgrave, pr.	Sussex.
C.	† Boxley, abb.	Kent.
+ (n.)	Boxwell	Gloucester.
H.	Boycodeswade, near Cokesford	Norfolk.
H.	Braceford	Yorks.
Cru.	Brackley	Northants.
H.	Brackley, St. John's St. Leonard's.	Northants.
H.	Bradebusk	Notts.
A.	* Bradenstoke, pr.	Wilts.
B.	Bradewell, pr.	Bucks.
+	Bradfield	Berks.
H.	Bradford	Wilts.
+	Bradford	Wilts.
A.	Bradley, pr.	Leicester.
	Bradsole (*see* St. Radegund's)	Kent.
H.	Bramber	Sussex.
A.	† Breamore, or Bromere, pr.	Hants.
Dom.	Brecknock	Brecon.
	* Brecknock, or Brecon (*see* Battle).	
	† Bredon (*see* Nostell).	
+	Bredon	Worcester.
A.	† Breadsall, pr.	Derby.
+	Brent, or East Brent	Somerset.
Hosp.	Bretesford	Suffolk.
B. (n.)	Bretford (removed to Kenilworth)	Warwick.
H.	Bretford	Warwick.
B. (n.)	Brewood Black Ladies	Stafford.
C. (n.)	† Brewood White Ladies	Salop.
H.	Breydeford	Yorks, E.R.
Franc.	Bridgnorth	Salop.

ORDER.	HOUSE.	COUNTY.
H.	Bridgnorth	Salop.
Franc.	Bridgwater	Somerset.
H.	Bridgwater, St. John's St. Giles'.	Somerset.
A.	* Bridlington, pr.	Yorks.
	Bridport	Dorset.
H.	Bridport	Dorset.
A.P.	Brimpsfield (cell to Fontenay, Norm.)	Gloucester.
Hosp.	Brimpton	Berks.
A.	* Brinkburne, pr.	Northumberland.
A.P.	Brisett (cell to Nobiliac)	Suffolk.
A.	* Bristol, Great St. Augustine's, abb.	Somerset.
B. (n.)	Bristol, St. Mary Magdalen's	Somerset.
	† Bristol, St. James' (see Tewkesbury)	Somerset.
Dom.	* Bristol	Somerset.
Franc.	Bristol	Somerset.
Carm.	Bristol	Somerset.
A. (fs.)	Bristol	Somerset.
H.	Bristol, St. Bartholomew's	Somerset.
H.	St. Catherine's.	
H.	Gaunts, or Billeswyke H.	
H.	Trinity H.	
H. (lep.)	St. Laurence's.	
H.	Lyons, or Lewins.	
H. (lep.)	St. John's.	
H.	St. Margaret's.	
H. (lep.)	St. Mary Magdalen's.	
H.	St. Michael's Hill.	
H.	Bartons.	
H.	St. Sepulchre's.	
H.	Temple Street.	
H.	Temple Gate.	
H.	Redcliff Hill.	

ORDER.	HOUSE.	COUNTY.
+	Brixworth . . .	Northants.
P.	Brockley, or Brocle, West Greenwich (removed to Bayham).	Kent.
P. (n.)	Brodholm . . .	Notts.
A.	Bromehill, pr. . . .	Norfolk.
	Bromere (*see* Breamore).	
	Bromfield (*see* Gloucester, St. Peter's).	
B. (n.)	Bromhall . . .	Berks.
A.	Bromhill	Norfolk.
Cl.	* Bromholm, pr. . . .	Norfolk.
	Bromley (*see* Stratford at Bow).	
	Bromwich, West (*see* Sandwell).	
A.	Brooke (*see* Kenilworth) . .	Rutland.
H.	Brough	Westmoreland.
H.	† Broughton, near Malton . .	Yorks.
H.	Broughton-under-Blean . .	Kent.
Hosp.	† Bruerne, or Temple Bruer .	Lincoln.
C.	Bruerne, or Brueria, abb. . .	Oxford.
+	Brunnesburg, or Bromburg .	Cheshire.
Fran.(n.)	Brusyard . . .	Suffolk.
A.	† Bruton, abb. . . .	Somerset.
H.	Bruton	Somerset.
A.	† Buckenham, pr. . . .	Norfolk.
C.	† Buckfast, abb. . . .	Devon.
H.	Buckingham . . .	Bucks.
C.	† Buckland, abb. . . .	Devon.
A. (n.)	Buckland Minchin . . .	Somerset.
Hosp.	Buckland Minchin . . .	Somerset.
H.	Buckstead . . .	Sussex.
C.	* Buildwas, abb. . . .	Salop.
	Bullington (*see* Bollington).	
B. (n.)	† Bungay (Bonna Gaie) . .	Suffolk.
M.	Burbach, or Eston, or Marlborough . . .	Wilts.

ORDER.	HOUSE.	COUNTY.
A.	Burchester, pr.	Oxford.
H.	Burchester	Oxford.
H.	Burford .	Oxford.
+	Burgh Castle	Suffolk.
A.(canon- esses)	* Burnham	Bucks.
Carm.	† Burnham Norton .	Norfolk.
	Burnham (see St. Mary de Pré).	
A.	* Burscough, pr.	Lancaster.
Fran.(n.)	Burshyard	Suffolk.
H. (lep.)	Burton Lazars	Leicester.
B.	† Burton-on-Trent, or Modwenstow, abb.	Stafford.
A.P.	Burwell (cell to St. Maria, Silvæ Majoris, Bordeaux)	Lincoln.
B.	* Bury St. Edmunds, abb.	Suffolk.
Franc.	Bury St. Edmunds	Suffolk.

H.	Bury St. Edmunds—
	    God's House, or St. John's.
	    † St. Nicholas'.
	    St. Peter's.
	    † St. Saviour's.
	    St. Stephen's.
		Suffolk.

A.	† Bushmead, pr.	Beds.
A.P.	Bustal, or Burstal Garth (cell to St. Martin d'Aley, Albemarle, Norm.)	Yorks.
A.	† Butley, pr. (Buteleia)	Suffolk.
C.	* Byland, abb.	Yorks.
A.	Byrkley, pr., now Butlehouse (in the parish of Merlynch)	Somerset.
+	Cadweli .	Carmarthen
+	Caerleon .	Monmouth.
+	Caistor, or Dormundescastre	Northants.

ORDER.	HOUSE.	COUNTY.
+ (n.) .	Calcaria, or Caelcacester . .	Yorks.
	Caldey (*see* Dogmael's, St.) .	Pembroke.
C. .	* Calder, abb. . . .	Cumberland.
A. .	Caldwell, pr. . . .	Beds.
A. .	† Calke (cell to Repton) . .	Derby.
H. .	Calne, St. John's . . .	Wilts.
A. .	Calwich, pr. . . .	Stafford.
B. .	Cambridge, Monks' or Buckingham College (now St. Mary Magdalen College) . .	Cambridge.
B. (n.) .	* Cambridge, St. Radegund's (now Jesus College) . . .	Cambridge.
G. .	Cambridge, St. Edmund's . .	Cambridge.
Dom. .	Cambridge . . .	Cambridge.
Franc. .	Cambridge . . .	Cambridge.
Carm. .	Cambridge . . .	Cambridge.
A. (fs.) .	Cambridge . . .	Cambridge.
S. .	Cambridge . . .	Cambridge.
B. (fs.) .	Cambridge . . .	Cambridge.
F.D. .	Cambridge . . .	Cambridge.
H. .	Cambridge, St. John Evangelist's	Cambridge.
+ (n.) .	Camestrune, or Camesterne .	Dorset.
A.P. .	Cammeringham (cell to Prem. abb. of Blanchland, Norm.) .	Lincoln.
A. (n.) .	Campsey . . .	Suffolk.
B. (n.) .	Cannington . . .	Somerset.
A. (n.) .	Canonleigh, or Mynchen Leigh .	Devon.
B. .	* Canterbury, St. Augustine's, abb.	Kent.
B. .	* Canterbury, Christ Church Cath. pr.	Kent.
B. .	* cells :—Dover, St. Martin's	Kent.
B. .	† Oxford, Canterbury College . .	Oxford.
B. (n.) .	Canterbury, St. Sepulchre's .	Kent.

ORDER.	HOUSE.	COUNTY.
A.	† Canterbury, St. Gregory's, pr.	Kent.
Dom.	† Canterbury	Kent.
Franc.	† Canterbury	Kent.
A. (fs.)	† Canterbury	Kent.
+	Canterbury, St. Mildred's	Kent.
H.	* Canterbury, St. John Baptist's	Kent.
H.	† Canterbury, Poor Priests	Kent.
H. (lep.)	Canterbury, St. Laurence's	Kent.
H.	Canterbury, St. Margaret's	Kent.
H.	* Eastbridge, St. Thomas Cant.	Kent.
H.	St. Nicholas.	
H.	St. Catherine.	
B.	Canwell, pr.	Stafford.
	Canyngton (see Cannington).	
+ (n.)	Carbroke (afterwards removed to Buckland)	Norfolk.
Hosp.	Carbroke	Norfolk.
Dom.	Cardiff	Glamorgan.
Franc.	† Cardiff	Glamorgan.
Carm.	† Cardiff	Glamorgan.
	Cardigan (see Chertsey).	
	Carham-on-Tweed (see Kirkham).	
A.P.	† Carisbrooke (cell to Lira)	I. of Wight.
A.	* Carlisle, Cath., pr.	Cumberland.
Dom.	Carlisle	Cumberland.
Franc.	Carlisle	Cumberland.
H. (lep.)	Carlisle, St. Nicholas'	Cumberland.
A.	Carmarthen, pr.	Carmarthen.
Franc.	Carmarthen	Carmarthen.
B. (n.)	* Carrow	Norfolk.
	Carswell (see Montacute).	
A.	* Cartmel, pr.	Lancaster.
Cl.	* Castleacre, pr.	Norfolk.
H.	Castle Donington	Leicester.

ORDER.	HOUSE.	COUNTY.
H.	Catchburne	Northumberland.
B. (n.)	† Catesby	Northants.
+	Cathall	Herts.
H.	Catterick	Yorks.
G.	† Cattley	Lincoln.
+ (n.)	Catune	Staffs.
B.	* Cerne, abb.	Dorset.
A.	† Chacomb, pr.	Northants.
A.P.	Charlton, near Uphaven (cell to Prem., abb., L'Isle Dieu)	Wilts.
A.P.	Charlton-on-Otmoore (cell to S. Ebrulf in Utica, Norm.)	Oxford.
H. (lep.)	Chatham	Kent.
B. (n.)	† Chatteris	Cambridge.
+	Chauce, or Charite	Sussex.
Dom.	Chelmsford	Essex.
+	Cheltenham	Gloucester.
B.	† Chepstow	Monmouth.
B.	† Chertsey, abb.	Surrey.
B.	cells :—Cardigan	Cardigan.
B. (n.)	Cheshunt	Herts.
B.	* Chester, St. Werburgh's, abb.	Cheshire.
B. (n.)	Chester, St. Mary's	Cheshire.
Dom.	Chester	Cheshire.
Franc.	Chester	Cheshire.
Carm.	Chester	Cheshire.
H.	Chester, St. John Baptist's	Cheshire.
H.	St. Giles'.	
H.	St. Michael's.	
H. (lep.)	Chesterfield	Derby.
A.	Chetwode	Bucks.
+ (n.)	Chewstoke, or St. Cross	Somerset.
	Chich (see St. Osyth's).	
Dom.	Chichester	Sussex.
Franc.	Chichester	Sussex.

ORDER.	HOUSE.	COUNTY.
+ .	Chichester . . .	Sussex.
H. (lep.)	Chichester, St. James' . .	Sussex.
	St. Mary Magdalen's	
	* St. Mary's . .	
G. .	* Chicksand . . .	Beds.
+ (n.) .	Chille, or Chiltre . . .	Herts.
A. .	Chipley (annexed to Clare) .	Suffolk.
Hosp. .	Chippenham . . .	Cambridge.
A. .	Chirbury, pr. . . .	Salop.
+ .	Cholsey	Berks.
H. (lep.)	Chosell	Norfolk.
	Chotes (see Croxden).	
A. .	* Christchurch, or Twyneham .	Hants.
+ .	Churchill . . .	Devon.
A. .	† Cirencester, abb. . .	Gloucester.
H. .	Cirencester, St. Thomas' .	Gloucester.
	St. John the Evangelist.	
	St. Laurence's.	
A.P. .	Clare (cell of St. Martin des	
	Champs) . . .	Carmarthen.
H. .	Clare	Carmarthen.
A. (fs.) .	* Clare	Suffolk.
A.P. .	Clare in the Castle (cell to Bec ;	
	removed to Stoke).	
A.P. .	Clatford (cell to Caux de Coleto,	
	Norm.) . . .	Wilts.
G. .	† Clattercote, pr. . . .	Oxford.
C. .	* Cleeve, abb. . . .	Somerset.
B. (n.) .	Clementhorpe . . .	Yorks.
A. (fs.) .	Cleobury Mortimer (see Wood-	
	house).	
B. (n.) .	Clerkenwell . . .	Middlesex.
Hosp. .	Clerkenwell (see London).	
H. .	Cleyhanger . . .	Devon.
Cl. .	Clifford, pr. . . .	Hereford.

ORDER.	HOUSE.	COUNTY.
+	Clive, or Wenlesclive . .	Worcester.
H.	Clothdale . . .	Herts.
B. (n.) .	Codenham (cell of Keyston) .	Suffolk.
C.	† Coggeshall, abb. . . .	Essex.
A.P.	Coggs (cell to Fecamp, Norm.)	Oxford.
C. (n.) .	Cokehill	Worcester.
+	Cokerham . . .	Lancaster.
P.	¦ Cokersande, abb . . .	Lancaster.
A.	† Cokesford, pr. . . .	Norfolk.
H.	Cokesford . . .	Norfolk.
	Coket (*see* Albans, St.).	
B.	† Colchester, St. John's, abb. .	Essex.
B.	cell :—Barrow . . .	Essex.
A.	* Colchester, St. Botulph's, pr. .	Essex.
Cru.	Colchester . . .	Essex.
Franc. .	Colchester . . .	Essex.
H. (lep.)	Colchester, St. Mary Magdalen's	Essex.
B.	† Colne Earls, pr. (cell of Abingdon)	Essex.
C.	† Combe, abb. . . .	Warwick.
Hosp. .	Combe (Temple) . . .	Somerset.
C.	† Combermere, abb. . . .	Radnor.
+	Congar's Mon. . . .	Glamorgan.
A.	Conishead, pr. . . .	Lancaster.
+	Constantine . . .	Cornwall.
H.	Cookham . . .	Surrey.
A. (n.) .	Cornworthy . . .	Devon.
A.P.	Corsham (cell to Caen) . .	Wilts.
H. (lep.)	Cotes, near Rockingham . .	Northants.
+	Cottingham (transl. to Haltem-price)	Yorks.
A.P.	Covenham (cell to Karilefus in diocese of Mains, afterwards to Kirksted) . . .	Lincoln.
B.	† Coventry, Cath., pr. . .	Warwick.

ORDER.	HOUSE.	COUNTY.
Carth. .	* Coventry, St. Anne's, near .	Warwick.
Franc. .	† Coventry . . .	Warwick.
Carm. .	† Coventry . . .	Warwick.
H. .	* Coventry, Bablake . .	Warwick.
	Grey Friars'.	
	Sponnes.	
	St. John Baptist's.	
P. .	* Coverham, abb. . . .	Yorks.
	Cowick (*see* Tavistock).	
A.P. .	Cowicke, or Cuich, near Exeter (cell to Bec) . . .	Devon.
Hosp. .	Cowley (Temple), or Sandford .	Oxford.
A. (n.) .	Crabhouse . . .	Norfolk.
	Cranborne (*see* Tewkesbury).	
+ .	Crawley	Bucks.
+ .	Crayke	Yorks.
H. .	Crediton	Devon.
Temp. & Hosp.	Cressing (Temple) . . .	Essex.
A.P. .	Cresswell, or Careswell (cell to Grandmont, Norm.) . .	Hereford.
A. .	* Creyk, abb. . . .	Norfolk.
A.P. .	Creting, St. Olave (a cell to Grestein) . . .	Suffolk.
A.P. .	Creting, St. Mary (a cell to Bernay) . . .	Suffolk.
H. .	Cricklade . . .	Wilts.
H. .	Crowmersh . . .	Oxford.
C. .	* Croxden, abb. . . .	Stafford.
P. .	† Croxton, abb. . . .	Leicester.
P. .	cell :—Hornby . .	Lancaster.
H. .	Croydon	Surrey.
B. .	* Croyland, or Crowland, abb. .	Lincoln.
B. .	cell :—Freston . .	Lincoln.
A.P. .	Cumbermere (cell to Savigny) .	Cheshire.

ORDER.	HOUSE.	COUNTY.
A.	Cumbwell, pr.	Kent.
A.	Custhorpe (cell to Westacre)	Norfolk.
C.	* Cwmhyre, abb.	Radnor.
	Cyrus, St. (*see* Montacute).	
+	Daeglesford, or Deilesford	Gloucester.
+	Dacor	Cumberland.
Hosp.	Dalby	Leicester.
P.	* Dale, or Stanley Park, abb.	Derby.
A.	† Darley, abb.	Derby.
Dom.(n.)	† Dartford	Kent.
H.	Dartford, Trinity H.	Kent.
H. (lep.)	Dartford, St. Mary Magdalen's.	
+	Dartmouth	Devon.
Cl.	† Daventry, pr.	Northants.
B. (n.)	* Davington	Kent.
	Deerhurst (*see* Tewkesbury).	
B. (n.)	De la Pré, or de Pratis	Herts.
Carm.	† Denbigh	Denbigh.
Fran.(n.)	* Denney	Cambridge.
H.	Denwall	Cheshire.
A.	Denys, St., Southampton	Hants.
	Deping (*see* Thorney)	Lincoln.
A.	Derby (*see* Darley)	Derby.
B. (n.)	Derby, King's Mead	Derby.
	Derby, St. James' (*see* Bermondsey).	Derby.
Dom.	Derby	Derby.
H. (lep.)	Derby, Maison Dieu	Derby.
H. (lep.)	Derby, St. Leonard's	Derby.
B.	Derent (cell to Rochester)	Kent.
+	Dereham, East	Norfolk.
P.	* Dereham, West	Norfolk.
H. (lep.)	Devizes	Wilts.

ORDER.	HOUSE.	COUNTY.
C.	† Dieulacres, abb.	Stafford.
Temp. & Hosp.	Dimsley (Temple) .	Herts.
Hosp.	† Dingley .	Northants.
Hosp.	Dinmore	Hereford.
A.P.	Docking (cell to Ivry, Norm.)	Norfolk.
+	Dodeling, or Dodelinch	Somerset.
P.	Dodford (see Halesowen) .	Worcester.
A.	Dodnash, pr.	Suffolk.
B.	Dogmael's, St., abb. cell:—Caldey.	Pembroke.
Franc.	Doncaster	Yorks, W.R.
Carm.	Doncaster	Yorks, W.R.
H.	Doncaster, St. James'	Yorks, W.R.
H.	Doncaster, St. Nicholas' .	Yorks, W.R.
H.	Donington	Leicester.
M.	Donnington, near Newbury	Berks.
H.	Donnington, near Newbury	Berks.
A.	* Dorchester, abb.	Oxford.
Franc.	Dorchester	Dorset.
H.	Dorchester, St. John Baptist's .	Dorset.
C.	* Dore	Hereford.
C. (n.)	Douglas .	Isle of Man.
	* Dover, St. Martin's (see Canterbury, Christ Church)	Kent.
H.	Dover, St. Mary's .	Kent.
H. (lep.)	Dover, St. Bartholomew's	Kent.
A.	Drax, pr.	Yorks.
A. (fs.) .	Droitwich	Worcester.
H.	Droitwich	Worcester.
	* Dudley (see Wenlock)	Stafford.
C.	† Dunkeswell, abb.	Devon.
A.	† Dunmow, pr.	Essex.
C.	Dunscroft, in Hatfield (cell to Rievaulx)	Yorks.

ORDER.	HOUSE.	COUNTY.
+ .	Dunscrofte . . .	Yorks.
A. .	* Dunstable, pr. . . .	Beds.
Dom. .	Dunstable . . .	Beds.
H. .	Dunstane, or Mere . .	Lincoln.
	† Dunster (*see* Bath) . . .	Somerset.
B. .	Dunwich (cell to Eye) . .	Suffolk.
Dom. .	† Dunwich . . .	Suffolk.
Franc. .	Dunwich . . .	Suffolk.
H. .	Dunwich, Maison Dieu . .	Suffolk.
H. (lep.)	† St. James'.	
Hosp. .	Dunwich	Suffolk.
P. .	† Dureford, abb. . . .	Sussex.
B. .	* Durham Cath., pr. . .	Durham.
B. .	cells :—† Farne Island . .	Northumberland.
B. . .	* Finchale . . .	Durham.
B. .	* Jarrow . . .	Durham.
B. .	* Lindisfarne . .	Northumberland.
B. .	Lytham . .	Lancaster.
B. .	Oxford, Durham Coll.	Oxford.
B. .	† Stamford, St. Leonard's	Lincoln.
B. .	* Monk Wearmouth .	Durham.
	Eagle, or Ocle (*see* Egle).	
P. .	* Easby (*see* St. Agatha's).	
B. (n.) .	* Easeburn . . .	Sussex.
	East Dereham (*see* Dereham).	
+ .	Eastry	Kent.
H. .	Eaton	Beds.
+ .	Ebbchester . . .	Durham.
A.P. .	Ecclesfield (cell to Fontanelle) .	Yorks, N.R.
H. .	* Edingdon (Bonshommes) . .	Wilts.
A.P. .	Edith Weston (cell to Bocherville)	Rutland.
B. .	Edwardstow (cell to Abingdon) .	Suffolk.

ORDER.	HOUSE.	COUNTY.
Hosp. .	† Egle, or Eycle . . .	Lincoln.
P. .	* Egleston, abb. . . .	Yorks.
+ .	Elfleet, or Elflit, Southminster .	Kent.
+ .	Ellenfordinmer . . .	Wilts, or Berks.
G. .	† Ellerton	Yorks.
H. .	Elleshaugh . . .	Northumberland.
A.P. .	Ellingham (cell to Le Vicomte, in diocese of Coutances) . .	Hants.
+ .	Elmet, or Leeds . . .	Yorks.
+ .	Elmham, North . . .	Norfolk.
C. (n.) .	† Elreton	Yorks.
B. (n.) .	† Elstow	Beds.
B. .	* Ely Cath., pr. . . .	Cambridge.
B. .	cell :—Holycourt . .	Norfolk.
H. .	Ely, St. John's . . .	Cambridge.
	St. Mary Magdalen's.	
+ .	Emmsay, or Emmesey . .	Yorks.
A.P. .	Endeston, or Eynestawe (cell to St. Server, Norm.) . .	Somerset.
Carth. .	Epworth, or Axholme . .	Lincoln.
A. .	Erdbury, pr., or Ardbury . .	Warwick.
C (n.) .	Esholt	Yorks.
	Eskdale (see Grosmont).	
M. .	Eston, or Burback, or Marl-borough . . .	Wilts.
A.P. .	Everdon (cell to Bernay, Norm.)	Northants.
B. .	* Evesham, abb. . . .	Worcester.
B. .	cells :—Alcester . . .	Warwick.
B. .	Penwortham . .	Lancaster.
H. .	* Ewelme	Oxford.
B. .	* Ewenny, pr. . . .	Glamorgan.
B. .	Exeter, St. Nicholas, pr. . .	Devon.
Dom. .	Exeter	Devon.
Franc. .	Exeter	Devon.

ORDER.	HOUSE.	COUNTY.
H.	Exeter, Bonvile's . . .	Devon.
	God's House.	
	St. Mary Magdalen's.	
	St. John's.	
Temp. & Hosp.	Eycle (*see* Egle) . . .	Lincoln.
B.	† Eye, pr.	Suffolk.
H. (lep.)	Eye	Suffolk.
B.	Eynesham, abb. . . .	Oxford.
B. (n.) .	† Fairwell	Stafford.
	Faith, St. (*see* Horsham).	
	Farendon (*see* Beaulieu).	
Cl.	Farleigh, or Farley . .	Wilts.
	Farne Island (*see* Durham) .	Northumberland.
B.	† Faversham, abb. . . .	Kent.
	Felixstow (*see* Rochester) . .	Suffolk.
A.	† Felley, pr. . . .	Notts.
A.	Ferreby (North), pr. (*ante* Temp)	Yorks.
A.P.	Field Dalling (cell to Savigny, Norm.) . . .	Norfolk.
	* Finchale (*see* Durham) . .	Durham.
A.	† Finneshed . . .	Northants.
A.	Fiscarton (cell to Thurgarton) .	Notts.
Dom.	Fisherton (*see* Salisbury) . .	Wilts.
+	Fladbury . . .	Worcester.
B. (n.) .	Flamstead . . .	Herts.
A.	Flanesford . . .	Hereford.
C.	* Flaxley, abb. . . .	Gloucester.
A.	† Flitcham, pr. . . .	Norfolk.
A. (n.) .	Flixton, South Elmham .	Suffolk.
H.	Flixton, or Carman's Spital .	Yorks, E.R.
A. (n.) .	Folkestone (cell to Lonley) .	Kent.
C.	* Ford, abb. . . .	Devon.

ORDER.	HOUSE.	COUNTY.
G.	† Fordham . . .	Cambridge.
H.	Fordingbridge . . .	Hants.
C.	Fors de Caritate, Wensleydale (translated to Jervaulx) . .	Yorks.
B. (n.) .	Fosse	Lincoln.
H.	Foulsnape . . .	Yorks, W.R.
C.	* Fountains, abb. . . .	Yorks.
H.	Fountains . . .	Yorks.
A.P.	Frampton (cell to St. Stephen's, Caen)	Dorset.
	Freston (*see* Croyland) . .	Lincoln.
Hosp. .	Friermagna (*see* Mayne) . .	Dorset.
A.	† Frithelstoke, pr. . . .	Devon.
+	Frome	Somerset.
+	Fruelege . . .	Hereford.
C.	* Furness, abb. . . .	Lancaster.
H.	Fyfield	Berks.
+	Galmanho, near York . .	Yorks.
+	Gare	Northumberland.
C.	† Garendon, abb. . . .	Leicester.
+	Gateshead . . .	Durham.
H.	Gateshead, St. Edmund's . .	Durham.
	Trinity H.	
A.	* Germans, St., pr. . .	Cornwall.
H.	Gild Martyn . . .	Cornwall.
+ (n.) .	Gilling	York.
A.	* Gisburn, pr. . . .	York.
Temp. & Hosp.	Gislingham . . .	Suffolk.
B.	* Glastonbury, abb. . . .	Somerset.
	cells :—Green Ore on Mendip	
B.	Basselech, or Basil .	Monmouth.
H.	* Glastonbury . . .	Somerset.
H.	Glenford Brigg . . .	Lincoln.

ORDER.	HOUSE.	COUNTY.
A.	† Gloucester, St. Oswald's . .	Gloucester.
B.	* Gloucester, St. Peter's abb. .	Gloucester.
B.	cells :—* Bromfield . .	Salop.
	* Ewenny . .	Glamorgan.
B.	Hereford, St. Guthlac's	Hereford.
B.	* Stanley, St. Leonard's	Gloucester.
Dom.	* Gloucester . . .	Gloucester.
Franc.	* Gloucester . . .	Gloucester.
Carm.	* Gloucester . . .	Gloucester.
H.	Gloucester, St. Bartholomew's .	Gloucester.
	St. Mary Magdalen's.	
H.	St. James'.	
H. (lep.)	St. Margaret's.	
Hosp.	Godesfield . . .	Hants.
B. (n.)	† Godstow	Oxford.
A.P.	Goldcliff (cell to Bec) . .	Monmouth.
A. (n.)	† Goring	Oxford.
A. (fs.)	Gorleston . . .	Suffolk.
H. (lep.)	Gorleston . . .	Suffolk.
Hosp.	Gosford (Kidlington) . .	Oxford.
C. (n.)	Goykwell, or Gowkeswell . .	Lincoln.
A. (n.)	† Grace Dieu, Belton . .	Leicester.
C.	Grace Dieu, abb. . . .	Monmouth.
A.	Grafton Regis (Hermitage) .	Northants.
Franc.	Grantham . . .	Lincoln.
Temp.	Grantham . . .	Lincoln.
H.	Great Hobbesse, or Hautbois .	Norfolk.
H.	Greatham . . .	Durham.
Cru.	Great Waltham . . .	Essex.
C. (n.)	Greenfield . . .	Lincoln.
Hosp.	Greenham . . .	Berks.
+	Greenore, on Mendip . .	Somerset.
Franc.	Greenwich . . .	Kent.
A.	† Gresley, pr. . . .	Derby.

ORDER.	HOUSE.	COUNTY.
B. (n.) .	Grimsby	Lincoln.
Franc. .	Grimsby	Lincoln.
A. (fs.) .	Grimsby	Lincoln.
B. .	† Grosmont, pr. (originally A.P., cell to Grandmont, Norm.) .	Yorks, N.R.
A.P. .	Grovebury, or De la Grove, in parish of Leighton (cell to Fontevrault) . . .	Beds.
Dom. .	Guildford (see Langley) . .	Surrey.
Cru. .	Guildford . . .	Surrey.
+ .	Guignes, or Gyones . .	Northumberland.
+ (n.) .	Hackness (cell to Whitby) .	Yorks.
+ .	Hadleigh . . .	Suffolk.
A.P. .	Hagham, or Hayham (cell to St. Sever, Coutances) .	Lincoln.
A.P. .	Haghe, or Howghe on the Mount (cell of St. Maria de Voto, Cherbourg) . . .	Lincoln.
A. .	* Haghmond, abb. . . .	Salop.
P. .	Hagneby, abb. . . .	Lincoln.
P. .	* Hales Owen, abb. . . .	Worcester.
P. .	cell :—Dodford . . .	Worcester.
B. (n.) .	Haliwell, or Holywell, London .	Middlesex.
Temp. & Hosp.	Halston	Salop.
A. .	Haltemprice, pr. . . .	Yorks.
A. .	Halywell on Watling St. (cell of Roucester) . . .	Worcester.
A.P. .	† Hamble (C), (cell to Tyronne, France) . . .	Hants.
+ .	Hambury . . .	Worcester.
+ (n.) .	Hamme	Berks.
C. (n.) .	Hampole . . .	Yorks.

ORDER.	HOUSE.	COUNTY.
Hosp. .	Hampton . . .	Middlesex.
+ .	Handbury . . .	Stafford.
B. (n.) .	Handale	Yorks.
+ .	Hanslope, or Gare . . .	Bucks.
H. (lep.)	* Harbledown . . .	Kent.
A. .	* Hardham, pr. . . .	Sussex.
H. (lep.)	Hardwick . . .	Norfolk.
A. .	† Hartland, abb. . . .	Devon.
Franc. .	Hartlepool . . .	Durham.
+ (n.) .	Hartlepool . . .	Durham.
A.P. .	Harmondsworth (cell to Rouen) .	Middlesex.
A. (n.) .	Harwood . . .	Beds.
A. .	Haselburg	Somerset.
C. .	Haselden in Rodmarton (removed to Kingswood) . . .	Gloucester.
A. .	† Hastings, pr. . . .	Sussex.
B. .	† Hatfield Regis, Broadoak, pr. .	Essex.
B. .	† Hatfield Peverel (*see* Albans, St.)	
A. .	† Haverfordwest, pr. . .	Pembroke.
Dom. .	Haverfordwest . . .	Pembroke.
G. .	† Haverholme . . .	Lincoln.
Hosp. .	Hawstone . . .	Salop.
C. .	* Hayles, abb. . . .	Gloucester.
A.P. .	Hayling (cell to Jumièges, Norm.)	Hants.
Cl. .	Heacham, or Hitcham (cell of Lewes) . . .	Norfolk.
B. (n.) .	Hedingham Castle . . .	Essex.
H. (lep).	Hedon, or Newton, St. Sepulchre's	Yorks, E.R.
A. .	Helagh Park, pr. . . .	Yorks.
Cl. .	Helen's, St. . . .	Isle of Wight.
H. .	Helston	Cornwall.
A. .	Hempton, pr. . . .	Norfolk.
H. .	† Henley	Warwick.

ORDER.	HOUSE.	COUNTY.
	Henton (*see* Hinton).	
B. (n.) .	Henwood . . .	Warwick.
	Hepp (*see* Shap).	
+ .	Hereford . . .	Hereford.
Dom. .	† Hereford . . .	Hereford.
Franc. .	Hereford . . .	Hereford.
H. .	Hereford, St. Anthony's . .	Hereford.
	St. Ethelbert's.	
	St. Giles'.	
	St. Giles' (lep.).	
	St. John's.	
	St. Thomas'.	
H. .	Heringby . . .	Norfolk.
A. .	Heringfleet, pr. . . .	Suffolk.
A. .	† Heringham, pr. . . .	Sussex.
	Hertford (see Alban's, St.).	
H. (lep.)	Herting	Sussex.
	Hertland (*see* Hartland).	
	Hether (*see* Hither).	
Carth. .	Hethorp, Locus Dei (removed to Hinton) . . .	Gloucester.
C. (n.) .	† Hevening, or Heyninges . .	Lincoln.
A. .	Heveringland (cell to Wymond-ham)	Norfolk.
A. .	* Hexham, pr. . . .	Northumberland.
A. .	cell :—Ovingham . .	Northumberland.
H. (lep.)	Hexham, St. Giles' . .	Northumberland.
H. .	Hexham, The Spittle . .	Northumberland.
	Heyninges (*see* Hevening).	
H. .	Heytesbury . . .	Wilts.
A. .	† Hickling, pr. . . .	Norfolk.
H. .	† Higham Ferrers . . .	Northants.
+ .	Hilbre Island, near Birkenhead, or Hilbury . . .	Cheshire.
B. (n.) .	Hinchinbrook . . .	Hunts.

ORDER.	HOUSE.	COUNTY.
A.P.	Hinckley (cell of Leyr)	Leicester.
Carth.	* Hinton (Locus Dei)	Somerset.
G.	Hitchin, or Newbigging	Herts.
Carm.	† Hitchin	Herts.
+	Hithe	Kent.
H. (lep.)	Hithe	Kent.
H.	Hithe, St. Andrew's.	
Hosp.	Hither, or Hether	Leicester.
H.	Hockliffe, or Hoccliffe	Beds.
H. (lep.)	Hoddesdon	Herts.
Hosp.	Hogshaw	Bucks.
H.	Holbeche	Lincoln.
B.	Holland, pr.	Lancaster.
G.	Holland Brigge	Lincoln.
C.	* Holm Cultram, abb.	Cumberland.
	Holme (*see* Montacute).	
+	Holmes, near Portbury	Somerset.
H. (lep.)	Honiton	Devon.
A.P.	Hooe (cell to Bec)	Sussex.
C.	Horewell (cell to Stonelegh)	Warwick.
Cl.	Horkesley Parva, pr.	Essex.
	Hornby (*see* Croxton).	
A.H.	Hornchurch, or Havering (cell to M. de Monte Jovis, Savoy)	Essex.
H.	† Horning	Norfolk.
+	Horningsea	Cambridge.
B.	† Horsham, St. Faith, pr.	Norfolk.
+ B.(n.)	Horsley	Surrey.
A.P.	Horsley, or Horkesley (cell to Troarn, Norm.)	Gloucester.
A.P.	Horsted (cell to nuns of Caen)	Norfolk.
	Horton (*see* Sherborne).	
Cl.	Horton, Monks (cell to Lewes) (*see* Monks Horton)	Kent.
M.	Hounslow	Middlesex.

ORDER.	HOUSE.	COUNTY.
	Hoxne (*see* Norwich Cath., pr.).	
Carth. .	Hull (Kingston-on-) . .	Yorks, E.R.
Dom. .	Hull	Yorks, E.R.
Carm. .	Hull	Yorks, E.R.
A. (fs.) .	Hull	Yorks, E.R.
H. .	Hull, God's House . . .	Yorks.
	Griggs.	
	Mariner's.	
	Pole's.	
	Selby's.	
	Hulme (*see* Benet's, St., of).	
Carm. .	* Hulne (Alnwick) . . .	Northumberland.
C. .	† Hulton, abb. . . .	Stafford.
B. .	Humberston, or Hunston, abb. .	Lincoln.
H. .	Hungerford . . .	Berks.
	Hunston (*see* Humberston).	
A. .	Huntingdon, pr. . . .	Huntingdon.
A. (fs.) .	Huntingdon . . .	Huntingdon.
H. (lep.)	Huntingdon, St. Margaret's .	Huntingdon.
H. .	Huntingdon, St. John Baptist's .	Huntingdon.
	Hurley (*see* Westminster).	
B. .	† Hyde, or Newminster, Winchester, abb. . . .	Hants.
	Hyrst in Axholme (*see* Nostell).	
+ .	Icanhoc	Lincoln.
A.P. .	Ickham	Lincoln.
B. (n.) .	Icklington . . .	Cambridge.
B. .	Ilbre Island (cell to Chester) .	Cheshire.
Dom. .	Ilchester	Somerset.
H. .	Ilchester	Somerset.
H. (lep.)	Ilford	Essex.
+ .	Indio	Devon.
A.P. .	Ipplepen (cell to Fulgers, Brit.) .	Devon.

ORDER.	HOUSE.	COUNTY.
A.	† Ipswich, Holy Trinity, pr.	Suffolk.
A.	† Ipswich, St. Peter's, pr.	Suffolk.
Dom.	† Ipswich	Suffolk.
Franc.	† Ipswich	Suffolk.
Carm.	† Ipswich	Suffolk.
H. (lep.)	Ipswich, St. Mary Magdalen's	Suffolk.
H. (lep.)	Ipswich, St. James'	Suffolk.
P. (n.)	Irford	Lincoln.
A.P.	† Isleham (cell to abb. of St. Jacutus, near Dol, Brit.)	Cambridge.
+	Ithancaester	Essex.
	Ives, St. (*see* Ramsey).	
B. (n.)	Ivinghoe	Bucks.
A.	Ivychurch, pr.	Wilts.
A.	Ixworth, pr.	Suffolk.
	† Jarrow (*see* Durham).	
+	Jerring	Sussex.
C.	*Jervaulx, or Jorvaulx, abb.	Yorks.
H.	Jesmont	Northumberland.
C. (n.)	Keldholme, Kirkby Moorside	Yorks.
+	Kempsey	Worcester.
A.	† Kenilworth, abb.	Warwick.
	cell :—Brooke	Rutland.
B.	Kersey	Suffolk.
	Kershall (*see* Lenton).	
A.	† Keynsham, abb.	Somerset.
+	Kidderminster, or Sture.	Worcester.
	Kidwelly (*see* Sherborne).	
B. (n.)	Kilburn	Middlesex.
Cru.	Kildale	Yorks, N.R.
H.	Killingwoldgrove	Yorks, E.R.
B.	† Kilpeck (cell to Gloucester)	Hereford.
B. (n.)	*Kington	Wilts.

ORDER.	HOUSE.	COUNTY.
Dom. .	* King's Langley . . .	Herts.
	Kingsthorpe (*see* Northampton, St. David's).	
H. .	Kingston . . .	Surrey.
C. .	† Kingswood, abb. . . .	Wilts.
H. (lep.)	Kirby in Kendale . . .	Westmoreland.
A. .	Kirby Beller, pr. . . .	Leicester.
A.P. .	Kirkby Monks . . .	Warwick.
A. .	* Kirkham, pr. . . .	Yorks.
C. (n.) .	† Kirkles . . .	Yorks.
C. .	* Kirkstall, abb. . . .	Yorks.
C. .	† Kirksted, abb. . . .	Lincoln.
M. .	† Knaresborough . . .	Yorks, W.R.
H. .	Knightsbridge . . .	Middlesex.
B. .	Kydwelly, Cadwell (cell to Sherborne)	Carmarthen.
A. .	Kyme, pr. . . .	Middlesex.
	† Kyme, South, pr. . . .	Lincoln.
C. .	† Kymmer, abb. . . .	Merioneth.
B. (?) .	Kynemark, St. . . .	Monmouth.
A. (n.). .	* Lacock, abb. . . .	Wilts.
A. .	Lacton, pr. . . .	Essex.
B. (n.) .	Lambley-on-Tyne . . .	Northumberland.
H. .	Lambourn . . .	Berks.
B. .	Lammona (cell to Glastonbury) .	Cornwall.
Dom. .	Lancaster . . .	Lancaster.
Franc. .	Lancaster . . .	Lancaster.
A.P. .	Lancaster (cell to St. Martin of Séez)	Lancaster.
H. .	Lancaster . . .	Lancaster.
A. .	* Lanercost, pr. . . .	Cumberland.
P. .	* Langdon, abb. . . .	Kent.
H. (lep.)	Langeport . . .	Somerset.
B. (n.) .	Langley	Leicester.

ORDER.	HOUSE.	COUNTY.
P.	† Langley, abb.	Norfolk.
Dom.	* Langley, King's (*see* King's Langley)	Herts.
Dom.	Langley (*see* Guildford)	Surrey.
H.	Langriph	Lancaster.
+	Langton Maltravers (*see* Wicheswood)	Dorset.
H.	Langwade	Norfolk.
A.	† Lantony, New, pr.	Gloucester.
A.P.	Lapley, or Lappele (cell to St. Remigius, Rheims)	Stafford.
B.	* Lastingham (cell to Whitby)	Yorks.
A.	Latton	Essex.
A.	† Launceston, pr.	Cornwall.
+	Launceston	Cornwall.
H. (lep.)	Launceston	Cornwall.
A.	Launde, or Landa, abb.	Leicester.
P.	Lavenden, abb.	Bucks.
A.P.	Lavenestre (cell of B. nuns for Almanesche, Norm.)	Sussex.
H.	Lawardyn	Pembroke.
A.P.	Leasingham (cell of Bec)	Norfolk.
H.	Lechlade	Gloucester.
H.	Ledbury	Hereford.
A.	Leedes, pr.	Kent.
+	Leeds (*see* Elmet)	Yorks.
A.	† Lees, or Leighs	Essex.
A.	Lees, St. Michael (cell of Roucester)	Stafford.
C. (n.)	† Legbourne	Lincoln.
A.	Leicester, St. Mary de Pré, abb.	Leicester.
Dom.	Leicester	Leicester.
Franc.	Leicester	Leicester.
A. (fs.)	Leicester	Leicester.
S.	Leicester	Leicester.

ORDER.	HOUSE.	COUNTY.
H. .	Leicester, St. John's . .	Leicester.
H. .	Leicester, St. Ursula's . .	Leicester.
H. (lep.)	Leicester, St. Leonard's . .	Leicester.
P. .	* Leiston, abb. . . .	Suffolk.
Cl. .	† Lenton, pr. . . .	Notts.
Cl. .	cell :—Kershall . . .	Lancaster.
Carm. .	Lenton	Notts.
H. .	Lenton, St. Antony's . .	Notts.
	* Leominster (see Reading).	
B. (n.) .	Leominster, or Nonne-minster .	Sussex.
A. .	† Lesnes, abb. . . .	Kent.
A.P. .	Lessingham (cell to Okeburn) .	Norfolk.
A. .	, Letheringham, pr. . . .	Suffolk.
H. .	Leverington . . .	Cambridge.
Cl. .	* Lewes, pr. . . .	Sussex.
Cl. .	cell :—Stanesgate . .	Essex.
Franc. .	Lewes	Sussex.
H. .	Lewes, St. James' . . .	Sussex.
H. .	St. Nicholas' . .	Sussex.
A.P. .	Lewesham (cell to St. Peter's, Ghent) . . .	Kent.
Franc. .	† Lichfield	Stafford.
H. .	Lichfield, St. John's . .	Stafford.
	Bacon Street H.	
	Poor Woman's H.	
B. (n.) .	† Lillechurch, Higham . .	Kent.
A. .	* Lilleshall, abb. . . .	Salop.
A.P. .	Limber Magna (cell to Aulnay, or Aveney, Norm). . .	Lincoln.
G. .	Lincoln, St. Catherine's . .	Lincoln.
	† Lincoln, St. Magdalen's (see York, St. Mary's).	
Dom. .	Lincoln	Lincoln.
Franc. .	† Lincoln	Lincoln.
Carm. .	Lincoln	Lincoln.

ORDER.	HOUSE.	COUNTY.
A. (fs.) .	Lincoln	Lincoln.
S. .	Lincoln	Lincoln.
+ .	Lincoln	Lincoln.
H. (lep.)	Lincoln, Holy Innocents' . .	Lincoln.
H. .	† Lincoln, St. Giles' . . .	Lincoln.
H. .	† Lincoln, St. Mary's . .	Lincoln.
H.G. .	Lincoln, Holy Sepulchre . .	Lincoln.
	* Lindisfarne (see Durham).	
B. (n.) .	Ling	Norfolk.
A.P. .	Linton (cell to Jacutus, St., Dol, Brit.)	Cambridge.
H. (lep.)	Liskard, or Minhelled . .	Cornwall.
B. (n.) .	Littlemore . . .	Oxford.
C. (n.) .	Llanclere . . .	Glamorgan.
A.P. .	Llangennith (cell to Evreux, Norm.) . . .	Glamorgan.
A.P. .	Llangkywan, near Gresmond (cell to abb. of Leyr, Norm.) .	Monmouth.
C. (n.) .	Llanleir	Cardigan.
C. (n.) .	Llanlurgan . . .	Montgomery.
C. .	† Llantarnam, or Caerleon, abb. .	Monmouth.
A. .	* Llantony, Old, pr. . . .	Monmouth.
Franc. .	† Llanvaise, near Beaumaris .	Anglesea.
A.P. .	Lodres (cell to Montisburg, Norm.) . . .	Dorset.
H. (lep.)	Locko[1]	Derby.
A. .	* London, St. Bartholomew's, pr.	Middlesex.
A. .	London, Holy Trinity, Aldgate, pr.	Middlesex.
C. .	London, St. Mary Graces, abb. .	Middlesex.
B. (n.) .	* London, St. Helen's . .	Middlesex.
Fran.(n.)	London,[2] the Minories . .	Middlesex.
Hosp. .	* London, Clerkenwell . .	Middlesex.

[1] A preceptory of Knights of St. Lazarus, temp. Edw. III.
[2] For London, see also Clerkenwell and Haliwell.

ORDER.	HOUSE.	COUNTY.
Carth. .	* London	Middlesex.
Dom. .	London	Middlesex.
Franc. :	London	Middlesex.
Carm. .	† London	Middlesex.
A. (fs.) .	† London	Middlesex.
Fran.(n.)	London	Middlesex.
Cru. .	London	Middlesex.
S. .	London	Middlesex.
H. .	London, St. Mary's, Spital, or New H. of our Lady, Bishopsgate .	Middlesex.
H. .	London, Elsing Spital, near Cripplegate . . .	Middlesex.
H. .	London, Charing Cross . .	Middlesex.
H. .	London, Denton's, near the Tower	Middlesex.
H. .	† London, Domus Conversorum (now Chapel of the Rolls) .	Middlesex.
H. (lep.)	London, St. Giles' . . .	Middlesex.
H. .	London, St. Giles', without Cripplegate . . .	Middlesex.
H. (lep.)	London, Highgate . . .	Middlesex.
H. B.(fs.)	London, St. Mary Bethlehem .	Middlesex.
H. .	London, St. Katherine's, near the Tower . . .	Middlesex.
H. .	London, The Papey . .	Middlesex.
H. .	London, St. Paul's . .	Middlesex.
H. .	London, Syon, or Brentford .	Middlesex.
H. .	† London, St. Thomas of Acres .	Middlesex.
H. .	London, Whitington . .	Middlesex.
A.P. .	Long Bennington (cell to Savigny, Norm.) . . .	Lincoln.
H. (lep.)	Long Blandford . . .	Dorset.
A. .	Longleat . . .	Wilts.
H. .	Long Stow . . .	Cambridge.
H. .	Lorwing	Gloucester.

ORDER.	HOUSE.	COUNTY.
Carm. .	Losenham, in Newenden . .	Kent.
Hosp. .	Louth, or Maltby . . .	Lincoln.
C. .	* Louth Park, abb. . . ,	Lincoln.
H. (lep.)	Lowcrosse . . .	Yorks.
A.P. .	Ludgarswell . . .	Bucks.
Carm. .	Ludlow	Salop.
H. .	Ludlow, St. John Baptist's .	Salop.
B. .	† Luffield (cell of Westminster) .	Northants.
H. .	Lutterworth . . .	Leicester.
A. (n.) .	Lymbrook . . .	Hereford.
H. (lep.)	Lyme (?)	Dorset.
B. .	Lyminge	Kent.
B. .	Lynge	Norfolk.
	Lynn (*see* Norwich Cath., pr.).	
Dom. .	† Lynn	Norfolk.
Franc. .	† Lynn	Norfolk.
Carm. .	* Lynn	Norfolk.
A. (fs.) .	† Lynn	Norfolk.
H. .	Lynn, St. John's . . .	Norfolk.
H. .	Lynn, St. Mary Magdalen's .	Norfolk.
H. (lep.)	Lynn, West Lynn . . .	Norfolk.
H. (lep.)	Lynn, Cowgate . . .	Norfolk.
H. (lep.)	Lynn, Setchhithe . . .	Norfolk.
H. (lep.)	Lynn, Mawdely . . .	Norfolk.
	Lytham (*see* Durham Cath., pr.).	
+ .	Magnusfield, or Mangotsfield .	Gloucester.
A. .	Maiden Bradley, pr. . .	Wilts.
Franc. .	Maidstone . . .	Kent.
G. .	Maimond, or Marmund . .	Cambridge.
Carm. .	Maldon	Essex.
H. (lep.)	Maldon, Little . . .	Essex.
B. (n.) .	* Malling, abb. . . .	Kent.
B. .	* Malmesbury, abb. . .	Wilts.
B. .	cell :—Pilton . . .	Devon.

ORDER.	HOUSE.	COUNTY.
	Malpas (*see* Montacute).	
A.	Malsingham (cell to Westacre) .	Yorks.
Temp. & Hosp.	Maltby, or Louth (*see* Temple Maltby) . . .	Lincoln.
G.	* Malton, Old . . .	Yorks.
B.	* Malvern, Great, pr. . .	Worcester.
	† cell :—Avecote . . .	Warwick.
	* Malvern, Little (*see* Worcester Cath., pr.).	
+	Mangotsfield (*see* Magnusfield) .	Gloucester.
A.P.	Manton (cell to Cluny) . .	Rutland.
H.	Manton	Rutland.
Hosp.	* Maplestead . . .	Essex.
C.	* Margam, abb. . . .	Glamorgan.
C. (n.)	† Marham	Norfolk.
A.	† Markby, pr. . . .	Lincoln.
G.	† Marlborough . . .	Wilts.
Carm.	Marlborough . . .	Wilts.
H.	Marlborough, St. John's . .	Wilts.
H.	Marlborough, St. Thomas of Canterbury . . .	Wilts.
B. (n.)	† Marlow, Little, Mynchen . .	Bucks.
G.	Marmond . . .	Cambridge.
B. (n.)	† Marrick	Yorks.
	Marsh, St. Mary de (*see* Plympton)	
B.	Marsh (cell to York) . .	Nottingham.
+	Marshfield . . .	Gloucester.
A.	Marton, pr. . . .	Yorks.
	Massingham (*see* Westacre).	
G.	† Mattersey . . .	Notts.
A.	* Maxstoke, pr. . . .	Warwick.
Hosp.	Mayne, or Friar Magna . .	Dorset.
C.	† Meaux, or Melsa, abb. . .	Yorks.
A.	Medmenham, abb. . .	Bucks.
Hosp.	Melchburne . . .	Beds.

ORDER.	HOUSE.	COUNTY.
Dom. .	Melcombe, or Milton, near Wey-mouth	Dorset.
Cl. .	† Mendham . . .	Suffolk.
Carth. .	Mendip (cell to Witham) . .	Somerset.
Temp. & Hosp.	Mere (*see* Temple Mere) . .	Lincoln.
C. .	† Merevale, abb. . . .	Warwick.
B. (n.) .	Merkyate, or De Bosco . .	Beds.
A.P. .	Mersea (cell to St. Ouen, Rouen)	Essex.
A. .	† Merton, pr. . . .	Surrey.
H. .	Merton	Wilts.
B. .	Michael, St. (cell to Malmes-bury)	Devon.
A.P. .	† Michael's Mount, St. (cell to Mont S. Michel) . . .	Cornwall.
A. .	† Michelham, pr. . . .	Sussex.
	Middlesborough (*see* Whitby).	
H. .	Middleham . . .	Yorks.
B. .	* Milton, or Middleton, abb. .	Dorset.
H. .	Milton, near Gravesend . .	Kent.
+ .	Milton	Oxford.
A.P. .	† Minster Lovell (cell to Ivry de Ibreio) . . .	Oxford.
A.P. .	Minting (cell to Leyr, France) .	Lincoln.
A. .	Mirdial	Herts.
A. .	† Missenden, abb. . . .	Bucks.
H. .	Mitton, near Kingston-upon-Hull	Yorks.
A.P. .	Modbury (cell to St. Pierre sur Dives)	Devon.
M. .	Modenden . . .	Kent.
	Modney (*see* Ramsey).	
B. (n.) .	Molesby, or Marton . .	Yorks.
	Molycourt (*see* Ely).	

ORDER.	HOUSE.	COUNTY.
Cl.	* Monk Bretton, pr.	Yorks.
A.P.	Monken Lane, Lena, or Monkland (cell to Conches and Wotton Wawen)	Hereford.
B.	Monketon (cell to Séez and then to St. Alban's)	Pembroke.
Cl.	† Monks Horton, pr.	Kent.
A.P.	Monks Kirby (cell to Angier)	Warwick.
A.P.	† Monks Tofte, or Tofte, near Beccles (cell of Preaux (de Pratellis), Norm.)	Norfolk.
B.	Monks Risborough (cell to Canterbury)	Bucks.
A.P.	Monkton Winterbourne (cell to Cluny).	Dorset.
B.	† Monmouth, pr.	Monmouth.
H.	Monmouth, Holy Trinity	Monmouth.
H.	Monmouth, St. John's	Monmouth.
Cl.	† Montacute, pr.	Somerset.
Cl.	cells :—Carswell	Devon.
Cl.	Cyrus, St.	Cornwall.
Cl.	Holme	Dorset.
Cl.	Malpas	Monmouth.
	Morfield, or Morville (see Shrewsbury).	
+	Morelynch, or Poledon Hill	Somerset.
H.	Morpeth .	Northumberland.
A.	* Motisfont, pr.	Hants.
Carth.	* Mountgrace	Yorks, N.R.
A.	† Mountjoy, or Heveringland, pr.	Norfolk.
Hosp.	Mount St. John	Yorks.
A.P.	† Mount St. Michael (see Michael)	Cornwall.
B.	* Muchelney, abb.	Somerset.
A.P.	Muckleford	Dorset.

ORDER.	HOUSE.	COUNTY.
	Mulebrok, or Millbrook (*see* Beaulieu).	
A.P. .	Munkland . . .	Hereford.
M. .	Muttlinden . . .	Kent.
H. .	Nantwich, St. Laurence's . .	Cheshire.
H. .	Nantwich, St. Nicholas' . .	Cheshire.
C. .	* Neath, abb. . . .	Glamorgan.
B. .	Neots, St., or Eynesbury, pr. .	Hunts.
B. (n.) .	Neseham . . .	Northumberland.
C. .	* Netley, Letley, or Edwardstow, abb.	Hants.
P. .	Neubo, abb. . . .	Lincoln.
Franc. .	† Newark	Notts.
A. (fs.) .	Newark	Notts.
H. .	Newark, St. Leonard's . .	Notts.
H. .	Newark, The Spital . .	Notts.
	Newbigging (*see* Hitchin).	
A. .	† Newburgh, pr. . . .	Yorks.
H. .	Newbury . . .	Berks.
B. (n.) .	Newcastle-on-Tyne, or Monkchester . . .	Northumberland.
Dom. .	Newcastle-on-Tyne . .	Northumberland.
Franc. .	Newcastle-on-Tyne . .	Northumberland.
Carm. .	† Newcastle-on-Tyne . .	Northumberland.
A. (fs.) .	Newcastle-on-Tyne . .	Northumberland.
S. .	Newcastle-on-Tyne . .	Northumberland.
H. .	Newcastle-on-Tyne—	Northumberland.
	St. Mary the Virgin.	
	St. Mary Magdalen's.	
	Maison Dieu.	
	Brigham's.	
	St. Catherine's, or Thorneton's.	
Dom. .	Newcastle-under-Lyme . .	Stafford.

ORDER.	HOUSE.	COUNTY.
C.	Newenham by Axminster . .	Devon.
+	Newent, or Newenton (cell of Corneilles) . . .	Gloucester.
P.	Newhouse, abb. . . .	Lincoln.
+ (n.)	Newington . . .	Kent.
A.P.	Newington Longueville (cell to Longueville, Norm.) . .	Bucks.
H.	Newington, Our Lady and St. Catherine's . . .	Surrey.
Hosp.	Newland . . .	Yorks.
C.	† Newminster . . .	Northumberland.
A.	Newnham . . .	Beds.
C.	Newnham . . .	Devon.
A. (fs.)	Newport . . .	Monmouth.
	Newport (see Tickford).	
H.	Newport, or Birchanger H. .	Essex.
H. (lep.)	Newport, near Launceston .	Cornwall.
H.	Newport Pagnell, St. John's .	Bucks.
	St. Margaret's.	
	New Hospital.	
	New Rumney (see Rumney).	
Temp.	Newsom Temple . . .	Yorks.
A.	Newstead (by Stamford), pr. .	Lincoln.
G.	† Newstead (in Lindsey) . .	Lincoln.
A.	* Newstead, in Sherwood, pr. .	Notts.
H.	Newton, St. Mary Magdalen's .	Yorks, E.R.
A.	Nocton, pr. . . .	Lincoln.
H.	North Allerton, St. James' .	Yorks.
	Maison Dieu .	Yorks.
Cl.	Northampton, St. Andrew's, pr.	Northants.
Cl. (n.)	† Northampton, De la Pré . .	Northants.
A.	† Northampton, St. James', pr. .	Northants.
Dom.	† Northampton . . .	Northants.
Franc.	Northampton . . .	Northants.
Carm.	Northampton . . .	Northants.

ORDER.	HOUSE.	COUNTY.
A. (fs.) .	Northampton . . .	Northants.
H. .	† Northampton, St. David's, or Holy Trinity . .	Northants.
H. .	† St. John Baptist's.	
H. (lep.)	St. Leonard's.	
H. .	St. Thomas'.	
A.P. .	Northile, or Ile (cell of Marmoutier) . . .	Beds.
A. .	Norton, pr. . . .	Cheshire.
H. .	Norton	Yorks.
A. .	Norton, or Cold . . .	Oxford.
B. .	* Norwich Cath., pr. . .	Norfolk.
	cells :—Aldeby . . .	Norfolk.
	Hoxne . . .	Suffolk.
	* Lynn . . .	Norfolk.
	Norwich, St. Leonard's	Norfolk.
	Yarmouth . .	Norfolk.
Dom. .	* Norwich	Norfolk.
Franc. .	Norwich	Norfolk.
Carm. .	Norwich	Norfolk.
A. (fs.) .	Norwich	Norfolk.
P. F. .	Norwich	Norfolk.
S. .	Norwich	Norfolk.
H. .	Norwich, St. Paul's . .	Norfolk.
H. .	St. Giles'.	
H. .	God's House.	
H. .	Hyldebronds Spittle.	
H. (lep.)	St. Mary Magdalen's.	
H. .	St. Saviour's.	
H. (lep.)	Without St. Austin's gate.	
H. (lep.)	Without Fibriggate, or Magdalen gate.	
H. (lep.)	Without Nedham, or St. Stephen's gate.	

ORDER.	HOUSE.	COUNTY.
H. (lep.)	Norwich, Without Westwyk, or St. Benet's gate.	
A.	† Nostell, pr.	Yorks.
A.	cells :—Bamburgh	Northumberland.
A.	† Bredon	Leicester.
A.	Hyrst, in Axholme	Lincoln.
A.	Tockwith	Yorks.
A.	Widkirk	Yorks.
Franc.	Nottingham	Notts.
Carm.	Nottingham	Notts.
H.	Nottingham, St. John's	Notts.
	St. Leonard's.	
	Plumtree's.	
C. (n.)	Nunappleton	Yorks.
B. (n.)	Nunburnholme	Yorks.
C. (n.)	Nuncoton	Lincoln.
B. (n.)	† Nuneaton	Warwick.
B. (n.)	Nunkeling, or Chilling	Yorks.
B. (n.)	† Nunmonkton	Yorks.
	Nun Ormesby (*see* Ormesby).	
	Nunthorpe (*see* Basedale).	
A.	* Nutley, abb.	Bucks.
+	Nyot	Cornwall.
+ H.	Oceleir	Beds.
A.P.	Ocle Livers', or Lyre Ocle (cell to Lyre, Norm.).	Hereford.
A.P.	Ogebourn (cell to Bec)	Wilts.
H.	Okeham	Rutland.
B.	Olave's, St.	Suffolk.
B. (n.)	Oldbury (cell of Pollesworth)	Warwick.
A.	† Olveston, abb.	Leicester.
A.	Orford	Suffolk.
H.	Orford, St. Leonard's	Suffolk.

ORDER.	HOUSE.	COUNTY.
G.	Ormesby, or Nun Ormesby	Lincoln.
A.	† Osney, abb.	Oxford.
H.	Ospring, Maison Dieu	Kent.
+	Oswestry	Salop.
A.	† Osyth, St., or Chich, abb.	Essex.
H. (lep.)	Otford	Kent.
P.	Otteham in Hailsham (transl. to Bayham)	Sussex.
H. (lep.)	Otteley	Yorks.
A.P.	Otterton, or Otterington (cell to Mt. St. Michael, Norm.)	Devon.
+	Oundle	Northants.
	Ovingham (*see* Hexham).	
G.	Ovingham, or Overton	Yorks.
+	Oxenford	Surrey.
A.	* Oxford, or Frideswide's, pr.	Oxford.
B.	† Oxford, Canterbury College (part of Christ Church).	Oxford.
B.	† Oxford, Durham College (now Trinity)	Oxford.
B.	† Oxford, Gloucester Hall (now Worcester)	Oxford.
A.	Oxford, St. Mary's College	Oxford.
C.	Oxford, St. Bernard's College	Oxford.
Dom.	Oxford	Oxford.
Franc.	Oxford	Oxford.
Carm.	Oxford	Oxford.
A. (fs.)	Oxford	Oxford.
Cru.	Oxford	Oxford.
S.	Oxford	Oxford.
+	Oxford, St. Aldate's	Oxford.
H.	Oxford, St. Bartholomew's	Oxford.
	Oxford, St. John's	Oxford.
	Oxney (*see* Peterborough).	
	Oxney (*see* Barlings).	

ORDER.	HOUSE.	COUNTY.
+	Padstow	Cornwall.
A.P.	Panfield (cell to Caen) . .	Essex.
	Parndon, Great (*see* Bileigh).	
A.P.	Patricksbourne, or Bourne (cell to Beaulieu, Norm.) . .	Kent.
+	Peakirk	Northants.
+	Peartan	Lincoln.
Hosp.	Peckham, Little, or West . .	Kent.
	Pembroke (*see* Alban's, St.).	
B. (?)	Penmon, pr. . . .	Anglesey.
+	Penrhys	Glamorgan.
A. (fs.)	Penrith	Cumberland.
A.	† Pentney, pr. . . .	Norfolk.
A.	† cell :—Wormgay . .	Norfolk.
	Penwortham (*see* Evesham).	
B.	* Pershore, abb. . . .	Worcester.
B.	* Peterborough, abb. . .	Northants.
B.	cell :—Oxney . . .	Northants.
H.	Peterborough, St. Leonard's .	Northants.
H.	* Peterborough, St. Thomas' .	Northants.
A.	Peterstone . . .	Norfolk.
+	Petrockstow, or Padstow . .	Devon.
H.	Pevensey, St. John Baptist's .	Sussex.
+	Peykirk	Northants.
H.	Pickering . . .	Yorks.
B.	Pille, pr.	Pembroke.
	Pilton (*see* Malmesbury).	
H. (lep.)	Pilton	Devon.
B. (n.)	† Pinley	Warwick.
C.	† Pipewell, abb. . . .	Northants.
H.	Pleydone . . .	Sussex.
Franc.	Plymouth . . .	Devon.
Carm.	Plymouth . . .	Devon.
H. (lep.)	Plymouth . . .	Devon.

ORDER.	HOUSE.	COUNTY.
A.P. .	† Plympton, pr. . . .	Devon.
A. .	cells:—St. Anthony in Roseland	Cornwall.
A. .	St. Mary de Marsh .	Devon.
H. (lep.)	Plympton . . .	Devon.
	Poling (see Arundel).	
B. (n.) .	† Pollesworth . . .	Warwick.
B. (n.) .	Polslo, or Polleshoo . .	Devon.
A.P. .	Ponington (cell of Bec) . .	Dorset.
Cl. .	Pontefract . . .	Yorks, W.R.
Dom. .	Pontefract . . .	Yorks, W.R.
Franc. .	Pontefract . . .	Yorks, W.R.
Carm. .	Pontefract . . .	Yorks, W.R.
H. .	Pontefract, St. Mary's . .	Yorks, W.R.
	St. Mary Magdalen's	
	St. Nicholas'.	
	Knowles'.	
+ .	Poole	Dorset.
Hosp. .	Pooling	Sussex.
A. .	† Porchester, pr. . . .	Hants.
H. .	† Portsmouth, God's House .	Hants.
A. .	Poughley, pr. . . .	Berks.
A.P. .	Povington (cell to Bec) . .	Dorset.
B. (n.) .	Pré, St. Mary de la (St. Alban's)	Herts.
Cl. .	Prene, or Preone (cell of Wen-	
	lock)	Salop.
Franc. .	Preston	Lancaster.
H. .	Preston	Lancaster.
Cl. .	Preston Capes (translated to	
	Daventry) . . .	Northampton.
Cl. .	† Prittlewell, or Pipwell, pr. .	Essex.
H. .	Puckeshall . . .	Kent.
G. .	Pulton	Wilts.
	Pulton (see Deulacres).	
	Pyling (see Cockersand).	

ORDER.	HOUSE.	COUNTY.
A.P.	Pylle, or Pulle (cell to St. Martin of Tours)	Pembroke.
A.	Pynham, pr.	Sussex.
C.	* Quarre, abb. (Isle of Wight)	Hants.
Hosp.	Queinington	Gloucester.
H. (lep.)	Racheness in Southacre	Norfolk.
P.	* Radegund's, St.	Kent.
	Radford (*see* Worksop).	
C.	Radmore in Cannock Chase (trans. to Stonleigh)	Stafford.
B.	† Ramsey, abb.	Hunts.
B.	cells :—Ives, St.	Hunts.
B.	Modney	Norfolk.
A.	Ratlincope (cell of Wigmore)	Salop.
A.	Raunton	Staffs.
A.P.	† Ravendale (P), (cell to Prem. abb. of Beauport, Brit.)	Lincoln.
A.	Ravenston, pr.	Bucks.
B.	* Reading, abb.	Berks.
B.	* cell :—Leominster	Hereford.
Franc.	† Reading	Berks.
H.	* Reading, St. Laurence's	Berks.
H. (lep.)	Reading, St. Mary Magdalene	Berks.
+	Readingham	Sussex.
Temp. & Hosp.	Rebston	Yorks, W.R.
+	Reculver	Kent.
+	Redbridge, or Redford	Hants.
	Redburn (*see* Alban's, St.).	
B. (n.)	† Redlingfield	Suffolk.
C.	Regill (cell of Flenley)	Somerset.
B. (n.)	Remsted	Sussex.

ORDER.	HOUSE.	COUNTY.
A.	* Repton, or Repingdon, pr.	Derby.
A.	cell :— Calk	Derby.
C.	† Revesby, or Rewesby, abb.	Lincoln.
C.	Rewley, abb.	Oxford.
A.	Reigate, pr.	Surrey.
Dom.	Rhuddlan	Flint.
H.	Rhuddlan	Flint.
Hosp.	Ribstone.	Yorks.
	† Richmond, St. Martin's (*see* York, St. Mary's).	
Franc.	† Richmond	Yorks, N. R.
Franc.	Richmond	Surrey.
+	Richmond	Yorks.
H.	Richmond, St. Nicholas'	Yorks.
C.	* Rievaulx, or Rievalle, abb.	Yorks.
H. (lep.)	* Ripon, St. Mary Magdalen's	Yorks.
H.	St. John Baptıst's.	
	† St. Anne's.	
	St. John's.	
A.P.	Riselipp, or Ruislip (cell to Bec).	Middlesex.
C.	* Robertsbridge, abb.	Sussex.
C.	* Roche, or De Rupe in Maltby, abb.	Yorks.
B.	* Rochester Cath., pr.	Kent.
	cell :— Felixstowe	Suffolk.
H.	† Rochester, St. Bartholomew's, Eastgate	Kent.
Hosp.	Rockley (Temple)	Wilts.
B.	Romberg (cell of Hulme)	Suffolk.
H. (lep.)	Romenale, or Rumney	Kent.
B. (n.)	* Romsey	Hants.
A.	† Ronton, pr.	Stafford.
B. (n.)	† Rosedale	Yorks.
Temp. & Hosp.	Rotheley.	Leicester.

ORDER.	HOUSE.	COUNTY
A.P.	Rotherfield (cell to St. Denis, France) . . .	Sussex.
A. (n.)	† Rothwell . . .	Northants.
A.	Roucester, abb. . . .	Stafford.
A.	Routon, or Mundene (cell to Haughmond) . . .	Stafford.
A.H.	Rouncevall, St. Mary, near Charing Cross (cell to Rouncevall, Navarre) . . .	Middlesex.
A.	Royston, pr. . . .	Herts.
H.	Royston, St. Nicholas' . .	Herts.
H.	Royston, St. John and St. James'	Herts.
C.	† Rufford, abb. . . .	Notts.
	Rumburgh (see York, St. Mary)	
A.P.	Rumney, New (cell to Pountney)	Kent.
	Runcorn (*see* Norton).	
C.	Rushen	Isle of Man.
B. (n.)	† Rusper	Sussex.
Carm.	Ruthin	Denbigh.
A. (fs.)	† Rye	Sussex.
H.	Rye	Sussex.
Temp.	Saddlescombe . . .	Sussex.
+	St. Benet's . . .	Cornwall.
A.P.	St. Clears (cell to St. Martin de Campis, Paris) . . .	Carmarthen.
A.P.	St. Cross (C), (cell to Tyronne) .	I. of Wight.
A.	St. Davy, or Dewe . . .	Northampton.
A.P.	† St. Helen's (cell to Cluny) . .	I. of Wight.
+	St. Keynemark . .	Monmouth.
+	St. Martin's, nunnery .	Cornwall.
+	St. Mawe's (?) St. Matthew's .	Cornwall.
A.P.	† St. Michael's Mount (cell of St. Michael's, Norm.) . .	Cornwall.
B.	Saintoft	Lincoln.

ORDER.	HOUSE.	COUNTY.
Franc. .	Salisbury . . .	Wilts.
Dom. .	Salisbury, Fisherton . .	Wilts.
H. .	Salisbury, Trinity H. . .	Wilts.
	† Harnham.	
	St. John's.	
+ .	Saltash	Cornwall.
C. .	* Salley, or Sawley, abb. . .	Yorks.
B. .	Samford (cell to Durham) . .	Durham.
Hosp. .	Sandford (*see* Cowley) . .	Oxford.
A. .	Sandford, or Newbury . .	Berks.
H. .	Sandon	Surrey.
B. .	† Sandwell, pr. . . .	Stafford.
Carm. .	Sandwich . . .	Kent.
+ .	Sandwich . . .	Kent.
H. .	* Sandwich, St. Bartholomew's .	Kent.
H. .	Sandwich, St. Thomas' . .	Kent.
+ .	Sapalanda . . .	Hants.
A. .	Sarra Isle, or Scarthe (cell of Gisburne) . . .	Yorks.
+ .	Sawbridgworth . . .	Herts.
C. .	Sawtre, abb. . . .	Hunts.
Dom. .	Scarborough . . .	Yorks, N.R.
Franc. .	Scarborough . . .	Yorks, N.R.
A. (fs.) .	Scarborough . . .	Yorks, N.R.
H. .	† Scarborough, St. Thomas' .	Yorks, N.R.
H. .	Scarborough, St. Nicholas' .	Yorks, N.R.
B. .	Scilly (cell of Tavistock) . .	Cornwall.
H. .	Seaford	Sussex.
H. (lep.)	Sedeberbrook (*see* South Weald)	Essex.
A. .	† Selborne, pr. . . .	Hants.
B. .	* Selby, abb. . . .	Yorks.
B. .	cell :—Snaith . . .	Yorks.
A.P. .	Sele, or Beeding (cell of St. Florent, Samur) . . .	Sussex.
Carth. .	Selwood (*see* Witham) . .	Somerset.

ORDER.	HOUSE.	COUNTY.
H. (lep.)	Selwood	Somerset.
G. .	Sempringham . . .	Lincoln.
B. (n.) .	Seton	Cumberland.
H. .	Sevenoaks, St. John Baptist's .	Kent.
C. (n.) .	† Sewardesley . . .	Northants.
B. (n.) .	† Shaftesbury . . .	Dorset.
H. .	Shaftesbury . .	Dorset.
P. .	* Shapp, or Hepp, abb. . .	Westmoreland.
+ .	Shapwick . . .	Dorset.
A. .	Shelford, pr. . . .	Notts.
Carth. .	† Shene	Surrey.
Hosp. .	Shengay	Cambridge.
B. (n.) .	* Sheppey (Minster in) . .	Kent.
B. .	* Sherborne, abb. . . .	Dorset.
B. .	cells :—Horton . . .	Dorset.
B. .	Kidwelly . .	Carmarthen.
H. .	Sherborne . . .	Dorset.
H. .	* Sherborne, St. John's . .	Dorset.
A.P. .	* Sherborne, West, or Monks (cell to St. Vigor's, Cerisy) . .	Hants.
H. (lep.)	Sherburn . . .	Durham.
H. .	Sherburn, St. Mary Magdalen's .	Yorks.
A. .	Sherringham (cell of Nutley) .	Norfolk.
Carm. .	† Shoreham, New . . .	Sussex.
H. .	Shoreham . . .	Sussex.
G. .	† Shouldham . . .	Norfolk.
B. .	* Shrewsbury, abb. . . .	Salop.
B. .	cell :—Morfield . . .	Salop.
Dom. .	Shrewsbury . . .	Salop.
Franc. .	† Shrewsbury . . .	Salop.
A. (fs.) .	Shrewsbury . . .	Salop.
H. .	Shrewsbury, St. Mary's . .	Salop.
	St. Giles'.	
	St. John Baptist's.	

ORDER.	HOUSE.	COUNTY.
A.	† Shulbrede, pr.	Sussex.
C.	* Sibton, abb.	Suffolk.
A.P.	Sidmouth (cell to Mont St. Michel, Norm.)	Devon.
C. (n.)	Sinningthwaite, or Senning-thwaite	Yorks.
	Sion (*see* Syon).	
G.	Sixhill	Lincoln.
Hosp.	Skirbeke	Lincoln.
A.	Skokirk, or Stowkirk (cell of Nostel)	Yorks.
Hosp.	Slanden	Herts.
Hosp.	Slebach	Pembroke.
Cl.	Slevesholme, or Methwold (cell of Castleacre)	Norfolk.
	Snaith (*see* Selby).	
B. (?)	Snape	Suffolk.
A.	Snede, or Snet (translated to Chirbury)	Salop.
B.	Snetteshall, pr.	Bucks.
	Snitterly, Blakeney	Norfolk.
+	Soham	Cambridge.
A.P.	Sompting	Sussex.
+	Sompting	Sussex.
B. (n.)	Sopwell	Herts.
B. (n.)	Sopwikes	Essex.
A.	† Southampton, St. Dennys, pr.	Hants.
Franc.	Southampton	Hants.
H.	† Southampton, God's House	Hants.
H. (lep.)	Southampton, St. Mary Magdalen's	Hants.
A.	† Southwark, St. Mary Overy, pr.	Surrey.
H.	Southwark, St. Thomas'	Surrey.
H.	South Weald, or Sedberbrook	Essex.
H.	Southwell, St. Mary Magdalen's	Notts.

ORDER.	HOUSE.	COUNTY.
A.	† Southwick (*see* Porchester)	Hants.
B.	† Spalding, abb.	Lincoln.
A.P.	Spettesbury (cell to Preaux, Norm.)	Dorset.
A.	Spinney	Cambridge.
H.	Spittle on the Peak	Derby.
H.	Spittle on the Street	Lincoln.
A.P.	† Sporle (cell to Saumur)	Norfolk.
H.	Sprotsburgh	Yorks.
A.	† Stafford, St. Thomas', pr.	Stafford.
Franc.	Stafford	Stafford.
A. (fs.)	Stafford	Stafford.
H.	Stafford, St. John's	Stafford.
H.	Stafford, St. Leonard's	Stafford.
B. (n.)	Stainfold, or Staynesfield	Lincoln.
	† Stamford, St. Leonard's (*see* Durham).	
B. (n.)	Stamford, St. Michael's	Northants.
Dom.	Stamford	Northants.
Franc.	Stamford	Northants.
Carm.	† Stamford	Northants.
A. (fs.)	Stamford	Northants.
H.	Stamford, St. John Baptist's and St. Thomas'	Northants.
H.	St. Giles'	Northants.
H.	St. Sepulchre (Pilgrim House)	Northants.
B.	Standon (cell of Stoke)	Herts.
B.	Stane, or Stave	Lincoln.
	Stanesgate (*see* Lewes)	Essex.
B. (n.)	Stanfield	Lincoln.
H. (lep.)	Stanford	Lincoln.
	Stanlaw (*see* Whalley).	
C.	Stanlegh, or Stanley, abb.	Wilts.

ORDER.	HOUSE.	COUNTY.
	* Stanley, St. Leonard's (see Gloucester, St. Peter's).	
	Stanley in Arden (see Stoneleigh).	
	Stanley Park (see Dale).	
A.	* Stavordale, pr.	Somerset.
A.	Stepholm	Somerset.
H. (lep.)	Steresbergh, or Sturbridge, near Cambridge	Cambridge.
A.P.	Steventon, near Abingdon (cell to Bec)	Berks.
A.P.	† Steyning (cell to Fecamp) .	Sussex.
C. (n.)	† Stixwold .	Lincoln.
B. (n.)	Stodley .	Oxford.
A.P.	† Stoke Courcy (cell to L'Onley, or Lolley)	Somerset.
+	Stoke-next-Nayland	Suffolk.
A.P.	Stoke by Clare (cell to Bec)	Suffolk.
H.	Stoke by Newark .	Notts.
B.	Stoke Courcy, or Stogursey (cell of Lonlay)	Somerset.
H.	Stokefaston	Leicester.
A.	Stoke Kirk (cell of Nostell)	Yorks.
A.	† Stone, pr.	Stafford.
C.	† Stoneleigh, or Stanley in Arden, abb.	Warwick.
A.	Stonely, pr.	Hunts.
H.	Stony Stratford	Bucks.
B. (n.)	Stoure .	Dorset.
+	Stourminster	Dorset.
Cl.	Stow (cell of Castleacre) .	Norfolk.
C.	* Strata Florida (Stratflour), abb. .	Cardigan.
C.	Strata Marcella (Strat Margel), abb.	Montgomery.
B. (n.)	Stratford at Bow, Bromley	Middlesex.

ORDER.	HOUSE.	COUNTY.
C.	† Stratford Langthorn, West Ham, abb.	Essex.
A.P.	Strathfieldsaye (cell to Vallemont, Norm.) . . .	Hants.
A.P.	Stratton, St. Margaret's . .	Wilts.
+	Strenshall . . .	Stafford.
H.	Strode, near Rochester . .	Kent.
B. (n.) .	Studley	Oxford.
A.	† Studley, pr. . . .	Warwick.
Dom.	Sudbury	Middlesex.
B.	† Sudbury (see Westminster) .	Suffolk.
H.	Sudbury	Suffolk.
P.	† Sulby, or Welford, abb. . .	Northants.
Hosp. .	Sutton-at-Hone . . .	Kent.
H.	Sutton-at-Hone . . .	Kent.
H.	Sutton	Yorks.
B. (n.) .	† Swaffham . . .	Cambridge.
P.	Swainby (trans. to Coverham) .	Yorks.
H.	Swansea	Glamorgan.
A.P.	Swavesey (cell to Angers) . .	Cambridge.
C. (n.) .	† Swine, or Swinhey . .	Yorks.
C.	† Swineshed, abb. . . .	Lincoln.
H.	Swinestre . . .	Kent.
Hosp. .	Swinford . . .	Leicester.
Temp. & Hosp.	† Swinfield . . .	Kent.
Brıdg. .	Syon	Middlesex.
A.P.	Takeley (cell to St. Valery, Picardy) . . .	Essex.
A.P.	Talcarn (cell to Angers) . .	Cornwall.
P.	† Talley, or Tallagh, abb. . .	Carmarthen.
H.	Tamworth . . .	Stafford.
B. (n.) .	Tamworth (trans. to Polesworth)	Stafford.

ORDER.	HOUSE.	COUNTY.
A.	Tandridge, pr.	Surrey.
H. (lep.)	Tanington, St. James'	Kent.
C. (n.)	Tarrent, or Kaines	Dorset.
H.	Tarent Rushton	Dorset.
H.	Tarvin	Cheshire.
A.	Taunton, pr.	Somerset.
Carm.	Taunton	Somerset.
H. (lep.)	Taunton	Somerset.
B.	† Tavistock, abb.	Devon.
B.	cell :—Cowick	Devon.
A. (fs.)	Tavistock	Devon.
H. (lep.)	Tavistock	Devon.
Temp. & Hosp.	* Temple Bruer (see Bruerne)	Lincoln.
Hosp.	Templecombe (see Combe)	Somerset.
Temp. & Hosp.	Temple Covele	Oxford.
Temp. & Hosp.	Temple Dynesley	Herts.
Temp. & Hosp.	† Temple Egle	Lincoln.
Temp. & Hosp.	Temple Hirst	Yorks, W.R.
Temp. & Hosp.	Temple Maltby	Lincoln.
Temp. & Hosp.	Temple Mere	Lincoln.
Temp. & Hosp.	† Temple Newsam	Yorks, W.R.
Temp. & Hosp.	Temple Rockley	Wilts.
Temp. & Hosp.	Temple Standon	Herts.
Temp. & Hosp.	Temple Witham	Lincoln.
Temp. & Hosp.	Temple Wilcketone	Lincoln.

ORDER.	HOUSE.	COUNTY.
H.	Tenby, St. Mary Magdalen's	Pembroke.
H.	Tenby, St. John Baptist's	Pembroke.
+	Terring	Sussex.
+	Tetbury, or Telton	Gloucester.
B.	* Tewkesbury, abb.	Gloucester.
B.	cells :—Bristol, St. James'	Gloucester.
B.	Cranborne	Dorset.
B.	* Deerhurst	Gloucester.
H. (lep.)	Tewkesbury	Gloucester.
C.	Thame, abb.	Oxford.
H.	Thame	Oxford.
+	Thanet Minster	Kent.
M.	† Thelesford	Warwick.
Dom.	Thetford	Norfolk.
A. (fs.)	Thetford	Norfolk.
Cl.	* Thetford, pr.	Norfolk.
A. (Sep.)	† Thetford, pr.	Norfolk.
Cl.	* Thetford	Norfolk.
B. (n.)	† Thetford	Norfolk.
H.	Thetford	Norfolk.
H.	Thetford, God's House	Norfolk.
H. (lep.)	St. John's.	
H.	St. Mary and St. Julian's.	
H.	St. Mary Magdalen's.	
H. (lep.)	St. Margaret's.	
B. (n.)	Thickhed	Yorks.
+	Thirling	Cambridge.
A.	† Thoby, pr.	Essex.
B.	* Thorney, abb.	Cambridge.
B.	cell :—Deping	Lincoln.
H.	Thorney	Cambridge.
A.	Thornham, or Thornholm, pr.	Lincoln.
A.	* Thornton, abb.	Lincoln.
H. (lep.)	Thrapston	Northants.
A.	† Thremhall, or Trenchale, pr.	Essex.

ORDER.	HOUSE.	COUNTY.
A.P.	Throwley (cell to St. Omers in Artois)	Kent.
A.	† Thurgarton, pr.	Notts.
A.H.	Thurlow, Great (cell to Hautpays, or De Alto Passu)	Norfolk.
M.	Thusfield, or Thuffield	Oxford.
A.P.	Thwaites	Bucks.
	Tickford (*see* York, Holy Trinity).	
A. (fs.)	Tickhill	Yorks, W.R.
H.	Tickhill	Yorks, W.R.
+	Tillaburg, or West Tilbury	Essex.
C.	† Tiltey, abb.	Essex.
H.	Tilton	Leicester.
C.	* Tintern, abb.	Monmouth.
A.	Tiptree, pr.	Essex.
+	Tisbury	Wilts.
P.	* Titchfield, abb.	Hants.
A.P.	Titley (cell to Tyronne)	Hereford.
	Tockwith (*see* Nostell).	
H.	Toddington	Beds.
	Toftes, Monks (*see* Monks Tofte).	
A.P.	Tolcarme (cell to Angers)	Cornwall.
A.P.	Tooting, or Tooting Back (cell to Bec)	Surrey.
A.	Torkesey, pr.	Lincoln.
P.	* Torre, abb.	Devon.
+	Torre, Glastonbury	Somerset.
A.	Tortington, pr.	Sussex.
B.	Totnes, pr.	Devon.
M.	Totnes, Little	Devon.
H. (lep.)	Towcester	Northants.
Hosp.	Trebigh, or Turbigh	Cornwall.
A.P.	Tregony (cell to de Valle, Norm.)	Cornwall.
A.	† Trentham, pr.	Stafford.
	Trew (*see* Letheringham).	

ORDER.	HOUSE.	COUNTY.
A.P.	Trewleigh (cell of St. Omer)	Kent.
Dom.	Truro	Cornwall.
A.	Tunbridge, pr.	Kent.
A.P.	Tunstall	Devon.
G. (n.)	Tunstall, near Redburn	Devon.
P.	† Tupholm, abb.	Lincoln.
	Turbigh (*see* Trebigh).	
B.	† Tutbury, pr.	Stafford.
H.	Twedemouth	Northumberland.
A.	* Twyneham, or Christ Church, pr.	Hants.
A.P.	Tykeford (cell to Marmoutiers, Tours)	Bucks.
B.	* Tynemouth (*see* St. Alban's)	Northumberland.
	Tytley (*see* Titley).	
B.	Tywardreath, pr.	Cornwall.
A.	* Ulverscroft, pr.	Leicester.
A.P.	Uphaven (cell to Fontenelle)	Wilts.
	Urford (*see* Irford).	
B. (n.)	Usk	Monmouth.
C.	† Vale Royal, abb.	Cheshire.
C.	* Valle Crucis, or De Valle Dei, abb.	Denbigh.
C.	Vaudey, abb.	Lincoln.
+	Vagnaleck, or Pegnalech	Northumberland.
A.	† Waburn, or Weybourn, pr.	Norfolk.
B.	Walden, abb.	Essex.
	Wallingford (*see* Alban's, St.).	
H.	Wallingford	Berks.
B. (n.)	Wallingwells, or St. Mary de Parco	Notts.
A.	* Walsingham, pr.	Norfolk.
A. (fs.)	* Walsingham	Norfolk.
H. (lep.)	Walsingham	Norfolk.

ORDER.	HOUSE.	COUNTY.
H.	Walsoken	Norfolk.
M.	Walknoll, near Newcastle	Northumberland.
A.	* Waltham, Holy Cross, abb.	Essex.
	Walton (*see* Felix Stowe).	
Cl.	Wangford, pr.	Suffolk.
C.	† Wardon de Sartis, abb.	Beds.
Franc.	Ware	Herts.
A.P.	Ware (cell to Utica, Norm.)	Herts.
A.P.	Wareham (cell to Lyra)	Dorset.
+	Wareham	Dorset.
A.P.	Warham, St. Mary's (cell to Mustrelle, Amiens)	Norfolk.
B.	Warmington, or Warrington (cell of York)	Northumberland.
A.P.	Warmington (cell to Preaux, or de Pratellis)	Warwick.
A. (fs.)	Warrington	Lancashire.
A.	† Warter, or Watre, pr.	Yorks.
A. (sep.)	Warwick, pr.	Warwick.
Dom.	Warwick	Warwick.
Temp. & Hosp.	Warwick	Warwick.
+	Warwick	Warwick.
H.	Warwick, St. John Baptist's	Warwick.
H. (lep.)	St. Michael's.	
H.	St. Thomas'.	
Fran.(n.)	Waterbeach	Cambridge.
G.	† Watton	Yorks.
C.	* Waverley, abb.	Surrey.
	Wearmouth, or Weremouth (*see* Durham).	
+	Weedon	Northants.
A.P.	Weedon Beck (cell to Bec)	Northants.
A.P.	Weedon Pinkney (cell to St. Lucian, near Beauvais, France)	Northants.

ORDER.	HOUSE.	COUNTY.
P.	† Welbeck, abb. . . .	Notts.
	Welhouse (see Wellow).	
H.	Welle	Yorks.
A.P.	† Welles, or Well Hall, in Geyton (cell to St. Stephen's, Caen) .	Norfolk.
G.	Welles	Lincoln.
H.	Wells, St. John's . . .	Somerset.
A.	† Wellow, abb. . . .	Lincoln.
+	Wendesclive, or Clive . .	Gloucester.
P.	† Wendling, abb. . . .	Norfolk.
A.P.	Wenge (cell to Angers) . .	Bucks.
A.P.	Wenghall, or Wenhall (see Crabhouse) (cell to Séez, Norm.) .	Lincoln.
Cl.	* Wenlock, pr. . . .	Salop.
Cl.	cell :—Dudley . . .	Stafford.
H.	Wenlock . . .	Salop.
M.	Werland, near Totnes . .	Devon.
A.	* Westacre, pr. . . .	Norfolk.
P.	† West Dereham, abb. . .	Norfolk.
B.	* Westminster, abb. . .	Middlesex.
B.	cells :—Hurley . . .	Berks.
B.	Sudbury . . .	Suffolk.
F.A.	Westminster . . .	Middlesex.
H. (lep.)	Westminster, St. James' . .	Middlesex.
H.	Westminster, Savoy . .	Middlesex.
H.	West Somerton . . .	Norfolk.
B. (n.) .	Westwood (originally A.P. for six nuns of Fontevrault) .	Worcester.
A.	Westwood . . .	Kent.
	† Wetheral (see York, St. Mary's) .	Cumberland.
A.	† Weybridge, pr. . . .	Norfolk.
	Weymouth (see Melcombe).	
C.	* Whalley, or Locus Benedictus, abb.	Lancaster.
C.	cell :—Stanlaw . . .	Cheshire.

ORDER.	HOUSE.	COUNTY.
.+ .	Whersted . . .	Suffolk.
B. (n.) .	† Wherwell . . .	Hants.
C. (n.) .	Whiston	Worcester.
B. .	* Whitby, abb. . . .	Yorks.
B. .	cell :—Middlesborough . .	Yorks.
H. .	Whitby, St. John Baptist's .	Yorks.
H. .	Whitchurch . . .	Salop.
C. .	* Whitland, or Blanchland, abb. . .	Carmarthen.
H. .	Whittlesford Bridge . .	Cambridge.
+ .	Wicheswood in Langton Maltravers . . .	Dorset.
B. (n.) .	† Wickes	Essex.
C. (n.) .	Wickham . . .	Yorks.
B. .	Wickham Skeyth . . .	Suffolk.
	Wickton (translated to Studley) .	Worcester.
	Widkirk (*see* Nostell).	
A. .	Wigmore, abb. . . .	Hereford.
H. .	Wigton	Cumberland.
B. (n.) .	Wilberfoss . . .	Yorks.
Temp. & Hosp.	Wilburgham, Great (Wilbraham)	Cambridge.
Hosp. .	Wilhelme . . .	Lincoln.
Hosp. .	Wilketon . . .	Gloucester.
A.P. .	Willesford (cell to Bec) . .	Lincoln.
A.P. .	† Wilmington (cell to Grestein) .	Sussex.
Hosp. .	Willoughton . . .	Lincoln.
B. (n.) .	Wilton, or Ellandune . .	Wilts.
Dom. .	Wilton	Wilts.
H. .	Wilton, St. Giles' . . .	Wilts.
	St. John's.	
	St. Mary Magdalen's.	
H. .	Winburn, or Wimborne . .	Dorset.
B. .	† Winchcombe, or Winchelcombe, abb.	Gloucester.
H. .	Winchcombe . . .	Gloucester.

ORDER.	HOUSE.	COUNTY.
Dom. .	Winchelsea . . .	Sussex.
Franc. .	* Winchelsea . . .	Sussex.
B. .	* Winchester, St. Swithun's Cath., pr.	Hants.
B. .	Winchester, Newminster (see Hyde)	Hants.
B. (n.) .	Winchester, St. Mary's, abb. .	Hants.
Dom. .	Winchester . . .	Hants.
Franc. .	Winchester . . .	Hants.
Carm. .	Winchester . . .	Hants.
A. (fs.) .	Winchester . . .	Hants.
H. .	* Winchester, St. Cross . .	Hants.
H. .	† St. John's.	
H. .	St. Mary Magdalen's	
H. .	Windeham, St. Edmund's . .	Sussex.
A.P. .	Winewale (cell of Mountsrol) .	Norfolk.
	Winterbourne (see Monkton).	
C. (n.) .	† Wintney	Hants.
A.P. .	† Winwaloe (cell of Mountsrol) .	Norfolk.
A.P. .	Wirham (cell of Mountsrol) .	Norfolk.
A. .	Wirksop, or Radford .	Notts.
A. .	Wirmegay (cell of Pentney) .	Norfolk.
+ .	Wirral-on-the-Hill . . .	Somerset.
H. .	Wisbech, St. John Baptist's .	Cambridge.
+ .	Wittering . . .	Northants.
Carth. .	† Witham, or Selwood . .	Somerset.
Temp. & Hosp.	Witham, or South Witham (see Temple Witham) . .	Lincoln.
A.P. .	Witherness (?) Withernsea (cell to Albemarle) . . .	Yorks, E.R.
+ .	Withington . . .	Worcester.
B. (n.) .	Wix	Essex.
C. .	† Woburn, abb. . . .	Beds.
+ .	Wockings . . .	Northants.
A. .	Wolinchmere, pr. . . .	Sussex.

ORDER.	HOUSE.	COUNTY.
A.P.	† Wolston (cell to St. Pierre sur Dives)	Warwick.
H.	Wolverhampton	Stafford.
A.	Wombridge, pr.	Salop.
A.	Woodbridge, pr.	Suffolk.
A. (fs.)	Woodhouse, near Cleobury Mortimer	Salop.
+	Woodchester	Gloucester.
A.	* Woodspring, or Worspring, pr.	Somerset.
H.	Woodstock, St. Mary the Virgin and St. Mary Magdalen	Oxford.
B.	* Worcester, Cath., pr.	Worcester.
	cell :—Little Malvern	Worcester.
Dom.	Worcester	Worcester.
Franc.	Worcester	Worcester.
M.	Worcester	Worcester.
S.	Worcester	Worcester.
H.	Worcester, St. Oswald's	Worcester.
H.	* Worcester, St. Wulstan's	Worcester.
A.	* Worksop, pr.	Notts.
A.	Wormley, or Wormesley, pr.	Hereford.
	† Wormgay (see Pentney).	
Cru.	Wotton-under-Edge	Gloucester.
A.P.	Wotton Wawen (cell to Conches, Norm.)	Warwick.
H.	Wotton Basset	Wilts.
H.	Wrauby	Lincoln.
A.H.	Writtle (cell to H. of Holy Spirit, Rome)	Essex.
A.	Wrongley, or Wrongay (cell of Pentney)	Norfolk.
B. (n.)	† Wroxall	Warwick.
A.	† Wroxton, pr.	Oxford.
+	Wudrandun	Worcester.
H.	Wybumbury	Cheshire.

ORDER.	HOUSE.	COUNTY.
H. (lep.)	Wycomb, St. Margaret and St. Giles'	Bucks.
H. .	* Wycomb, St. John Baptist's .	Bucks.
C. (n.) .	† Wykeham . . .	Yorks.
H. .	Wykes, or Wyken . .	Cambridge.
B. .	* Wymondham, abb. . .	Norfolk.
H. .	Wymondham . . .	Norfolk.
A. .	Wymondley Parva, pr. . .	Herts.
B. (n.) .	Wyrthorp . . .	Northants.
A.P. .	Wytchingham (cell of Longueville)	Norfolk.
A.P. .	Wytherness (cell of Albemarle) .	Yorks.
Dom. .	Yarm, or Yarum . . .	Yorks, N.R.
H. .	Yarm	Yorks, N.R.
Dom. .	† Yarmouth . . .	Norfolk.
Franc. .	Yarmouth . . .	Norfolk.
Carm. .	Yarmouth . . .	Norfolk.
H. .	Yarmouth, St. Mary's . .	Norfolk.
H. (lep.)	Yarmouth . . .	Norfolk.
H. (lep.)	Yarmouth . . .	Norfolk.
A. (fs.) .	Yarmouth, Little (see Gorleston)	Suffolk.
B. (n.) .	Yedingham, or de Parvo Marisco	Yorks.
Hosp. .	† Yeveley, or Stede . . .	Derby.
+ .	Yodby (?) . . .	Devon.
B. .	* York, St. Mary's, abb. . .	Yorks.
B. .	* cells :—St. Bees . . .	Cumberland.
B. .	† Lincoln, St. Mary Magdalen's . .	Lincoln.
B. .	† Richmond, St. Martin's	Yorks.
B. .	Rumburgh . .	Suffolk.
B. .	† Wetheral . .	Cumberland.
B. .	† York, Holy Trinity, pr. . .	Yorks.
B. .	cell :—Tickford . . .	Bucks.

ORDER.	HOUSE.	COUNTY.
G. .	York, St. Andrew's . .	Yorks.
Dom. .	York	Yorks.
Franc. .	York	Yorks.
Carm. .	York	Yorks.
A. (fs.) .	York	Yorks.
Cru. .	York	Yorks.
+ .	York (cell to Whitby) . .	Yorks.
H. .	York, St. Anthony's . .	Yorks.
H. .	† York, St. Peter's, alias St. Leonard's . . .	Yorks.

Counties
⌂ Abbey
✚ Cathedral Priory
♦ Conventual Priory
○ Cell

Houses
of the
Black Monks
(Benedictines
and Cluniacs)

Lindisfarn
Farn Island
Coquet
Tinmouth
Jarrow
Wetheral
Wearmouth
Finchale
Durham
St Bees
Middlesborough
Grasmont
Richmond
Whitby
York H.Trinity
York St Mary
Selby
Lytham
Pontefract
Smith
Penworthan
Holland
Monk Bretton
Humberston
Kershallo
Birkenhead
Blyth
Bardney
Premon
Lincoln St Mary Magd
Chester St Werburgs
Freston
Belvoir
Binham
Bromholm
Derby St Jones
Lenton
Spalding
Brawth of Holme
Shrewsbury
Tutbury
Croyland
Lynne
Castleacre
Norwich
Horm
Yarmouth
Burton on Trent
Depois
Wymondham
Norwich St Leonard
Aldeby
Bardsey
Wenlock
Sandwell
Stamford
Thorney
Molycourt
Canwell
Alvecote
Oxney
Modney
Aldeby
Morfield
Peterboro
Ely
Thetford
Bromfield
Dudley
Coventry
Ramsey
Bury St Edmunds
Horne
Leominster
Worcester
Daventry
Northampton
St Ives
Mendham
Langford
Clifford
Alcester
St Andrews
Cambridge
Bury St Edmunds
Rumburgh
Snape
Gt Malvern
Evesham
Buckingham
College
Sudbury
Hertford
L Malvern
Tickford
Walden
Felixstow
Brecknock
Pershore
Bradwell
Barkenley
Abergavenny
Gloucester
Snetteshall
Redburn
Earle Colne
Colchester
St Kynemark
Winchcombe
St Peter
Hatfield Peveral
St Johns
Monmouth
Eynsham
Oxford
Gloucester Hall
Hatfield
Chepstow
Stanley
Oxford
Canterbury Coll
Broadoak
Stanesgate
Malpas
St James
Abingdon
Durham College
Prittewell
Cardigan
Bristol
Malmesbury
Wallingford
St Albans
Westminster
St Doginael's
Swenny
Hurley
Bath
Farleigh
Bermondsey
Rochester
Canterbury Cath
Pille
Kidwelly
Reading
Chertsey
Faversham
St Andrews
Pembroke
Glastonbury
Horton
Dover
Milton
Muchelney
Athelney
Hyde
Winchcombe
Folkstone
St Martins
Barnstaple
Dunster
Montacute
Boxgrave
Lewes
Battle
Cowick
Exeter
Sherborne
Cranborne
Carswell
St Nicholas
Cerne
Holton
Milton
Tavistock
Abbotsbury
Tywarareath
Totnes
Holme
St Cyrus

Houses
of the
Cistercians
(White Monks)

.... Counties
Abbey
Cell

Newminster

Holm Cultram

Calder
Furness

Byland   Rivaulx
Jervaulx
Fountains

Sawley
Whalley
Meaux

Kirkstall

Roche
Louth Park

Basingwerk
Abercomen   Stanlaw   Vale Royal
Valle Crucis   Combermere   Dieulacres   Rufford   Kirksted
Hulton   Revesby
Croxden   Swineshead
Strata Marcella   Carendon   Vaudey
Wigmore
Buildwas   Merevale   Pipewell   Sawtre
Combe   Sibton
Strata Florida   Cumbhire   Bordesley   Stoneleigh
Dore   Biddlesden   Warden
Grace Dieu   Flexley   St Bernard's Coll:e   Woburn   Tilty
Whitland   Tintern   Hayles   Oxford   Coggeshall
Neath   Llantarnam   Bruerne   Thame   Stratford Langthorne
Margan   Kingswood   Sibley   Medmenham   London
Stanley   Waverley   Boxley
Cleeve   Robertsbridge
Dunkeswall   Ford   Netley   Quarr
Newenham   Beaulieu
Bindon
Buckfast   Buckland

...Counties
ꝼ Abbey
+ Conventual Priory
○ Cell

Houses of
Regular Canons
Black (Austin)
and
White (Premonstr.)

Nunneries.

...... Counties
. Benedictine
o Cistercian
⊙ Gilbertine
+ Augustinian
+ Premonstratensian
× Minoresses

Halystan

Newcastle
Lambley
Armthwaite

Seton

Ovingham · Nessham
Basedale
Marryck
Hartlale
Arden Rosedale
Elreton Keldholme Wykeham
Yedingham
Molesby
Malton
Nunmonkton Watton
Sinningthwaite York St Andrew Nunkeling
Eshol Clementhorpe Ormingham
Thickhed Arthington Wilberfosse
Ellerton Nunburnholme
Kirklees Hampole Swine

Nuncotton
Gokewell Irford Grimsby
Newstead Ormsby
Mattersey Greenfield Sixhills
Wallingwells Fosse Bollington Legbourne
Brodholm Stainfeld Greenfield
Lincoln Stixwold
Catherine
Haverholme
Calterlen
Holland Bridge

Blackborough
Derby de Pre Sempringham Marham
Langley Shouldham
Grace Dieu Crabhouse Carrow
Fairwell Stamford Marmond Bungay
Brewood Brewood Pollesworth St Michael Thetford Flixton
Llanllugar White Black Nuneaton Hinchinbrook Chatteris Bedingfield
Ladies Henwood Rothwell Denny Fordham Brusyard
Lymbrook Wroxall Pinley De la Pre Gurwood Waterbeach Swaffham Campsey
Llanlier Westwood Catesby Orwahsley Cambridge St Edmund
Whiston Cokehill Chicksand Icklington Yedingham
Aconbury Hitchin Wyke
Usk Godstow Ivinghoe Merkyate
Shuley Flamstead Sopwell
Pulton Littlemore Cheshunt
Little Marlow De la Praye
Kington Gorinet Burnham Barking
Bristol Ankerwyk Syon Waltham
St Mary Stratford Lillechurch
Barrow Gurney Laycock Marlborough Bromhall Sheppey (minster in)
Cannington Amesbury Witney Davington Canterbury
Wilton Minchin Wherwell Rusper Malling
Canonleigh Buckland Winchester St Mary Easeburn
Shaftesbury Rumsey
Polslo Tarrant

Cornworthy

London Clerkenwell
Halwell
St Helen
Minoresses ×
Kilburn
Stratford

INDEX

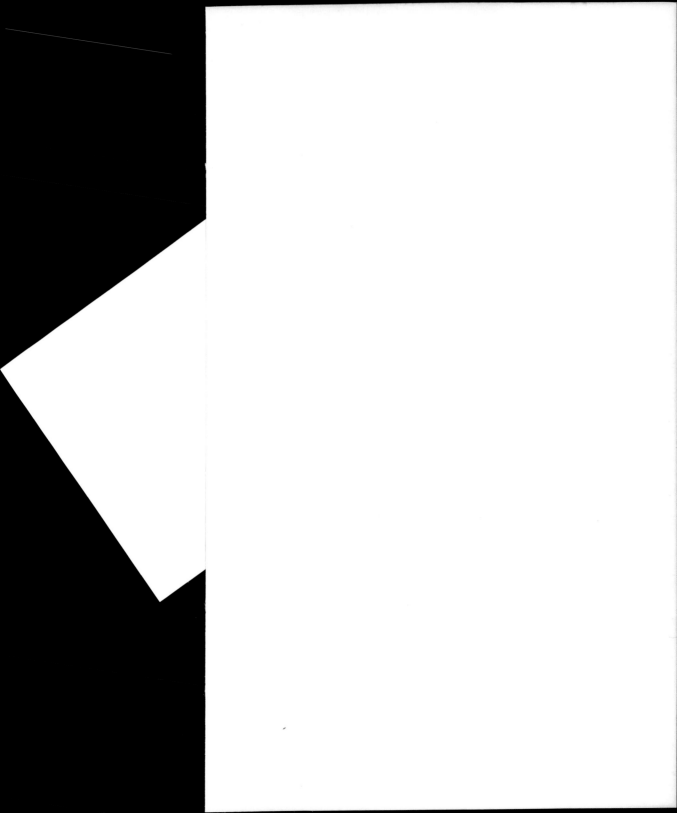

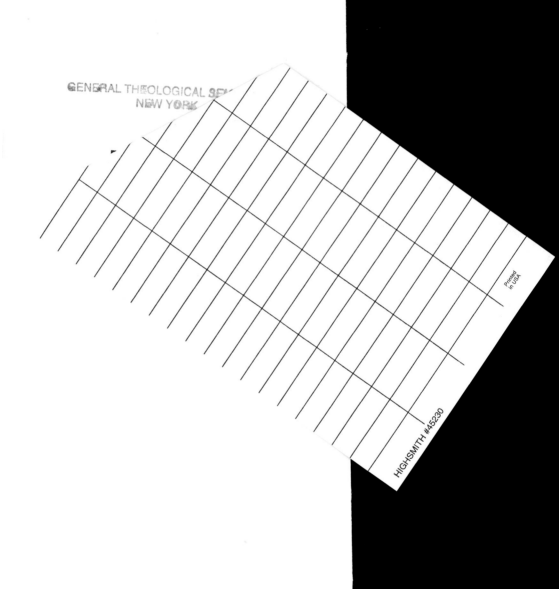